DAYS OF SLAUGHTER

DAYS OF SLAUGHTER

*Inside the Fall of **Freddie Mac***
and Why It Could Happen Again

SUSAN WHARTON GATES

Johns Hopkins University Press • Baltimore

Johns Hopkins University Press
2715 North Charles Street
Baltimore, Maryland 21218-4363
www.press.jhu.edu

A catalog record for this book is available from the Library of Congress

ISBN 978-1-4214-2193-3 (hardback; alk paper)
ISBN 1-4214-2193-3 (hardback; alk paper)
ISBN 978-1-4214-2194-0 (ebook)
ISBN 1-4214-2194-1 (ebook)

A catalog record for this book is available from the British Library.

Special discounts are available for bulk purchases of this book. For more information, please contact Special Sales at 410-516-6936 or specialsales@press.jhu.edu.

Johns Hopkins University Press uses environmentally friendly book materials, including recycled text paper that is composed of at least 30 percent post-consumer waste, whenever possible.

For my "old Freddie" colleagues

and in memory of
Freddie Mac Interim Chief Financial Officer
David Kellerman
1968–2009

Justice is turned back, and righteousness stands far away;
for truth has stumbled in the public squares.

Isaiah 59:14

Contents

Acknowledgments

Bringing a book to life—one's first—is no picnic, nor is it a private endeavor, nor is it done on a whim. When I left Freddie Mac in 2009 shaken and disillusioned, but with a story burning to be told, I never imagined that it would take eight years for *Days of Slaughter* to be published. We should all be thankful for the delay, as the story greatly benefited from the passage of time, the wise guidance of mentors, and the critical eye of reviewers. Yet the gestation was not so long that stories of misguided public policy, the foibles of leaders, and the dangerous brew of ideology and politics cannot speak to present-day concerns.

I am indebted to a wide range of people, many of whom I will undoubtedly fail to acknowledge as it has been nearly a decade since I began ruminating on this story. Thank you for your ear and early encouragement. Guiding the overall shape and development of the book, writing coach David Hazard lent needed confidence during the long years of marketing the manuscript to scores of uninterested agents and publishers, saying, "Someday it will go." And he was right.

My agent, Ron Goldfarb, deftly shepherded the manuscript to success, fully confident in the importance of the work to enhancing public understanding of the collapse of the housing market. His assistant, Gerri Sturman, worked efficiently to push out queries and pester publishers (in a nice way). I could not be happier to work with Kerry Cahill, Elizabeth Demers, Hilary Jacqmin, Mary Lou Kenney, Meagan Szekely, Gene Taft, and others at Johns Hopkins University Press. Copyeditor Kira Bennett Hamilton smoothed countless wrinkles in the text.

I received excellent review and guidance from top scholars and practitioners: Scott Frame, Vanessa Perry, Edward Pinto, Philip Swagel, and Barry Wides. My former "old Freddie" colleagues provided both insight and encouragement, especially Dave Andrukonis, Cindy Gertz, Richard Green, Alan Hausman, Hyacinth Kucik, Craig Nickerson, Chris Morris, Ann Schnare, and Brian Surrette. I am thankful for the support and prayers of many friends, including Mark and Grace Andringa, Roland and Mary Jo Binker, Kevin and Cheryl Buford, Sue Hardman, Sara Hoyt, Erica Kenney, Nancy Le Sourd, Clancy Nixon, Debbie Rivera, Anjeanette Roberts, Ann Simeone, Phil and Deonne Snare, Martin and Iveta Steinhobel, Eldon Stoffel, Kim and Penelope Swithinbank, Katie Wang and the sweet women in her destiny prayer group, Scott Ward, and John and Susan Yates.

Over the years I have been challenged by passionate policy discussions with my very smart siblings, David and Betsy Wharton, who will recall our father's sad finale with another big corporation. And for sustaining me through long months of writing and difficult setbacks, I am forever grateful to my steady and long-suffering husband, Peter, and our three children, none of whom wants a career in finance. Ultimately, I give thanks to God: muse, friend, goad, and joy. All errors are mine. All glory his.

DAYS OF SLAUGHTER

ACKNOWLEDGING THE OBVIOUS

Early one Monday morning in late August 2008, I walked into another vice president's office and shut the door. I needed to know how bad things were. He was more knowledgeable about where Freddie Mac stood in the capital sense, that is, whether the company was still solvent.

I cleared my throat. "There is a lot of talk going around," I said softly. "Is it true what I'm hearing—about conservatorship?"

He was staring at his computer. Then he turned and faced me hard.

"We're in a shit-load of trouble." He returned to the screen.

My throat felt dry. "Oh" was all I managed to say. Years of bad premonitions rose like ghosts in my head.

Less than two weeks later, in early September 2008, Freddie Mac was taken away from its shareholders and placed in government conservatorship along with its sibling, Fannie Mae. Both government-sponsored enterprises, or GSEs, were on the brink of insolvency as a result of mounting losses on higher-risk mortgages and related mortgage securities and dwindling capital. The specter of a sudden collapse of confidence in the twin pillars of the US housing market loomed. Policy makers feared that the GSEs could not refinance the hundreds of billions in GSE debt securities sitting in investment portfolios around the world. To stave off a disaster, the US government essentially nationalized Freddie Mac and Fannie Mae.

Nine years after those fateful days, the US housing market continues to stabilize. Firmly under government control, the GSEs still play a vital role in attracting mortgage money from around the world to fund residential homes and apartment buildings. In fact, because so many private sources of mortgage money have vanished, the GSEs are even more critical to the nation's housing markets than before. But it is a fragile arrangement. For many complicated reasons, which this book hopes to illuminate, lawmakers have yet to agree on a comprehensive reform plan for putting the nation's housing finance system, with or without the GSEs at its core, on a more stable footing. Yet the task is critical.

From 2008 to 2012, taxpayers provided $187.5 billion to keep the GSEs afloat while massive losses on defaulted mortgages ran through their balance sheets. In return, the GSEs had paid $241.2 billion in dividends to their senior preferred shareholder, the US Treasury, as of December 31, 2015.[1] In 2012, the government amended its original bailout agreement with the GSEs, changing the required 10 percent dividend it was to receive to a near 100 percent income "sweep" of GSE profits. Today the GSE spigot continues to flow towards its largest shareholder. The president's 2017 budget is counting on a steady stream of GSE dividends through 2026—an additional $151.5 billion beyond what already has been paid.[2]

Although the GSEs have repaid their emergency infusions—and then some—they remain very much under government control, even as other financial bailout recipients have been released from their government obligations. This stalemate greatly aggravates current GSE shareholders, many of whom purchased the grossly undervalued stocks in recent years, in hopes of a GSE revival and massive multi-billion-dollar windfall. Since 2013, myriad shareholder lawsuits have been filed against the government, alleging unlawful "takings" of GSE profits. Bringing their case to all three branches of government, an unlikely coalition of hedge funds, banking trade groups, and housing trade groups have called for the government to "recapitalize and release" the GSEs from their purgatory status.

Their efforts have been to no avail. A number of shareholder lawsuits have been dismissed, and the Obama administration seemed relieved to leave the hornet's nest of GSE reform to the next president. Congress has the power to make the important changes but remains hamstrung by lingering mistrust, ideological divide, fear of upending the uneven housing recovery, and the daunting operational challenges of reconfiguring a $5 trillion market with tentacles reaching into every corner of the world. To prevent the US

Treasury or the GSE conservator from taking independent action, Congress passed a law in 2015 prohibiting the executive branch from divesting of the GSEs for two years without congressional approval.

In the absence of reform, billions of GSE profits continue to flow from the GSEs to the US Treasury rather than to shareholder equity. Innovation is stalled, market discipline is adrift, key personnel have left, and morale languishes. Having only a small and declining capital cushion, and lacking the ability to retain earnings, the GSEs may be forced to return to taxpayers for another infusion of public funds. Such was the warning of the GSE regulator cum conservator Melvin L. Watt in February 2016. Was anyone listening?

Need for Contrition

In 2007 before the housing crash, shares of Freddie Mac were in the $60 range, and the market capitalization of the firm was more than $40 billion. Thousands of individual and institutional investors, large and small, saw their supposedly safe investments wiped out in a matter of weeks. Nine years later, in March 2016, a share of Freddie Mac stock sold for $1.71; the firm was valued at a mere $1.4 billion.

The stock collapse was particularly acute for banks. According to researchers at the Federal Reserve Board (FRB), more than six hundred depository institutions holding worthless GSE preferred stock, much of it issued just a year before, suffered paper losses of $8 billion, and 15 banks actually went under. In turn, exposed community banks experienced a sudden diminishment of their capital and contracted lending by $4 billion in the first quarter following the government takeover of the GSEs.[3]

In addition to direct infusions of funds, the government started buying GSE securities to shore up investor confidence and keep mortgage rates from skyrocketing. From September 2008 to December 31, 2009, the Department of the Treasury purchased $226 billion of GSE mortgage-backed securities (MBSs).[4] In its largest provision of credit during the financial crisis, the FRB purchased even greater quantities of MBSs. In the 14-month period between January 2009 and March 2010, the FRB bought a combined $1.1 trillion in GSE securities.[5] As of June 2016, $1.76 trillion of these and other mortgage-related securities remain on the FRB balance sheet, constituting nearly 40 percent of total Federal Reserve assets.[6]

Other costs of the GSE demise and broader mortgage market collapse are incalculable. Since the takeover, the US government now directly insures the risk on the vast majority of new mortgages because private investment has fled the US housing market. Families are still struggling, and so are their communities. Millions of homeowners lost their homes to foreclosure or are still "underwater," pondering hard futures without the ability to sell their homes because they now owe more than their homes are worth.

Memories fade of how bad things were—and how much it cost to stabilize the housing market—but the lack of contrition on the part of the former GSE regulator and top executives is shocking. Nor has there been any real remorse from the big banks, the brokers, consumer advocates, homebuilders, or real estate agents. In fact, nobody in the housing finance industry wants to talk about the past. But they have a lot to say about the future of housing finance: keep it pretty much the same. That is why I wrote this book—to tell an ugly story that everyone would like to forget.

Truth and Truce

I believe it is important to give an insider account of not simply *what* happened but *why*, and to admit the mistakes and hubris of a company that can't or won't admit its own. Freddie Mac failed in its public mission to provide stability to the US mortgage market. Period. The fateful choices of the company's leaders may have seemed right to some at the time, but history has proved otherwise. As a former employee—and executive—I give voice to that.

To the extent that it means anything, coming not from the company per se but from a single former employee, I express deep regret to American taxpayers for such an unfortunate state of affairs. As well as to homeowners, investors, and all those everywhere whom Freddie let down.

For nearly two decades my job essentially was to write Freddie's story—that's what a humanities major does at a financial services company. Following graduate school, I became a presidential management intern and spent five years as a budget examiner at the Office of Management and Budget. One of the budgets I oversaw was the VA home loan mortgage program, an entitlement program that guaranteed zero-down-payment loans to the nation's veterans. In 1990, I left OMB and took a job as a Freddie Mac economist. Over the next 19 years, I had jobs in a variety of different departments that gave me a unique perspective on Freddie Mac's competing objectives and the external ideological gridlock in which the firm operated. I was editor of the company's research magazine, compiler of credit risk data for the Board of Directors, policy director for Freddie Mac's top lobbyist, coordinator of the reputation risk group, and primary writer of CEO congressional testimony. In 2004, I was promoted to vice president of public policy, joining the ranks of some 250 officers striving to manage a 5,000-person firm and admired Fortune 50 company.

For most of my tenure, I loved Freddie Mac. I worked with some amazing colleagues, whom I call "old Freddie." They were smart, hard-working, and committed to the success of Freddie Mac's mission. Unfortunately, most were eventually driven out—or co-opted—by a new regime that was both arrogant and incompetent. These new leaders were the ones who chose to gamble the company's future for short-term gain.

Nine months before the government takeover in September 2008, I changed jobs and became vice president of corporate strategy. Severe external pressures, competing visions of Freddie Mac's role in the deepening housing crisis, and warring factions within the firm made that job impossible. The publicly held corporation known as Freddie Mac was already on a collision course with disaster.

In this book, I have assembled the backstory as best I can recall and make sense of it. You won't find a lot of accounting terms, Wall Street lingo, or complex economic equations. Rather, consider this unofficial account an explanation and a lament. I began working for Freddie Mac at a time when it was easy—for me at least—to admire both its mission and its prudent business approach. When I left in June 2009, a few months after acting CFO David Kellerman took his life, I was as devastated as I was disillusioned.

For federal investigators, litigators, GSE watchers, and other inside-baseball types, there is not much new in these pages. Top GSE executives have had their grilling in Congress and before the SEC, and a trove of internal documents has been splayed over public websites. But at least one untold tale will titillate the Washington crowd: the fact that Freddie Mac had *a lot* to do with the idea of including minority homeownership in former president George W. Bush's State of the Union Address in 2002.

Some people may disagree with my assessment of events. That's fair. We all view events from different vantage points. Others may agree with my assessment but believe what I have to say should not be aired but buried. That's *not* fair. Truth can only be a redemptive and restorative force when it is set free, however ugly or painful that is. Urgently needed GSE reform measures must be based on a complete understanding of what happened and why.

My sincere hope is that this account will help explain to American homeowners what happened to the "greatest housing finance system in the world"—and to them, as well. And ultimately to keep us from reliving it.

RECKONING DAY

Midafternoon on Friday, September 5, 2008, while the rest of official Washington raced to beat weekend rush hour traffic, Richard Syron, Freddie Mac CEO and board chairman, and his Fannie Mae counterpart, Daniel Mudd, met their fates in a conference room in an obscure office building not far from the White House. Across the table were the nation's top financial regulators. It would not be a good day for either man.

Reminiscent of the scene in the movie *Mary Poppins*, where rueful board members relieved George Banks of his banking duties and plucked the poppy off his lapel, their regulator, James Lockhart, joined by Treasury Secretary Henry Paulson and Chairman of the Federal Reserve Ben Bernanke, summarily fired the two executives sitting at the twin helms of disaster. The leaders of two of America's most successful companies, then hopelessly insolvent by the government's reckoning, signed over control of their firms to their federal regulator, the Federal Housing Finance Agency (FHFA), which would take on the added role of conservator going forward. Rather than liquidate the two firms, FHFA's job was to keep them running, rebuild financial strength, and shrink their outsized mortgage portfolios. Directed to "preserve and conserve" the public's newly acquired assets, FHFA acts as a steward for US taxpayers until Congress decides what to do with the failed GSEs. For the past eight years, the firms have not been able to amass capital, lobby Congress, or undertake new ventures as they did in the past.[1] Practically speaking, the GSEs are tied, gagged, and stuck. Yet they remain absolutely critical to the stability of US housing markets.

At the time of the takeover, the outstanding amount of GSE debt and MBS amounted to about $5.5 trillion. To put that number in perspective, on the day of the takeover, the amount of outstanding GSE securities exceeded the $5.3 trillion in public debt held by the US Treasury.[2] Like US Treasury securities, GSE obligations were spread all over the world, held by central banks and investors who had bought them in good faith and counted on stable returns.[3] Therein was the problem. As George Banks was reminded, "When fall the banks of England, England falls."[4]

On Sunday, September 7, the government take-over was announced, and markets rallied around the globe. Monday morning, September 8, Treasury Secretary Paulson summoned all 5,000 Freddie Mac employees—of which I was one—to an all-hands meeting. No rally there. The grim event was held at the company's McLean, Virginia, headquarters in a cavernous room generally used for divisional meetings and the executive holiday party.

On that fateful morning we stood woodenly at attention and learned that Freddie Mac was now under government control and that Paulson had hand-picked a new CEO to replace the outgoing Syron. Paulson was no-nonsense and firm. Despite the ousters at the top of Freddie Mac, he implored employees to remain at their jobs. Freddie Mac needed to keep buying mortgages as fast as it possibly could to keep the housing market afloat, even as house prices were sinking to an unthinkable nadir. The 30 percent decline in home values was setting off a tsunami of mortgage defaults in communities across the nation.

Employees also were told of the stiff, strong-armed agreement Paulson had wrested out of the departing executives. To assure investors that the US government would honor the massive quantity of outstanding GSE securities, thereby assuaging the very real concern that global panic would ensue, the US Treasury took drastic measures. In bailing out each GSE, Treasury required the GSEs to issue $1 billion in preferred stock, giving the US government a near 80 percent stake in each company.[5] This massive issuance of new shares diluted the value of everyone else's shares and essentially wiped out common shareholders. In return, the government gave each GSE access to $100 billion in capital, which was later raised to $200 billion when losses skyrocketed. Both entities were levied a hefty 10 percent quarterly dividend on the government's considerable stake in the firms.[6]

Employees would later learn that Paulson designed the stringent terms to ensure that the two companies would not be able to grow out of their problems without significant reform. In this way, Paulson sought to force Congress to deal, at long last, with some of the worst skeletons in its closet—the powerful and politically connected GSEs, which had been created by congressional decree decades earlier. At the time of the government takeover, the firms were known in some quarters as the bastards of politics and finance. As Paulson recounts in his 2010 memoir, *On the Brink*, "Working nearly nonstop to stave off disaster for the crippled housing markets and US economy, we had, within a few months, managed to force massive changes at these troubled but powerful institutions that had stymied reformers for years."[7]

The Treasury chief's announcement was brief, and we left in silence. Back in our offices across the street, I called a staff meeting. There wasn't much to say or do. Nine months later, I resigned. I had worked for Freddie Mac for nearly two decades.

Several years later, a man knocked on the front door of my home and handed me an envelope. I opened it as he sprinted away. It was a subpoena, and my hands went cold.

Fatal Fault Lines

Since leaving Freddie Mac, I have thought a lot about my experiences there, about the things Freddie Mac did right and wrong, and more broadly about the strengths and weaknesses of the GSE model of housing finance. I've looked at respected analyses of mortgage defaults, considered the various "who-dunnit" arguments, and read the popular books. As a financial policy consultant and academic, I closely track the current state of new mortgage regulations being implemented and those still on the drawing board. I have watched countless congressional hearings on the subject.

My overall conclusion is that although the GSEs made serious mistakes, the financial crisis was not brought about by one single company (or two) operating in a single slice of the mortgage market. The causes are far broader and more complex than that. Expansive Federal Reserve monetary policies, loosely regulated subprime mortgage brokers, unregulated and rapacious Wall Street investors seeking high-yielding assets, conflicted credit rating agencies that failed to accurately assess the risk of subprime securities, millions of suckered, naïve, or conniving borrowers, and widespread regulatory lapses have all been nominated for best actor. Nevertheless, the fact remains that the GSEs' purchase and mismanagement of higher-risk mortgages inflamed an already vulnerable mortgage landscape. And that's what this story is about.

Within the mortgage market, the disaster resembled a high-stakes game of musical chairs, with multiple entities piling on business and warily competing with each other as the mortgage music played on and on, and then greedily grabbing chairs when it ended, attempting to stick each other with the losses. This game did not occur in a vacuum; it was heartily cheered on by the homebuilders and real estate trade groups and well-intended nonprofit organizations, such as consumer and housing groups. Unfortunately, as has been well documented, regulators were lounging on the sidelines and did little to set the terms of engagement or to enforce existing rules—much less develop new ones in a timely fashion.

Like fault lines under major cities, other unseen dimensions of the crisis make true recovery elusive and unsustainable. Beneath the mortgage game is a maze of competing philosophies and ideologies that has yet to be untangled and addressed. These include outsized government investments in homeownership at the expense of rental housing and other more productive investments society could be making; the unresolved tension between free markets and government support for housing, and between safety and soundness of the system and broad access to homeownership. These issues are hard and make for painful conversations, which is why there's been little progress toward addressing them.

Ethics is another fault line that has received little scrutiny. How could this industry—with teams of lawyers checking every jot and tittle for regulatory and statutory purity—not have been attuned to the ethical pitfalls associated with an unregulated market on financial steroids? While it is comforting to think that notorious cases of personal greed and fraud are the exception, they are simply the tips of deep cultural icebergs. Greed is gas to capitalism, but how much profit maximization is safe? And at what cost?

The antithesis of patient capital, the insatiable desire for more—whether for property, sales, commissions, returns, market share, or even political power—easily overcame the weak collective conscience, defiled the mortgage industry, and brought the nation to its knees.

As obvious as an indictment of greed might be, it is not the official view. In the 2011 report of the Financial Crisis Inquiry Commission (FCIC), the government said that "to pin this crisis on mortal flaws like greed and hubris would be simplistic. It was the failure to *account* for human weakness that is relevant to this crisis" (emphasis added).[8] Translation: regulations failed, and we need more of them.

A fair point: people will be people, which makes such accounting systems necessary. But let me be simplistic. Focusing solely on tightening regulations without a concomitant call for greater civic virtue will fail to bring about the results we desire. An extrinsic regulatory structure, however perfectly calibrated, is a poor substitute for conscience and good judgment; without temperance and other qualities, leaders will always choose to exploit regulatory loopholes, which can undercut a regulation's effectiveness and lead to unintended negative consequences. Burdensome, punitive, and arbitrary regulations also impose a high cost on efficiency and innovation.

To function well, to attract necessary capital to US housing, and to be able to serve qualified borrowers, a housing finance system requires spotless financial integrity. Law, regulations, and compliance programs have their roles, but they are not enough. The 2008 financial crisis was an unlovely display of the backside of American capitalism. It is critical that we hold each other—and our commercial transactions—to higher ethical standards.

A second fault line is moral cowardice. From my vantage point as a policy communicator at Freddie Mac, the crisis was as much a result of sins of omission as of commission. For every bad decision financial companies like mine made, I would guess there were a dozen in-the-know employees who swallowed their reservations and said nothing. Within that group, six probably had the power to do something but sat on their hands instead. Yes, issues were ambiguous at times, but sometimes they were not. There were far more bystanders than whistleblowers.

In an October 2011 House subcommittee hearing, Richard Dorfman, Managing Director and Head of Securitization Group of the Securities Industry Financial Markets Association, commented wryly that the GSEs were not the only ones in the housing finance system that had "lost all discipline [such that] success went to their heads and then some." Elaborating his point that something had gone inexplicably wrong, Dorfman concluded, "It is not necessarily true that the fundamental architecture of Fannie Mae and Freddie Mac is useless and decrepit, but how did something good become so bad?"[9]

Third is the problem of myopia. While companies sacrificed long-term returns for short-term gains, and trade groups shamelessly pushed their individual agendas at the expense of the health of the broader industry, special blame is reserved for the policy makers and politicians charged with the care of the public interest. More often than not, their focus was on their own pet projects or party grievances. Whether it was hammering the GSEs while turning an ideological blind eye to Wall Street or satisfying consumer calls to liberalize underwriting over the objections of wizened risk stalwarts, many elected officials got caught in the thicket of interests and failed to think holistically about the good of the system.

The fourth fault line is the lack of true leadership. Notwithstanding well-documented regulatory failures, business leaders failed to exert restraint and sound judgment and lacked an innate sense of "the right thing to do" in the face of tempting regulatory loopholes, a supervisory vacuum, and exploitable political advantage. Quoting again from the government's 2011 report, "We do place special responsibility with public leaders charged with protecting our financial system, those entrusted to run our regulatory agencies, and the chief executives of companies whose failures drove us to the crisis. The individuals sought and accepted positions of significant responsibility and obligation. Tone at the top does matter, and, in this instance, we were let down. No one said 'no.'"[10]

To a large extent, these fault lines lie beyond the scope and reach of law and regulation. Hence, unless we want to repeat recent history, the debate about what to do going forward must move beyond Washington all the way to our schools and communities, our places of worship, and our very homes and hearts.

Counting the Cost

Damaging effects of the crisis continue to reverberate through communities. For most middle-income families, a home is the largest single investment they will ever make. Homes truly are the national nest egg. That's why the near 30 percent decline in house values was so devastating. As reported by the Government Accountability Office (GAO) in 2013, Americans suffered a loss of $9.1 trillion in home equity (in constant 2011 dollars) from 2005 to 2011, largely attributable to the decline in house values.[11] Over a similar period, the Federal Reserve's Survey of Consumer Finances found that US households experienced a 39 percent decline in household net worth—an astounding $49,100 per family.[12]

These paper losses became real for the roughly 20 million borrowers who could not keep up with mortgage payments, or who no longer wanted to, given that they owed more than their home was worth. High levels of foreclosures have continued for years, moving through the system like a pig in a snake. In September 2015, CoreLogic reported that the nation's serious delinquency rate of 3.4 percent had fallen to pre-crisis levels. Even so, there were 55,000 foreclosures settled in that month alone, well above pre-crisis levels of 21,000 monthly foreclosures between 2000 and 2006.[13]

Falling house prices can decimate entire communities. When one household experiences the loss of a home through foreclosure, the values of other surrounding homes and businesses are weakened. On top of the estimated $7 trillion in lost home equity, the Center for Responsible Lending (CRL) estimated additional "spillover" costs totaling $2 trillion for families living in proximity to foreclosed properties, with minority communities suffering the most.[14]

An earlier CRL study looked at initial foreclosure patterns by racial composition. From 2007–2009, foreclosure rates were widely disproportionate; of 10,000 mortgages, 790 foreclosures were for African Americans, 769 for Hispanics, and 452 for non-Hispanic whites. The spillover costs would be similarly uneven. CRL estimated that "between 2009 and 2012, $194 and $177 billion, respectively, will have been drained from African-American and Latino communities in these indirect spillover losses alone."[15]

Despite gradual upturns in national house prices, thousands of families remain underwater. In December 2015, 13.4 percent of homes were still in negative equity territory, down from 31.4 percent at the peak of the crisis.[16] Negative equity adds considerable drag to economic recovery efforts, as underwater homeowners are less able to sell their homes and, due to a reverse wealth effect, are more likely to constrict spending.[17]

In the years before the crash, many homeowners took advantage of rising house prices and low interest rates to extract money from their homes for improvements, children's education, vacations, and other uses. Like a generous credit card, these home equity lines of credit, or HELOCs, allowed for borrowing up to the limit while making minimum interest-only payments, with repayment of principal not due for a decade. That decade has come and gone, and experts report that consumers are facing $265 billion in HELOC debt coming due over the next few years. Delinquencies have started to spike.[18]

As go property values, so goes the solvency of localities, as local governments are largely funded by property tax revenue. Falling house prices decimated local government coffers, and many localities had to cut services drastically to stay afloat. A few even declared bankruptcy.[19]

Like a rock thrown in a pond, mortgage pain trickled further out. Cutbacks in consumption and job losses gutted state government finances, heavily dependent on sales and income taxes. And federal coffers lost personal and corporate income tax while laying out billions for bailouts, stimulus packages, and higher unemployment benefits.

In terms of the hit to economic growth, the financial crisis resulted in output losses, or reductions to economic growth, of between several trillion to over $10 trillion—as much as a full year's worth of gross domestic product (GDP).[20] Other tallies are equally staggering. In 2013, researchers at the Dallas Federal Reserve estimated that the crisis cost individual Americans between $20,000 and $120,000, taking into account both direct and indirect costs.[21]

The huge tab could not help but exacerbate the fiscal imbalance between revenue and spending. From the end of 2007 to the end of 2010, federal debt held by the public increased from around 36 percent to 62 percent of GDP.[22] It is fair to say that the housing crisis and attendant fiscal stimulus costs and reduced revenues—plus a complete lack of confidence in the US political system's ability to deal with burgeoning deficits—were responsible for the nation losing its prized AAA credit rating in August 2011.[23]

The burning mortgage telephone wires stretched around the globe. In the United States, we call what happened in 2007–2008 simply the financial crisis; overseas, it's known as the global financial crisis. Because of a domino effect, other countries with housing bubbles lost billions in household wealth, doled out costly financial stimuli, or endured painful years of fiscal austerity. Foreign investors, including many sovereign central banks, absorbed billions in US mortgage losses. A tiny town in Norway was nearly wiped off the Arctic Circle for having invested in Florida's overheated real estate market.[24] The cumulative hit to global economic growth is likely incalculable.

Slow and Uneven Recovery

If the wealth effect was real during the run-up in house values, causing Americans to spend more because their homes were appreciating in value, then the opposite has played out since. For many years, people felt poorer because their homes had lost value and intuitively tightened their belts, apparently even more than they had previously loosened them.[25] This negative wealth effect has had a cataclysmic impact on an economy addicted to some of the highest levels of consumption in the world.

The house-price bubble also led to reduced savings rates, particularly for the lowest-income families. In 1999, families saved about 3 to 4 percent of disposable income, on average. As house prices rose, families tended to save less as their homes swelled in value and could be monetized for consumption purposes. By 2007, the average savings rate had fallen to about 1 percent. For those with the lowest income growth, however, the savings rate actually went negative. According to the International Monetary Fund (IMF), "households experiencing lower income growth during 1999–2007 saw a sharper decline in their saving rates and a larger rise in their indebtedness before the crisis, contributing significantly to the decline in the overall saving rate. These households were less able to reduce their debt and raise their net worth after the crisis."[26]

After the bubble popped, the Department of Treasury and FHFA, the GSE regulator, established two new programs to assist affected borrowers. The Home Affordable Modification Program (HAMP) authorized the GSEs to modify the terms of qualifying borrowers' existing loans to enable them to remain in their homes and eventually reinstate their loans. Under HAMP, investors, mortgage servicers, and borrowers receive incentive payments to lower borrower monthly payments to affordable levels. The GSEs absorb the cost of the incentives for the mortgages held on their books; the government's Troubled Asset Relief Program (TARP) covers the rest. At the end of 2015, the government reported that "nearly 2.4 million trial modifications have been initiated, resulting in more than 1.6 million homeowners entering permanent mortgage modifications."[27]

The Home Affordable Refinance Program (HARP) helps underwater borrowers obtain more favorable mortgage interest rates and terms. As house prices collapsed, the GSEs were guaranteeing millions of mortgages with unpaid principal balances (UPBs) greater than the homes were worth. To stave off more losses, it was good for all parties—GSEs, borrowers, and taxpayers—to create a streamlined way to get underwater borrowers on a better footing. Modified several times, HARP permits participating lenders to offer low-cost refinances to borrowers who remain current on their loans—even if their mortgage is more than 125 percent of the value of their home. Since 2009, HARP has helped over 3.4 million borrowers get better financing.[28] The work done under these programs was commendable, but millions more lost their homes altogether.

Nine years after the housing collapse, the pain continues for Main Street America. Borrowers with the slowest-growing incomes, little or no home equity, and perhaps less awareness of government assistance programs bore the brunt of the crisis and will be the last to recover. As of this writing, some 367,000 underwater borrowers qualify for HARP refinances but have yet to apply; the program closes at the end of 2016.

Another troubling aftershock is that, at the behest of FHFA, the GSEs have begun selling thousands of troubled mortgages to private investors in order to reduce taxpayer risk. Scooping up the delinquent loan pools at bargain prices, the purchasers are supposed to adhere to government guidelines about helping borrowers reinstate their mortgages, if possible. Nonprofit housing groups participate in these sales to help stabilize communities but are often out-bid by investment firms and hedge funds. Fearing that hedge funds are more likely to foreclose on seriously delinquent borrowers, some are urging the GSEs to give preferential treatment to the nonprofits in the sales. GOP lawmakers overseeing the GSEs strongly oppose this move, citing the conservator's bounden duty to maximize loss recoveries given "the almost $200 billion in taxpayer expenditures needed to prevent the collapse of the GSEs."[29]

While borrowers and communities continue to struggle, banks and other financial firms have seen the quickest recovery. Thanks to massive government bailouts, higher consumer fees, employee layoffs, and the sale of capital-intensive mortgage assets, the largest firms appear to have put the worst behind them, financially speaking. Many banks continue to suffer from damaged reputations, particularly as they appeared to hoard their bailout funds rather than lend them out and rewarded themselves with large salaries and bonuses once again. Even the insurance company AIG is out of hock, having repaid its massive $182 billion government loan.[30] Only the GSEs remain stuck in the events of 2008, and their future is anything but certain.

Who Gets the Spoils?

From 2008 to 2012, the GSEs borrowed a total of $187.5 billion from taxpayers to cover a torrent of mortgage-related losses.[31] For a number of quarters, the GSEs hemorrhaged so much money that they had to borrow money from the Treasury just to pay the Treasury its required 10 percent dividend. To stop that insanity, in August 2012 the Treasury amended its bailout contract with the GSEs, known as the Preferred Stock Purchase Agreements (PSPA), to eliminate the 10 percent dividend. The so-called Third Amendment did not lower it—but increased it.

The move to capture all GSE profits essentially completed the nationalization process begun in 2008. The GSEs, for all practical concerns, today are as governmental as the Department of Agriculture, except that their massive mortgage liabilities remain off the government balance sheet—lest the firms tip the entire US budget deeper into the fiscal ocean.

After the first few turbulent years, the GSEs seemed to turn a corner. With the worst of the foreclosure wave behind them and safe, profitable mortgages going on the books, the GSEs reported several years of record-breaking profits. Many breathed a sigh of relief: problem solved. But it wasn't. The large profits were driven by large nonrecurring adjustments, such as reductions in loan loss reserves, reclaimed tax assets, which became essentially worthless during the crisis, and legal settlements paid by banks that sold the GSEs noncompliant high-risk mortgages. Once those adjustments worked through their balance sheets, GSE profits sank, particularly for Freddie Mac. From 2013 to 2014, Freddie Mac's net income fell from $48.7 billion to just $7.7 billion, and it's been a bumpy ride since. Following a net loss of $475 million in the third quarter of 2015, Freddie Mac posted a still lower $6.4 billion in net income for 2015.[32] In the first quarter of 2016, it reported a net loss of $354 million, which sent housing bloggers into a tizzy.[33]

Many blame Treasury's net worth sweep (NWS) for current GSE instability. As reported by FHFA in its *2015 Annual Report to Congress*, "Freddie Mac reported positive net worth of $2.9 billion at the end of 2015, $1.7 billion of which represented a dividend obligation to the US Department of the Treasury that was paid on March 31, 2016."[34] Fannie Mae paid $2.9 billion.[35] All in, as of the end of 2015, the two firms have paid $241.3 billion in dividends on the senior preferred stock, but this amount does not reduce the outstanding $187.5 billion in funds already drawn.[36]

The NWS also has come under tremendous legal pressure. At issue is whether the government overstepped its authority by placing the GSEs in conservatorship in 2008—and who will control their profits in the future. As described in Bethany McLean's second book on the financial crisis, *Shaky Ground: The Strange Saga of the US Mortgage Giants*, the lawsuits pit the government against deep-pocketed hedge funds hungry for a killing—to the tune of $90 billion.[37]

The crux of the issue rests on the government's motive behind its controversial take-over moves. According to FHFA, the government's stated rationale for taking excess profits was to ensure investors remained confident in GSE solvency—and to ensure that "all the Enterprises' earnings are used to benefit taxpayers."[38] But is there more? Ascribing darker motives, McLean suggests that Treasury had to squash the GSE return to profitability "because no one wanted to read headlines about hedge funds making fortunes." Another theory is that government has come to enjoy the sizeable contribution of GSE profits to deficit reduction, while others think letting the GSEs return to profitability would make congressional reform efforts that much more impossible. As McLean wryly notes: "One might expect that Republicans would be upset about the government nationalizing an industry, confiscating its profits, and using the money to help a Democratic administration improve its budget deficit. But this is not the case, because hatred of Fannie and Fannie seems to trump all else."[39]

In April 2016, a judge presiding over shareholder litigation unsealed a handful of government documents showing that, in summer 2012, the GSEs were not in a "death spiral" as government lawyers had argued—nor was that possibility on the horizon. Instead the documents reveal that in the days leading up to the NWS announcement, government officials had been apprised by Fannie Mae management that the outlook was bright; because of profitable new business and tax adjustments, the GSEs were entering an eight-year period of "golden earnings." Other documents suggest that the government's ultimate motive was not so much financial stability but to keep the GSEs from recapitalizing themselves. On the day before the government changed the bailout terms, Jim Parrott, then White House economic advisor and now with the Urban Institute, sent an e-mail that said as much: "We've closed off the possibility that they every [sic] go (pretend) private again."[40]

But the spoils may be slim going forward. At this writing, some have raised the specter of a fresh cycle of GSE bailouts.[41] According to FHFA's *2015 Annual Report to Congress*, the GSE "Capital Reserve Amount" was set at $3.0 billion in 2013 with mandated declines of $600 million each subsequent year. Accordingly, the capital reserve will be $1.2 billion for 2016 and decline to zero by January 1, 2018.[42] That's right: zero.

In February 2016, FHFA director Mel Watt gravely warned that the scheduled depletion of GSE capital buffers demanded congressional action. "An eight-year conservatorship is unprecedented, and managing the ongoing, protracted conservatorships of Fannie Mae and Freddie Mac poses a number of unique challenges and risks," he said. "I can assure you that these challenges are certainly not going away, and some of them are almost certain to escalate the longer the Enterprises remain in conservatorship."[43]

Watt succeeded in getting his point across. The increasingly dire situation has riled both political parties. The National Taxpayers Union and other conservative groups rallied behind legislation introduced in May 2016 that would require FHFA to overrule the NWS by directing the GSEs to keep their earnings until they have replenished their capital, also blocking any affordable housing commitments until then.[44] In June 2016, 32 House Democrats wrote to the FHFA and Treasury chiefs, arguing that the NWS runs counter to the dictates of 2008 GSE reform legislation, which requires the entities to be allowed to return to capital adequacy. Predictably, their arguments emphasize the importance of GSE solvency to keep liquidity flowing to underserved borrowers, particularly minority housing consumers.[45] Small banks and consumer groups support this approach, known as "recapitalization and release," creating an unlikely pairing with the hedge funds (yes, really). From this point of view, despite their warts, the GSEs looked after small banks, developed innovative programs, did good things for affordable housing, and stupidly got hoodwinked by the Wall Street banks who sold them terrible loans. Let them get back to work.

But that's not the view of the nation's largest banks. In contrast to the litigating hedge funds—the nouveau GSE shareholders ready to profit from a GSE rebound—the banks and their powerful trade group, the Mortgage Bankers Association (MBA), support reform models where the GSEs are eliminated and replaced by a new insuring entity. Under that approach, the job of financing the $5.7 trillion mortgage market would fall to institutions now known as "too big to fail." According to Gretchen Morgenson, author of *Reckless Endangerment*, who since has looked deeply into the revolving-door efforts of the MBA to influence the debate, the Obama administration and leading reformers in Congress have tacitly embraced this "bank centric model."[46] Unlike the "recap and release" crowd, the MBA opposes knee-jerk reactions to fears of depleted GSE capital, arguing that the firms still have access to remaining bailout funds, if needed. Better for Congress to do the hard work and fix the badly tattered system, they claim.[47]

These contentious fault lines are the grown-up versions of the ones we dealt with every day at Freddie Mac a decade ago. The only new stakeholder—and a very large one at that—is the US taxpayer, who now owns the GSEs and is on the hook for all their future losses. This book is written for you.

Illusion: Search for a Single Scapegoat

Since 2008, over a dozen books about the financial crisis include references to the role of Fannie Mae and Freddie Mac. Written primarily by journalists, these accounts paint a uniformly negative picture of the two GSEs. They overstated their case.

While the journalists were looking for headline-grabbing, silver bullet explanations, the FCIC took a more equivocal view. Among its many findings (and many pages), the commission concluded that the GSEs "contributed to the crisis but were not a primary cause." Rather, the government commission laid the lion's share of the blame at the feet of the shadow banking system that had come to operate outside of the rules, patchwork-y and inadequate as they were. This assessment comports with the widely held view, among political liberals anyway, that it was unregulated Wall Street firms—not the GSEs—who were at the epicenter of the crisis. Most housing economists, and certainly the rank and file of the housing lobby, readily subscribe to this interpretation of events. As evidence, they point to the fact that mortgages purchased by the GSEs in the years leading up to the crisis have performed significantly better than mortgages originated for private-label securities.[48]

There is truth to this. But there is another side of the story.

Several members of the commission dissented strongly from the majority view that financial deregulation was the primary culprit. In the back pages of the FCIC report, Commissioner Peter Wallison of the American Enterprise Institute (AEI) laid the blame squarely on Freddie Mac and Fannie Mae. Since the GSEs were created by a stroke of government social engineering and had to meet strenuous affordable housing goals, Wallison forcefully asserts that the "sine qua non of the financial crisis was government housing policy."[49]

Wallison's point is strengthened by the murky, government-like nature of the GSEs. The uniquely chartered entities existed in a netherworld where it was unclear to anyone outside the proverbial Washington, DC, beltway whether the GSEs were government agencies or private corporations—or both. This confusion led to the highly profitable notion (for the GSEs, anyway) known as the implicit guarantee, which meant that the GSEs could borrow money from investors around the world at rates almost as low as those enjoyed by the US Treasury itself. The implicit guarantee was not based on the GSEs' extraordinary level of capital, or stunning regulatory oversight, or crack management. Rather, it existed despite the lack of all those things. Low GSE borrowing costs resulted from the shrewd assessment on the part of global creditors that, despite all protestations to the contrary, the US government would come to the aid of the GSEs rather than let them collapse. Of course, no one knew, for sure, if this would be proven true. But in September 2008, Treasury Secretary Paulson made it true.

Important policy ramifications flow from the different explanations of what or who caused the financial crisis, and why. Democrats tend to draw a direct line from the deregulation that began under President Reagan to the Wall Street firms that pushed bad mortgages to unsuspecting borrowers and sold complex mortgage-related instruments to unsuspecting global investors. Their policy prescription, it follows, is a clamp-down on banks in terms of greater oversight and accountability, enhanced investment disclosures, and the institution of consumer protections, including greater legal recourse. In short, more regulation.

Many of these changes are well underway. In 2010, Congress passed the Dodd-Frank Wall Street and Consumer Protection Act (DFA), the most mammoth reconstruction of the US financial services system since the Great Depression. The hundreds of regulations spawned by the watershed legislation took years to develop, promulgate, and implement. Some have yet to go into effect. At this juncture, the full impact on mortgage lending of these complex and interactive regulations is still unknown.

On the other side of the aisle, Republicans generally despise the DFA and have vowed to rescind it if they ever reclaim the White House. They tend to agree with Wallison that government intrusion into the housing market distorted market incentives, creating a government-sanctioned erosion of underwriting standards and subsequent bubble as mortgages went for a song and house prices soared. House Financial Services Committee (HFSC) Chairman Jeb Hensarling (R-TX) and Senate Banking Committee (SBC) Chairman Richard Shelby (R-AL) have bitterly blamed the Democrats for shielding the GSEs from strong reform in the years leading up to the crisis. These reforms, they allege, would have raised GSE capital levels and required the GSEs to dismantle their astonishingly large on–balance sheet mortgage portfolios.

Led by retired Representative Barney Frank (D-MA), Democrats largely opposed these reforms (along with the GSEs, of course) as unnecessary and even harmful; a common concern was that shrinking the companies would effectively dampen homeownership opportunities for lower-income and minority communities. As has been often quoted, in 2003, Frank responded to then-Treasury Secretary John Snow that "The more people, in my judgment, exaggerate a threat of safety and soundness, the more people conjure up the possibility of serious financial losses to the Treasury, which I do not see . . . then the less I think we see in terms of affordable housing."[50]

As we will see later, Frank did support bipartisan reform legislation, working in 2005 with the HFSC chair, Rep. Michael Oxley (R-OH), and sponsoring his own reform bill in 2007.[51] But since that legislation ducked the issue of systemic risk and contagion should the GSEs ever fail, it failed to garner GOP support. A bipartisan solution was elusive then—and still is, unfortunately.

Given these largely irreconcilable viewpoints, it is no wonder that congressional hearings designed to sift through difficult and complex restructuring choices invariably end up in shouting matches, where Republicans blame Democrats and Democrats blame Republicans for their role in the crisis. It has become a national sport to blame the GSEs.

The truth is somewhere in between these two views. Government indicia and intervention (at times well intended and at times not) did complicate, incent, and reward some of the worst behavior on the part of the GSEs. But it is equally true that had fly-by-night brokers been regulated and Wall Street firms been prevented from jumping headlong into the riskiest mortgages, Freddie Mac, at least, would have been far less inclined to abandon tried and true mortgage underwriting standards in the name of market share. Hence, both sides of the aisle have something important to contribute to our understanding of how things got so badly out of control—and how to see our way forward.

Former Freddie Mac economist Arnold Kling chalks things up to more prosaic concerns. Rather than viewing the GSEs as "delinquent teenagers" playing with matches, Kling suggests the companies' fateful decisions reflected a lack of knowledge, or foresight, complicated by competing views of risk and mission. And they were not alone. Very few individuals, firms, or even policy makers perceived—or were prepared to admit—the dangers of the growing national house-price bubble. Nearly everyone was basing decisions on false propositions.[52]

Reality: Three-Dimensional Chess

While it is natural to seek a simple scapegoat—and the GSEs are a huge and easy target—most people realize that the US financial system is broader, deeper, and more complicated than that. The GSEs and broader housing market comprise a highly complex and interrelated system crisscrossed by very serious political and ideological fault lines. The refusal to acknowledge, at a minimum, or preferably to seek to reconcile these fault lines, spelled the doom of the entire system.

These rifts were keenly felt at Freddie Mac. Nearly every major business decision required managing competing politics and players, reconciling jarring differences in public policies, and bridging deep ideological divides between supporter and naysayer, friend and foe. In the years leading up to the crisis, managing the company was a constant game of three-dimensional chess.

Politics and Players

From the vantage point of one who worked at Freddie Mac on both the political and risk management sides of the company, the fact is, both political parties had vested interests in GSE success, and both parties benefitted from GSE profiteering and politicking. However, their divergent views—and pressures—regularly created angst for top management. How to please a powerful representative who wanted the firm to invest in higher-risk apartment buildings? Or a senator who wanted Freddie Mac to hold more capital?

The massive housing lobby—an extremely well-financed group of builders, real estate agents, brokers, bankers, and appraisers, to name a few players—also owns a piece of this sad story. Like remoras, they rode the back of the GSEs, hungrily supporting anything that grew the industry, their businesses, and American homeownership. Since most industry participants were paid on a percentage basis, the larger the mortgage a borrower took out, the more money the players made.

Not that everybody played well together. There were all sorts of spats in the housing family: between banks and the real estate lobby, between mortgage insurers and the GSEs, and between the GSEs and the nation's largest banks. But everyone sought to appease the Democrats on the House Financial Services committee because they kept the whole thing going, and growing. It was simply impossible to please those Republicans who would not be satisfied with any solution short of GSE privatization.

Many have pointed fingers at the phalanx of drowsy, nonexistent, overlapping, and co-opted regulators. Former Federal Reserve Chair Alan Greenspan, the nation's most important financial regulator, failed to use regulatory authority dating from 1994 to govern subprime mortgages and protect consumers. Others point to federal preemption of tough state laws against predatory lending as contributing to the astonishing growth in subprime lending. The Office of Thrift Supervision was essentially shut down for being so inept. Freddie Mac's own regulator at the time, the Office of Federal Housing Enterprise Oversight (OFHEO), constantly sought additional legislative authority over the GSEs while failing to use the authority it already had to oversee and limit the types of mortgages the company insured. From the perspective of many employees, OFHEO was still checking compliance reports dating back to 2003 when the company blew up in 2008.

As the saying goes, while their regulator was straining a gnat, the GSEs swallowed camels.

Housing Consumers

On the other hand, well-intentioned (but sometime militantly self-righteous) consumer groups pushed hard for greater homeownership equality while turning a blind eye when the low-documentation, nontraditional mortgages hit the market. Many types of people took out these loans for myriad reasons, and not everyone over-extended themselves. But these mortgages held special appeal to key constituent groups, many of whom operated in the cash economy and lacked the traditional documentation required for a mortgage, such as tax returns and a social security number. Adding to the lackluster, late-to-the-party response of regulators, the lack of unified opposition to nontraditional mortgages on the part of the consumer and minority groups hindered companies like mine from taking a strong stance against those products.

Although it is extremely unpopular to mention personal responsibility these days, it is hard to excuse the homeowners who got caught up in the housing frenzy, whether by willful intent to defraud or by their passivity or ignorance in the face of considerable risk. It is patently wrong to blame every mortgage default on a bad or predatory lender. Or on Wall Street, for that matter. Or on the GSEs.

But by the same token, key individuals in the top ranks of the nation's largest financial institutions did make some very bad choices. Were their actions illegal, or simply unethical, or stupid? What about the midlevel employees of financial firms, people like me who watched the whole bad movie in slow motion? Very few spoke up. Was everyone blind or duped? Or afraid?

Tangled Policy Jungle

Another layer on the high-stakes GSE chess board was the slate of competing policy and business agendas. The most obvious of these required satisfying the housing mission contained in the GSE congressional charter without jeopardizing the financial safety of the firm, or, I might add, shareholder interest in profitable growth.

As long as the GSEs could operate as a government-sanctioned duopoly with little direct competition, and as long as they made lots of money, it was possible to solve these dilemmas and keep the varied constituent groups happy to some degree. For many years, Freddie Mac employees felt proud to work for a company that did well while doing good. But once things got tight and GSEs lost market share to Wall Street firms, Freddie Mac's ability to triangulate the competing business and policy objectives greatly diminished.

A lot of this had to do with the unusual GSE business model, designed by Congress, which required the GSEs to remain in one slice of the residential housing market. If a firm can only do one thing—forever and ever—but is expected by shareholders to grow and make lots of money, the playing field will be over-plowed, if not destroyed.

At a broader level, bad structures almost always lead to bad outcomes, particularly when there is some underlying dishonesty. The fact that GSE activities were off budget, notwithstanding an implicit government guarantee, tainted the whole system from the get-go. Given this weak foundation, it is unsurprising that a web of complex structures, unusual freedoms, daring political escapades, and moral lapses would eventually emerge.

Competing Ideologies

Taking another stab at the causes of the crisis, a layer of ideologies and philosophies lies beneath the surface of each policy debate about housing.

In calling for greater fairness and access to mortgage markets via strenuous housing goals and relaxed underwriting standards, the Democrats and consumer groups embraced a normative preference for fairness and equal opportunity, important national ideals. On the other hand, Republican calls for downsizing or even privatizing the GSEs belie a preference for free, competitive markets and a limited government role—other important ideals.

The tug between freedom and equality is quintessentially American. That conflict was, at core, the GSE conflict. The GSE leaders, Syron and Mudd, operated at the fateful intersection of these two opposing ideologies. Their inability to manage this great schism, to bridge this enormous ideological fault line, in my mind, contributed to the undoing of both firms.

While the GSE leaders clearly should have done things differently, certain political appeasements would have helped them steer clear of the more dangerous shoals. The GSEs needed Congress to provide bipartisan support for the GSE housing mission while upholding traditional strong underwriting standards. Instead of taking a balanced approach, the political parties moved to the edges like two boats widening. The GSEs tried unsuccessfully to straddle both norms—and fell in the drink. The divided Congress became the GSE divide, and management struggled to balance these two important (and sometimes competing) objectives.

The GSEs also needed a single regulator, rather than one devoted to mission and another focused on safety and soundness. Prior to 2008 GSE reform legislation, the US Department of Housing and Urban Development (HUD) oversaw GSE goal performance, while OFHEO oversaw capital adequacy and other indicators of financial strength. A single regulator could have tempered the overly creative measures the GSEs took to reconcile the ideological divide to meet the ever-rising affordable housing goals. A single regulator could have ensured an integrated GSE role and reduced opportunity for regulatory capture. (Even as I write this, I wonder if the GSEs had lobbied for a divided regulator in order to weaken it. This wouldn't surprise me.)

Finally, the GSEs needed a plausible exit strategy. Certainly there was a time when Freddie Mac might have been open to privatization, as long as it wasn't being shoved down the company's throat. A bipartisan Congress could have put forth a phased privatization plan that did not rip the carpet out from under existing shareholders. And much suffering could have been avoided.

But Congress didn't do any of these things. The deep political and philosophical divide over housing created opportunities for the GSEs—and others in the industry—to play different political cards, thus ensuring that reform efforts were stymied. A divided Congress is dangerous to the national interest.

Taken together, the politics, policies, and philosophies embedded in US housing policy complicate the search for a single scapegoat. While GSEs certainly made bad choices, as this book will show, they did not single-handedly bring down the housing finance system, nor will simply changing the structure of the GSEs fix the deep rifts in US housing markets going forward.

Philosophical differences over fairness and free markets spawn a whole other set of questions that we have yet to address, let alone answer. How much homeownership should we support as a nation? Should homeowners be able to borrow money more cheaply than the nation's healthiest corporations? To what extent should we craft a safe housing finance system at the expense of limiting access to homeownership for first-time homebuyers or higher-risk borrowers? How should we deal with the fundamental racial disparity in wealth and income that inevitably results in homeownership disparities?

Interest groups and lobbyists still prey on the different ideologies, making compromise and forward movement nearly impossible. This state of affairs is compounded by the fact that Americans haven't begun to acknowledge our addiction to homeownership, or the ethical lapses of our institutions or of ourselves.

Conclusion

Despite unprecedented government action and financial support, the US housing market remains at risk. The GSEs appear to be stable for the time being, but they are treading water in dangerous ideological currents. Their capital is depleting steadily while lawsuits are waged over their heads that cast fresh doubt on government intervention. New mortgage regulations will help maintain decent underwriting standards, although key regulations already have been watered down significantly. Both Democrats and Republicans recognize the looming dangers of depleted GSE capital. Will it take another crisis to bring the sides together to stabilize the US housing market? Will the next generation of financial leaders find the temperance and moral courage to resist short-term gains at the expense of sustainable returns? Will political leaders work to unify their views in support of the nation's homeowners and the institutions that serve them?

These are the questions I raise in this book. While I don't purport to have all the answers, we are fooling ourselves if we don't even try to come to grips with these questions. The mortgage delivery system that is gradually coming into focus shockingly resembles the system that threw the world into economic chaos only a few years ago, and that's frightening.

Speaking to a group of investors in March 2015, Michael Stegman, counselor to the Treasury secretary for housing finance policy, said: "The status quo is unsustainable. Taxpayers remain at risk . . . Let's be prudent; let's have foresight; let's find a bipartisan pathway to preventing another GSE bailout, which continuation of the status quo guarantees. We can do this, and we must do this."[53]

CHAPTER 2

HOMEOWNERSHIP: DREAM OR NIGHTMARE?

In 2007, Joseph and Suzanne moved from Nashville, Tennessee, to Washington, DC, for a job change. House prices were beginning to soften in the South but were still strong in the nation's capital. When their home in Tennessee wouldn't sell, the couple faced an all-too-common dilemma: how to finance a modest home in a decent school district in a high-cost area, while continuing to pay the mortgage on an empty home hundreds of miles away. Their solution was a new-fangled mortgage that allowed them to pay only the interest on the new loan at a somewhat higher interest rate. Then they crossed their fingers and waited for a buyer of their former home. After nearly two years of juggling a double debt load, with no buyer in sight, things got pretty dire. Eventually the Tennessee house sold (albeit at a loss) and the family was able to right itself financially. But it was close.

An Ivy-League-trained professor, Alison bought her first home in Charlottesville, Virginia, at the height of the housing boom. Her predominately minority neighborhood was within walking distance of campus, and townhomes were comparatively affordable. She got a low-down-payment mortgage, which seemed to be a great deal at the time. But by 2008 the property lost value, and the mortgage quickly slid underwater. After several difficult years, house prices began to recover. Only through the government's flagship mortgage refinancing program—and the slimmest of positive equity positions—was she able to refinance. Her employment contract with the university ended, and she took a job out of state. The townhome remains vacant. The pipes burst last winter, creating unexpected expenses. And she still hasn't been able to sell it. She wishes she had never become a home-owner.

An immigrant from South America and talented optician, Eleanor talked about her mortgage woes while fitting me for glasses. With little money down, she had bought a condominium in an overbuilt suburb of Washington, DC. In 2009, she lamented that her mortgage was vastly underwater and asked why Freddie Mac, who "owned her loan," couldn't simply "write down" the loan amount? I explained that it was not that simple—that her monthly payment was owed to some investor halfway around the world. I didn't have the heart to tell her that her mortgage probably had counted for one of Freddie Mac's strenuous housing goals designed to help people just like her.

Everyone has heard stories like this. Or far worse. Five years into the crisis, I recall a sad newspaper article with a photo of a child playing in a crib while a local sheriff prepared the home for a foreclosure sale.

But here's another perspective. Don and Bethany and their four sons have lived in a small town in Connecticut for 15 years. Years ago they purchased a modest home and made improvements as the family grew. The economic downturn reduced sales opportunities for Don, and he eventually found himself out of work. Buoyed by their characteristically strong Yankee work ethic, they struggled to make ends meet, commuting to another state to find employment. It makes them angry to think of the government assisting people who made poor choices with their money and now want a bailout. What about the people who borrowed conservatively and have always played by the rules?

While joined by a single thread—the negative impact of the 30 percent decline in national house prices—these stories demonstrate the vast differences in perspectives about what caused the financial crisis and how to make sure it doesn't happen again. Although national nerves remain raw, it is vitally important that we examine our inordinate love for homeownership.

American Castles

The adage "home sweet home" is embroidered on pillows because it is deeply ingrained in the national psyche. In designing one of the greatest

American homes, Monticello, Thomas Jefferson sought refuge away from the "great cities," which he viewed as "pestilential to the morals, the health, and the liberties of man." One of the most famous lines to ever come out of Hollywood was on the lips of Judy Garland, who played Dorothy in *The Wizard of Oz*: "There's no place like home." American poet Maya Angelou wrote, "The ache for home lives in all of us, the safe place where we can go as we are and not be questioned."[1]

For much of US history, homeownership has been synonymous with the frontier and boot straps, freedom and autonomy, and securing a future for our children. In *Gone with the Wind*, Gerald O'Hara chides his daughter for not valuing Tara, the family homestead. "Do you mean to tell me, Katie Scarlett O'Hara, that Tara, that land, doesn't mean anything to you? Why, land is the only thing in the world worth workin' for, worth fightin' for, worth dyin' for, because it's the only thing that lasts." In the aftermath of the Civil War, Scarlett raises a clod of soil to heaven and makes a vow that she will never be hungry again.[2]

Notwithstanding fortunes earned during the so-called Gilded Age of the late 1800s, which gave rise to some spectacular urban homes, most people inhabited more humble dwellings. Many people were born, were raised, and died in the same house. By the turn of the century, millions of immigrants had found their way into US cities and crowded into tenement housing, often at their peril. That's when Topeka minister Charles Sheldon used the problems of substandard housing to ignite a brush fire of progressive reform in his runaway bestseller, *In His Steps* (1896). The book opens when an unemployed tramp, whose wife had recently died in a New York City tenement "gasping for air," ignites the moral imagination of small town churchgoers and propels them into social action.[3]

In the 1920s, rising property values led to the increasing use of mortgage debt to secure property. In the absence of a national mortgage market, many mortgages had one- to three-year terms and were due in full. Because the loans could only be used to finance up to 50 percent of a home's value, borrowers had to assemble several short-term mortgages with increasing interest rates. When real estate values plummeted in 1929, the layers of mortgage debt collapsed, causing foreclosures to rise dramatically.[4]

Resurrecting the housing market by providing a stable source of mortgage money was a key objective of many New Deal reforms, including the creation of the Federal Housing Administration (FHA) in 1934. FHA was particularly novel because it was the first entity to provide long-term mortgages with a federal backing. The loans had to be safe, though. The new FHA mortgages required a 20 percent down payment; that may seem high by today's standards, but it was a lot better than the traditional 50 percent equity stake. Subsequent legislation eased FHA down-payment levels and other mortgage terms, transforming the program over time into a low-down-payment program geared primarily for first-time home-buyers.[5]

In addition to providing insurance to back long-term mortgages, the government also set up a mechanism to insure private deposits so that financial institutions, particularly savings and loans, could attract funds for housing. Such was the impetus for the creation of another New Deal agency, the Federal Savings and Loan Insurance Corporation. Together the new institutions paved the way for a national mortgage market. Within six years, FHA sponsored a "Town of Tomorrow" exhibit at the World's Fair in New York in 1940. Resembling a tiny green Monopoly house, the $2,500 home was emblematic of the types of homes built en masse in newly created subdivisions springing up around the country.[6]

Homebuilding dropped precipitously during World War II as resources were directed to the war effort. As the war wound down, returning veterans often could not find suitable homes in which to live. In 1944, a mortgage program for veterans was created under what was then the Veteran's Administration. The Home Loan Guaranty Program went a step further than the FHA's government mortgage insurance. The VA would provide a "full faith and credit" guarantee on a veteran's mortgage, essentially turning the benefit into an entitlement program. Moreover, the VA program did not require a down payment at all, one of the first instances of direct government subsidies for housing.

In the latter part of the twentieth century, homeownership took on added dimensions. Owning a home was now not just about shelter; homes became first nest eggs and then trophies. The ability to finance a home with debt allowed a borrower to leverage a relatively small down payment to purchase a comparatively large asset. Long-term, fully amortizing mortgages allow families to incrementally pay off the debt over 30 years. The process of wealth-building through amortization takes a long time, however. These days, few people actually keep their homes for 30 years. When the economy is healthy, they may trade up for a bigger home or refinance to obtain better mortgage terms; the ease of these transactions has reduced the average life of a mortgage to between four and seven years.

The demise of high-flying technology stocks during the late 1990s soured many people's view of the stock market. By comparison, real estate was poised for growth, and investors poured in. When house prices began to take off, as they did from 2004 to 2007, many first-time homebuyers entered the market, while others rushed to trade up or buy multiple homes. At Freddie Mac, there were reports of individual borrowers having six to eight mortgages at a time.

Around this time Americans began to think of our homes not simply as places to live but also as investment vehicles. According to Yale's Robert Schiller, father of the Case-Shiller home price index, this is not always wise. Taking a very long view, and considering all the costs of maintaining a home, real returns to homeownership have been slim to nothing. Adjusting for inflation, from 1890 to 1990 home prices have experienced zero appreciation. It was only in the past few decades that housing demand took off—and prices with them. According to Shiller, just because house prices are starting to recover does not mean they will reach the levels they achieved in 2006.[7]

Of course, homeownership is also synonymous with a sense of making it, of display, and of keeping up with the Joneses. Average square footage peaked at around 2,500 in 2008, more than double the size of the average home in the 1950s.[8] Reality TV shows feed our lust for ownership, self-determination, and autonomy, not to mention the latest features and gadgets. Whereas earlier generations lived in one, perhaps two, homes in their adult lifetime, today homebuyers trade in their homes for better ones (or ones in different locations) far more frequently. On the other hand, millennials are reportedly delaying homeownership, possibly due to weak job prospects or stifling student-loan debts. Or is it because they simply don't want to join the ranks of the snow-shoveling, grass-cutting, DIYing, keeping-up-with-the-Joneses crowd?

During the run-up to the crash, the meaning of homeownership changed once again. A home became an ATM not only for long-term investments but for short-term purchases as well. As house prices rose, the home equity that used to be saved for retirement could suddenly be extracted via a cash-out refinance. Many people took advantage of this option, converting housing equity into college education, cars, and vacations. One of the saddest examples of predatory lending involved a man who agreed to refinance his house so he could purchase frozen meats from a travelling salesman. He was one of millions who lost their homes.

Since the crisis, it is not surprising that many are thinking twice about becoming homeowners—or about how much house they really need. The financial crisis revealed a sad truth: Many Americans did not really own much of their homes at all. Suddenly the tables were turned, and their homes owned them.

Do the Math

Mystique aside, homeownership is a serious financial undertaking. Consumers need to squint hard at the numbers to avoid getting in over their heads. A mortgage is a promise to repay, pure and simple, even if the home serving as collateral for the loan declines in value. Millions of underwater homeowners have wanted lenders to reduce their principal payments, but precious little principal has been forgiven. It is generally not a forgiving system. Not if you want investors to provide the money so consumers can get the homes they want or expect. Would you lend hundreds of thousands of dollars to a complete stranger—and then say don't worry about it?

The first illusion to dispel is the romantic idea of what constitutes ownership. Lawyers and economists define ownership in terms of rights; when you buy a home, you are buying a bundle of rights to do with your property as you please, subject to superior rights such as local zoning laws, tax liabilities and liens, covenants, and so on. These technicalities are lost on most of us, who simply want to take possession of brick and mortar, regardless of how little money we actually had to part with to purchase it. For example, if a borrower makes a down payment of 5 percent at origination, the bank owns 95 percent of the home. That's an indisputable fact, not to mention a pretty lopsided arrangement. We think that we are the proud owners of our own home, our castle. The truth is that we own the front door and a few feet inside—plus the right to do just about whatever we want with it. The rest of the house belongs to a bank, or, in many cases, a pension fund or foreign investor halfway around the world. Remembering these things when we are being driven around by a rapturous real estate agent would serve us all well.

The second illusion is the dominant view that the more we can borrow, or leverage, the better. That's why many people strive to get the biggest house and mortgage they can possibly afford, assuming the returns will be greater. This is a great strategy for people with deep pockets or a crystal ball that guarantees that house prices will be high when they need to sell the house—and pay off the creditor. Just because a real estate agent or bank lending officer says a particular house is affordable (based on simplistic government regulations and ratios) does not mean it actually is. Only the individual buyer knows if he or she can handle the mortgage payment—and don't forget about taxes and insurance. For most of us, it's not wise to take out the largest possible mortgage if it means committing to a radically lower level of living, with fingers crossed that house prices rise and quickly. The better choice is to pare down our expectations, purchase a smaller home, and start saving for a larger down payment. This is particularly good advice if the property is located in a neighborhood with lower house-price growth than surrounding areas.

The third illusion is a narrow focus on the monthly payment. When financing a home with a mortgage, the main thing consumers want to know is, "What is the monthly payment?" Homebuyers generally care much less about the cost of borrowing the money (the interest rate) or how many years are required to pay it back (up to one-third of the average human life span). We really don't want to know about the total amount of interest we'll be paying over that time.

Refusing to take into account the big, scary numbers is a way of denying the immensity and risk of the undertaking. For example, for a 30-year mortgage with a principal balance of $200,000 and an interest rate of 3.5 percent, a borrower will pay a total of $123,312 in interest over the life of the loan, assuming she keeps the mortgage to maturity. Including the principal owed, the total indebtedness is $323,312. That's a lot of money to pay for a $200,000 home, not to mention another 30 percent in taxes and insurance.

Over the past three decades, mortgage interest rates have been on a downward trajectory, so hardly anyone kept a mortgage for the full 30 years. But with mortgage interest rates at all-time lows, the tendency to stay with the same mortgage for many years will increase. When rates eventually rise, people may be less willing to move or trade up because they would have to borrow money for the new house at a higher interest rate.

Or maybe not. Using the prior example, and only considering the monthly payment, as most borrowers do, raising the interest rate by a full percentage point to 4.5 percent would increase the payment by around $115 a month. This may or may not be a deal breaker for some borrowers. But that full percentage point increase adds $41,512 over the life of the loan, bringing the total to $364,814.

Maybe it doesn't seem like a lot at the individual level. But in the aggregate, numbers like this add up quickly—and hugely.

In fact, the US housing finance system is the world's biggest, topping the scales with $10 trillion in single-family mortgage debt outstanding. How big is that? Quoting from the 2012 report of the Bipartisan Housing Commission, "The size of the US single-family mortgage market exceeds the entire European market and is nearly six times larger than that of the United Kingdom, which is home to the world's second-largest single-family market."[9]

In the years leading to the crisis, subprime mortgages carried very high interest rates. Many borrowers got into trouble with these loans. Shopping around for the best deal and looking at all the mortgage terms—not just the monthly payment—could have meant the difference between having a smaller home then or a foreclosed mortgage today.

If the financial crisis has taught us anything, it is that having a mortgage entails risk. Hopefully, borrowers who are old enough to remember the crisis think differently about their homes and debts. The place to begin is realizing that homeownership is a legally binding arrangement with a creditor who holds more cards than you do.

Transaction Costs and Profits?

Wherever there is a strong consumer demand, supply will rise to meet it. Along with a strong homebuilding industry, where breaking ground on less than a million new homes each year is cause for serious teeth-gnashing, there is a whole other set of characters catering to housing consumers. As anyone who has bought a home knows, the players' bench is wide and deep, including real estate brokers, loan officers, appraisers, title insurers, document preparers, and mortgage insurers. Everyone is ultimately paid by the homebuyer in the form of a fee, a higher mortgage rate, or a higher house price.

The regular churning of mortgages produces a lot of money in transaction costs for the mortgage industry. Every time a loan is refinanced and a new one is originated, most of the players on the bench get to play again (and get paid again). Of course, transaction costs reduce whatever savings the borrower gains through refinancing to a lower rate loan. Moreover, most borrowers refinancing their homes follow their broker's easy talk and roll the transaction costs into their loan amount, driving up their indebtedness even more.

And that's just the beginning. Money spent on maintaining and repairing a home can be considerable. The independence of homeownership is great until the furnace fails and you are your own landlord.

The big hoped-for payoff comes, of course, when a home is sold at profit. In the past, this was all but guaranteed to happen because the home had been purchased decades before, and often neighborhoods (and the homes within) had improved with age. But in the go-go days preceding the crash, a huge number of new homes were built and sold that were not quality construction or didn't have a lot of time to appreciate in value. Overbuilding was particularly acute in Florida, California, and the southwestern states. The spike in home prices was quickly followed by a steep and painful decline.

Benefits of Homeownership

Notwithstanding the uncertainty of monetary gain, there are a number of nonfinancial benefits of homeownership, such as safety and a desire for a good neighborhood and schools. Homeownership also is seen as a means of forced savings, whereby families can tap equity for future needs, such as starting a business or sending kids to college. These factors are very important (and personal) and are often cited by politicians as adequate justification for maintaining the existing pro-homeownership system.

Nearly synonymous with democracy and freedom, homeownership has easily crossed the political aisles. In the wake of the 1929 stock market crash, Republican President Herbert Hoover said, "A family that owns its own home takes pride in it and has a more wholesome, beautiful and happy atmosphere in which to bring up children." His Democratic successor, Franklin D. Roosevelt, echoed a similar theme, saying, "A nation of homeowners is unconquerable." In the early 1990s, Jack Kemp, former US Department of Housing and Urban Development (HUD) secretary under President George H. W. Bush, said, "Democracy can't work without the component that goes to the heart of what freedom is all about—the chance to own a piece of property."[10]

In the decade leading up to the financial crisis, there was a lot of research demonstrating the benefits of homeownership, known as positive externalities. These include higher educational attainment (and fewer antisocial outcomes) by children reared in home-owning families.[11] Homeownership also has been correlated with higher civic participation and neighborhood stability, as measured by turnover and stable or rising home values. In this way, homeownership tends to have a conservatizing influence. If the home is one's largest financial asset, then policies to protect and enhance its value will become a top priority. In short, homeowners tend not to rock the boat.

Politically speaking, more homeownership has generally been seen as better than less. Homeowners in stable and rising housing markets spin off a lot of tax revenue for governments; they spend billions in goods and services to furnish and care for their homes; and they tend to require fewer governmental resources, such as fire and police.

As a sizeable share of national economic output, housing also tends to be a big source of jobs. Before the crisis, housing accounted for approximately 5 percent of GDP, or between 17 and 19 percent if housing services are included. According to research by the National Association of Homebuilders, "the construction of a typical 100-unit multifamily development creates 80 jobs directly (through construction) or indirectly (through the supply chain), plus another 42 jobs in a range of local occupations as a result of construction workers spending their wages."[12] Single-family construction and renovation also provide substantial employment, as does the provision of services, such as house maintenance and repair. Following the crisis, housing's contribution has fallen to about 15 percent of GDP, weighing down economic recovery.[13]

Finally, it's worth acknowledging the link between supporting homeownership and getting reelected. Americans are attached to their homes, and homeownership is a huge industry, broadly dispersed across the country. Therefore, maintaining a nation of homeowners and extending the dream to more people—most of whom are also voters—has drawn intense attention from politicians and legislators.

The Blind Side

A homeownership society has its hidden costs, particularly when sprawl happens. These costs include heavy infrastructure investments for roads and other transportation systems, as well as utility lines and more and better schools. There is also a heavy toll on the environment, as private residences account for the bulk of greenhouse gases, and highly treated and irrigated lawns and paved surfaces produce unhealthy runoff into nearby streams and rivers. Although people have to live somewhere, many are giving thought to environmental considerations when they go to buy a home.

Homeownership entails social costs as well. Since the 1950s, the pathologies of homeownership have included racial redlining, segregation, NIMBY-ism, mortgage discrimination, and tax revolt. Cultural observers have documented the architectural changes of our homes that correspond with changing social mores. Front porches, which contributed to a sense of community and safety (if not small-town gossip), were moved to the rear of homes, emblematic of the inward turn of homeowners. Gated communities, largely unheard of in this country until the 1980s, have become increasingly prevalent. Some of the nation's wealthiest homeowners have sought to opt out of the social compact by refusing to pay for police and fire services supporting the entire community. Ironically, the country with some of the most expensive homes (and generous homeownership subsidies) in the world is also plagued by the deep-seated problem of poverty and homelessness.[14]

Another problem with a homeownership society is declined labor mobility. Classical economists tend to bemoan high homeownership rates as a drag on the economy. As in the case of Alison's townhouse, the time it takes to sell one's home (and sometimes it takes a very long time) greatly limits one's ability to pursue new employment opportunities, which, in turn, dampens economic growth. In the words of a British economist, homeownership acts as a gooey "treacle blanket" over the US economy. ("Molasses" would be our word for it.) Preference for single-family homeownership tends to diminish funding for rental housing options, which facilitates labor market flexibility and adaptation.[15]

Former Federal Reserve Chairman Alan Greenspan often testified that the United States had "over-invested" in housing, compared to other more productive sectors of the economy. Many in the housing industry viewed this as absolute heresy. He was referring primarily to all the tax preferences benefiting housing, as well as the enormous implicit subsidies going to the GSEs. Although the housing lobbyists bristled indignantly every time he said it, Greenspan was making an important point. What might the nation look like if we shifted tax preferences to stimulate investments in factories or farms, or even higher education, rather than our homes? As an economic sector, housing is pro-cyclical, which means that it has the propensity to be the first sector to swoon, dragging the rest of the economy into a recession. All the more reason not to overstimulate it.

How Much Should We Spend?

Despite these problems, homeownership remains a highly valued good, which explains the broad political support for tax policies that favor it. According to official US budget documents, the revenue lost to the federal government as a result of combined preferential tax treatment for housing—a budget concept known as a tax expenditure—is estimated to exceed $250 billion in 2016.[16] Over 91 percent of this amount directly subsidizes homeownership, leaving just 9 percent of the nation's total housing tax expenditure for rental housing.[17]

The largest pro-homeownership subsidy is the mortgage interest deduction (MID). The Center for American Progress provides this example of how the MID works to benefit homeowners over renters.

> Consider two families with equal incomes of $100,000. One family owns its house and pays $2,000 in interest on its mortgage each month, or $24,000 annually. The other pays $2,000 a month to rent an apartment. The family that owns its home can deduct $24,000 from its taxable income and pay taxes as if it only earned $76,000. The renter family is taxed on all $100,000 of its income. The homeowners pay about $6,000 less in taxes a year.[18]

Contrary to what the housing cheerleaders want everyone to believe, the MID was not designed to support homeownership; rather, it is an artifact of the nation's tortured history of tax policy. It was not explicitly created; rather, in 1986 it became the sole remaining consumer tax loophole when Congress eliminated the deductibility of all other forms of consumer interest. Largely unchanged since then, the MID permits homeowners to deduct interest on up to $1 million in mortgage debt on a first and second home each year, plus up to $100,000 in home equity debt.[19]

One consequence of eliminating exemptions for other types of consumer debt—auto loans, for example—has been to shift that debt onto our homes, where the interest we pay receives favorable tax treatment. Other things being equal, a borrower in good standing can extract home equity through the use of a cash-out refinance or, in a rising interest rate environment, a home equity line of credit. As house prices begin to recover, some are starting to invoke the concern that our homes are becoming ATMs once again.[20] The exclusive deductibility of mortgage interest contributes greatly to this phenomenon.

Not surprisingly, the MID has become the crown jewel of the housing and mortgage industry, and any attempt to minimize it is fought tooth and nail. It is the quintessential sacred cow. Economists assert that the value of the MID is capitalized—or baked—into home prices, so a complete or sudden removal of the deduction would be painful to say the least. Property values would surely decline in the short run. There is also an entitlement mentality around any loophole that has been around for a hundred years. Often referred to as the tax break of the middle class, the MID has long been considered an important counterweight to tax shelters employed by wealthier individuals who have more of their nest egg in financial assets than in their homes.

On the other hand, a growing array of detractors want to see the MID capped, reduced, or outright eliminated. Aside from the very real budgetary issues involved with the costliness of the subsidy and questions about its efficacy, there is the issue of fairness. Estimated to top $62 billion in 2016, the nation's largest housing subsidy flows only to homeowners—and the wealthiest ones at that. Homeowners also may deduct state and local property taxes ($33 billion) and capital gains on certain home sales ($41 billion).[21] Higher-income homeowners are more likely to itemize on their taxes than lower-income homeowners, which is the key to using the various deductions. Second, wealthier homeowners tend to have a larger mortgage, which means they receive a larger benefit from the deduction, dollar for dollar. Even as a percentage of one's income, the benefit from the MID rises with income for all but the wealthiest homeowners. According to the Center for Tax Policy, "households with cash incomes between $75,000 and $500,000 (27 percent of all tax units) will earn 48 percent of all cash income in 2015 but will receive 77 percent of the tax savings from the mortgage interest deduction."[22] Finally, the capitalization of the MID into house prices makes homeownership that much more expensive for lower-income borrowers. US homeowners tend to see the MID as a God-given right. But that's not how it is viewed abroad.

United States Outspends on Housing

For some time now, the IMF—the international agency that helps arrange emergency financing packages for debt-strapped nations—has been critical of the US housing market, particularly the MID. According to a 2010 report, "The US housing finance system is very complex, expensive, and mostly benefits middle- and high-income households, without raising homeownership rates significantly when compared to other countries."[23] The report is highly critical of the MID, calling it unfair and unnecessary to support a strong US housing market. The report notes that the US homeownership rate is actually lower than in other countries that have simpler and less generous housing subsidies.

Compared to the 17 other countries that make up the Organisation for Economic Cooperation and Development, the United States spends more money on housing but gets less bang for the buck. For example, neither Australia nor Canada has something akin to the MID, yet both countries enjoy higher homeownership rates than we do. The IMF concludes that the MID does less to promote homeownership than to encourage housing consumption and indebtedness. To make a simple comparison, the size of the average Australian mortgage is 40 percent less than the average US mortgage.[24]

Granddaddy of All Subsidies

Perhaps the largest—but least visible—way the US government has supported homeownership is through the use of government-sponsored enterprises to "intermediate" mortgage risk through the financial system. Government support for the GSEs has become very visible since the government takeover of the firms in 2008. What was implicit and "free" has become explicit and costly. The $187 billion in cash infusions far exceeds the large implicit government subsidies estimated over a decade ago.

In 2001, the Congressional Budget Office (CBO) did a study that estimated the present value of government subsidies directed to Freddie Mac and Fannie Mae. It was a very big number—$10.4 billion in 2000. This money was not appropriated by Congress or funded by taxpayers. Rather, it reflected the implied "cost" to taxpayers of the GSEs borrowing money at preferential rates, simply because the rest of the world could not conceive that the US government would not rescue them when push came to shove.[25]

Where did the $10 billion go? The CBO calculated that a large share of the subsidy—$7 billion—was passed along to borrowers in the form of lower mortgage interest rates.[26] The rest? A good bit of the subsidy gravy was clearly locked up in the GSEs themselves, earning the firms the moniker "spongy conduit."

Indeed, the subsidy—evidenced by the level of underpriced borrowing—was seen as the golden goose of GSE stock returns. Testifying before a congressional panel in 2005, Greenspan had this to say about the fabulous GSE profits: "Their annual return on equity, often exceeding 25 percent, is far in excess of the average approximately 15 percent annual returns achievable by other large financial competitors holding substantially similar assets. Virtually none of the GSE excess return reflects higher yields on assets; it is almost wholly attributable to subsidized borrowing costs."[27]

The size of the GSE subsidy—and how much (or how little) they passed along to borrowers and how much of an advantage it gave the GSEs over other firms—would become one of the key points of attacks against the GSEs.[28] Conservatives wanted to privatize the firms to rid the system of the subsidy and all its distortions, while liberals primarily wanted to squeeze the GSEs financially in order to shift the subsidy away from shareholders to affordable housing and other priorities.

Who Gets to Be a Homeowner?

Given the tax preferences and all the other generous subsidies for homeownership, including subsidies flowing in and through two very unique and well-endowed companies, it is no wonder that housing is a key political battleground. The disproportionate flow of US housing subsidies to the relatively well-housed is a flashpoint—as is the disparate rate of homeownership among different racial and ethnic groups. Prior to the crisis, the national homeownership rate peaked at 69.2 in 2004. The rate for non-Hispanic whites averaged around 70 percent, while the rates for African Americans and Hispanics were around or below 50 percent. For the first quarter of 2016, eight years after the crisis, the overall homeownership rate was 63.5 percent, a 48-year low. Rates for non-Hispanic whites, African Americans, and Hispanics were 72, 42, and 45 percent, respectively, suggesting that white homeowners weathered the crisis best, and then some. In terms of income, the homeownership rate for families with incomes at or greater than the median is 78 percent.[29] Clearly, there are disparities.

In the past, researchers looking into issues of disparity generally concluded that much of the gap in homeownership rates was attributable to demographic factors, such as age and income. In other words, some disparity in rates will arise simply because the average age of certain racial or ethnic groups may be lower than others or because their income is lower. On the other hand, not all the differences in homeownership rates can be explained by statistical inference and analysis. Many suspected racial discrimination was the reason for higher denial rates for minority mortgage applicants. Other nondemographic explanations for the lower-than-expected minority homeownership rates could include a lack of financial literacy, language and cultural barriers, and underwriting standards that were geared to mainstream borrowers. Mortgage applicants who were self-employed or reported seasonal income, or those without the standard elements of a strong credit history, were thought to be disadvantaged by the standardized system. To address these concerns, the wheels of mortgage research and public policy began to turn to address the question of unfairness—and the impact of low homeownership rates on wealth disparities between racial and ethnic groups.

As we will see later, concern about the difference in homeownership rates reached a fevered pitch starting around 2000, when mortgage defaults were very low and the outlook for housing was very bright. The thought of a disaster of the magnitude we have just witnessed was the farthest thing from any policy maker's mind. Amid a period of largely stagnant income growth, and following the downturn in the technology stocks, attention turned to the wealth gains from homeownership. But the gains were accruing primarily to white homeowners. Minority families, on the other hand, may have had adequate income to handle monthly mortgage payments but lacked funds for down payments, possibly due to little or no generational wealth transfers. The already skewed distribution of wealth was becoming more unbalanced. Consumer groups took these concerns to lawmakers and found strong support among Democrats for expanding access to homeownership.

With their large free subsidy, the GSEs were a lever policy makers could pull relatively effortlessly. And so they did.

Where Things Stand

An elderly, sick, foreign-born, and very poor woman I know lives in a one-bedroom apartment on the top floor of a three-story apartment building in Arlington, Virginia, a high-cost urban suburb of Washington, DC. She is a lucky holder of a Section 8 rental voucher, and because she struggles to walk up stairs, she is entitled to a unit with a washer and dryer. Under the government's Section 8 program—with its massive waiting list—participating landlords agree to accept greatly subsidized rental payment from tenants, with HUD picking up the remainder. My friend has lived there over a decade.

Recently, as a result of budget cutbacks, she faced eviction because HUD lacked the budgeted funds to pay its share of the annual rental increase of $41 a month. The new subsidized rent is a shocking $1,500 a month. In a last-minute reprieve, the landlord agreed to waive the increase for a year. Such are the hard times in low-income rental housing.

In striking contrast, mortgage money remains near historic lows, and in many areas, houses are still underpriced. The monthly mortgage payment on my comparatively palatial 1964 rancher 10 miles away is only several hundred dollars more than my friend's rent on a one-bedroom walk-up in an aging apartment building. And that's before I deduct the interest from my taxes.

This sort of disparity is crazy and unjust. While economists will shrug and point to issues of supply and demand, claiming that high-end building replenishes the housing stock and eventually trickles down to people of modest means, the fact remains that as a matter of policy we subsidize homeownership far more than we do rental housing, and yet that's where the greater need is.

No wonder homeownership looks comparatively cheap compared to renting—and no wonder consumer advocates and others fight hard to expand homeownership opportunities. That's where the subsidies are.

In her book *The Submerged State: How Invisible Policies Undermine Democracy*, Suzanne Mettler takes on the upwardly redistributive policies like the MID for exacerbating inequality and rewarding those "third-party organizations and businesses that benefit from the economic activities such policies promote."[30] The policies of the submerged state are undemocratic because they undermine citizenship; they hide the true nature of government benefits and costs, which inculcates "passivity and resentment."[31]

In February 2013, the Bipartisan Commission (BPC) for housing released a long-awaited report entitled "Housing America's Future: New Directions for National Policy." The commission was headed by illustrious retired policy makers from both political parties—former senators Christopher S. "Kit" Bond and Mel Martinez, also a former HUD secretary, Henry Cisneros, former HUD secretary, and George J. Mitchell, former Senate majority leader and co-founder of the BPC. The purpose of the commission was to "help set a new direction for federal housing policy." The culmination of 16 months of hard work, including field hearings around the country, the bipartisan effort to "provide a blueprint for an entirely new system of housing" contains a number of thoughtful observations and policy recommendations.[32]

The report's weakness is in its failure to question our fundamental assumptions about homeownership. Rather, the presumption of the distinguished panel is that public policy merely needs to figure out how to return to the large, complex, and high-debt system we had before the crisis with some added safety features. The report contains no serious assessment of how our obsession with homeownership might need to be tempered or our expectations of financial gain reined in. The report also fails to take a hard look at the uneven distribution of government subsidies and the disastrous effects of overindebtedness, particularly for lower-income borrowers.

While creating a new GSE-type structure may be an effective way to attract private capital and minimize government losses going forward, the ground underneath the proposed structures and policies remains rife with unresolved conflict—and difficult tradeoffs that go unaddressed in the report. Without addressing these hard questions, the prescriptions in the BPC report are like building a new house on some rather old and unstable sand.

Conclusion

In 1931, James Truslow Adams coined the phrase "American Dream" in his book *The Epic of America*. The original definition is sweeping:

> The American dream is that dream of a land in which life should be better and richer and fuller for everyone, with opportunity for each according to ability or achievement. It is a difficult dream for the European upper classes to interpret adequately, and too many of us ourselves have grown weary and mistrustful of it. It is not a dream of motor cars and high wages merely, but a dream of social order in which each man and each woman shall be able to attain to the fullest stature of which they are innately capable, and be recognized by others for what they are, regardless of the fortuitous circumstances of birth or position.[33]

Truslow's American Dream is about human flourishing—regardless of class, achievements, or possessions. Somewhere along the way it narrowed considerably to mean not just having a decent home but owning it—or, rather, financing it. And then refinancing it, upgrading it, or trading it for something better. The bigger the debt the better, given the sizeable tax write-off.

The US housing market has suffered a terrible self-inflicted blow that sent severe financial shock waves around the world. While most of the accusations and recriminations have been deflected outward—toward the GSEs, Wall Street, and regulators—mortgage borrowers have some owning up to do as well. The national preoccupation with obtaining larger and fancier homes, while carrying large amounts of debt levered on slim margins, is still alive and well. It seems somehow un-American to put limits on the dream of homeownership or to question its value.

But as great as homeownership is, there are dangers in over-investing in this sector. The penchant for large, reality-TV homes with manicured lawns comes with a cost—economic, environmental, and social. Some people should slow down and save more money before buying a house. Some should lower their sights and buy a smaller or existing home. Some people should rent. Taking into account all the money poured into a home to maintain and improve it, borrowers should be shrewdly realistic about expecting to profit from homeownership. House prices are not guaranteed to rise faster than inflation, particularly in areas where new and better homes are being built.

By over-exalting homeownership, we remain fiercely wedded to outdated exemptions that distort consumer behavior, encourage consumption, favor the wealthy, and reward increased indebtedness—all while contributing to budget deficits with little gain in homeownership rates.

In terms of housing finance, policy makers struggle today with how to resurrect the status quo: a system that provides low-cost mortgage money on demand (like the system we all are used to) but that is safer and less susceptible to political influence. On the other hand, many fear that the reformed system will be so cautious that it will exclude a significant share of the population. Supporting a stronger rental market should also be part of that deliberation. Weaning the country off such rich tax preferences for housing is another good idea that is long overdue. There are more productive sectors for our nation to invest in.

CHAPTER

3

SECURITIZATION BREAKDOWN

Every Christmas millions of Americans watch the Frank Capra film *It's a Wonderful Life*, starring Jimmy Stewart and Donna Reed. The movie is endearing because it takes us back to a time and place where things were simpler and the difference between right and wrong a little clearer; and where neighbors supported each other, even when times got rough. The film also shows the benefits—as well as the limits—of the pre-GSE mortgage market.

In the movie classic, George Bailey, the reluctant, though dutiful, president of the town's savings and loan (S&L), which financed "dozens of the prettiest little homes you ever saw," finds himself pitted against the greedy banker and slumlord Henry F. Potter.[1] A financial crisis is in the making when hazy-headed Uncle Billy loses a day's worth of financial deposits, causing a near-run on the tiny institution. To quiet his anxious, confused depositors, George explains that he can't give them all their savings because the money isn't actually available: it's been loaned out for homeownership. It's in "Joe's house." He then doles out his own hard-earned honeymoon cash to tide people over. The S&L makes it through that fateful day with just two dollars left in the vault that night.

In terms of financial epochs, today's world of automated underwriting, securitization, and global investors is light-years away from the Bailey

S&L. Despite notions to the contrary, that really is a good thing. To take the example from the movie, if Joe's mortgage had been sold to Freddie Mac, then the S&L would have had enough cash on hand—or liquidity—to survive the run, and George could have taken his honeymoon as planned. As it was, the S&L had no other source of ready cash than old man Potter, the local loan shark.

A society like ours with high rates of homeownership needs a constant supply of liquidity. When the S&L model essentially collapsed in the 1980s, the mortgage giants, Freddie Mac and Fannie Mae, took over the job of making mortgage money available everywhere, all the time. It is sadly ironic that these two entities, born in the ashes of the 1929 Great Depression, collapsed decades later amid another calamitous liquidity crisis, this one with global proportions.

Special from the Start

How did we get the GSEs in the first place? In the highly politicized years before the crisis, pundits often made sport of Fannie Mae and Freddie Mac's cute and seemingly benign company pen names. One political cartoon depicted the two firms as pudgy siblings wearing beanie caps, sitting in a sandbox trying to beat each other up.

That comical—if sadly accurate—depiction belies the well-intended, high-toned public policies surrounding their creation. Created in 1934 by the same government stroke as the Federal Housing Administration (FHA) and Federal Savings and Loan Insurance Corporation, Fannie Mae's job was to further bootstrap the mortgage market by providing an outlet for loans originated by private lenders and insured by FHA. In purchasing FHA-insured mortgages from lenders, Fannie Mae replenished lender funds for housing. This new outlet—known as a secondary market—made mortgage money more readily available by adding another source of mortgage capital above and beyond deposits in the nation's S&Ls. In purchasing the loans, Fannie Mae—with its full faith and credit imprimatur—provided a guarantee against borrower default. This government guarantee boosted investor confidence, attracting a steady supply of private capital to the residential housing market. Fannie Mae's national stature enabled funds for housing to flow across state lines, to small towns and urban areas alike, overcoming prohibitions on interstate banking that had previously hampered housing market growth.[2]

In 1968, Fannie Mae was converted to a publicly traded, shareholder-owned company. According to Washington lore, President Lyndon B. Johnson moved the lion's share of Fannie's debt obligations off budget to help rein in soaring deficits arising from the war in Vietnam. Not surprisingly, the submerged, off-budget treatment of so large an enterprise gave Fannie Mae a sense of entitlement, if not illegitimacy, right from the start.

The remaining portion of the entity was renamed the Government National Mortgage Association, or Ginnie Mae, which maintained the original task of providing a secondary market for FHA and later VA loans. Reflecting its stronger tie to governmental housing policy, Ginnie Mae remained on budget as part of HUD.

Released from official government status—but still retaining its original federal charter—Fannie Mae's new job was to buy conventional (that is, nongovernmental) mortgages originated by mortgage bankers, thereby ensuring a stable supply of financing to a broader swath of homebuyers. Unlike banks and other depositories, which could attract funds through deposits, mortgage bankers had no ready supply of cash for originating mortgages. Fannie Mae provided a secondary market where they could sell their mortgages and use the proceeds to originate new ones.

Another set of mortgage originators craved an outlet for their loans. In 1970, Congress created Freddie Mac to securitize mortgages originated by S&Ls—and to give Fannie Mae some competition. Initially capitalized by the twelve Federal Home Loan Banks (FHLBs), Freddie Mac was a private company for the first two decades of its existence. The three directors of the Federal Home Loan Bank Board, which was the S&L regulator, did double duty on Freddie Mac's board of directors. Freddie Mac's motto back then was "Owned by America's Savings Institutions."

It would be a temporary arrangement, as it turned out. In 1989 Freddie Mac shed its governmental status, paid off the FHLBs, and became a shareholder-owned corporation just like its big sib, Fannie Mae.[3]

Strange but Efficient

Publicly traded companies are incorporated in a particular state; many choose to base their operations in Delaware because of its favorable corporate tax environment. As publicly traded, government-sponsored enterprises, Freddie Mac and Fannie Mae rode above the fray. They were incorporated in Washington, DC, by the United States Congress. It was the first distinction among many that led to competitor complaints about an unfair playing field.

Over the decades following Freddie Mac's creation, the market distinctions between the two GSEs blurred, and both competed vigorously to purchase mortgages from any entity with loans to sell. Enjoying significant competitive advantages arising from their unique status, Freddie and Fannie operated on an exclusive playing field. In the words of GSE critics, Fannie and Freddie inhabited a quasi-quasi world that was neither fish nor fowl. Because of their low borrowing costs, arising from their government ties, no other firm could gain entry to their privileged space.

Unfair playing field aside, GSE support for the nation's mortgage market was lauded as a great improvement over the old geographically bound system, where lenders were constrained by the level of deposits they held. With a national secondary market now in place, mortgage originators could make loans regardless of the deposits on hand, knowing that one or the other GSE would buy the loan if it complied with GSE purchasing requirements. Over time, this movement of mortgage money became standardized and very efficient. It gave consumers nearly instant access to a ready—and relatively low-cost—supply of mortgage money. Another prized benefit of the system was the ability to lock in an interest rate in the early stages of applying for a loan.

The GSEs developed standard mortgage documentation, employed leading researchers on mortgage credit risk, developed safe and predictable mortgage securities, and pioneered the use of automated systems for underwriting, valuation, and developing "work outs" for troubled loans.

GSE mortgage-financing activities benefited the whole American economy. The advent of the secondary mortgage market through securitization attracted new money to the US housing market. Institutional investors, including pension and mutual funds, liked the higher yields—at low levels of risk—they received on GSE securities compared to ultra-safe (but low yielding) Treasury bonds. By making low-cost mortgage money broadly available—and the process of obtaining it increasingly efficient—the GSEs helped lessen homeownership's drag on labor mobility.

GSE activities in the secondary mortgage market caused the US housing market to grow. And grow. More houses were built. More houses traded hands. More mortgages were made. Houses rose in value, and more and more people became homeowners.

Most everyone—especially those of us working inside a GSE—thought we had licked the problem of the Bailey S&L. The system dominated by the GSEs was a safe, highly efficient, and highly liquid system.

Or so it seemed. The GSEs did not simply have a monopoly power over the mortgage market—they were a duopoly designed to compete with each other to make the mortgage market more efficient. However, no one ever envisioned how the protected system would hold up if other participants—with no public mission, scant regulation, and a massive global appetite for high-yielding investment assets—found a way to penetrate the GSE market.

Early Days

"Drink, ma'am?" said a smiling man in a white jacket. He gestured toward a makeshift bar as a second waiter popped a champagne bottle. The room was full of celebrating employees.

Accompanied by my new economist colleagues, I had just come up the back staircase from the low-lit basement cubicles where economists scrutinized and forecasted national house-price trends. The year was 1990. A junior economist, I had been at Freddie Mac all of two weeks, and already a major celebration was underway. Employees were invited to toast the launch of Freddie Mac's newest securities innovation—the Gold Participation Certificate, or Gold PC for short.

Wow, I remember thinking as we entered my new employer's "front office" on the third floor of Building Five, Freddie Mac's then-headquarters in Reston, Virginia. The spacious suite was festooned with gold banners and gold balloons. Alongside the well-stocked bar were several white-clothed tables laden with trays of hot appetizers. Keeping with the "Go Gold" theme, there were neat rows of little gold plates and napkins and mesh bags of gold-foiled chocolate coins. Drinks in hand, rank-and-file employees mingled easily with the top executives, and the mood was light.

I accepted the champagne served in a plastic flute and looked around. I had just arrived from the Office of Management and Budget, where we took pride in lording it over government agencies—and in our dour austerity. I thought back to the farewell party that was held for former OMB Director David Stockman. That party had been held in the wide hallways of the Victorian-era Old Executive Office Building in Washington, DC. Employees consumed soft drinks and potato chips served unceremoniously—and we budget examiners had felt honored by that.

But things were clearly different here at the Federal Home Loan Mortgage Corporation. Notwithstanding the sound of its official name, Freddie Mac was in its second year as a publicly traded *corporation*. And it was doing what corporations often do: celebrating its accomplishments, especially those that took months of work and millions of dollars to achieve, like the Gold PC, the hoped-for silver bullet to catapult the firm ahead of the competition.

What company was that? Freddie Mac's much larger and storied competitor, the other government-sponsored enterprise: Fannie Mae.

Battle for Security Dominance

In the early 1990s, the main locus of competition between the GSEs was in the realm of securities issuance. Freddie Mac created the first conventional mortgage-backed security (MBS), known as a participation certificate, or PC. Packaging together the different mortgages into commodity-like securities and selling them to private investors launched the modern system of housing finance.

Under Freddie's original PC security, the lender servicing a borrower's mortgage account sent the borrower's monthly principal and interest payment to Freddie Mac, net of a servicing fee. After Freddie's fee for guaranteeing the mortgage over its life had been subtracted, the remaining funds were forwarded to the investor. This process took about 75 days to complete, so a borrower's June payment, for example, would not be received by the actual investor until mid-August. In this arrangement, the GSEs earned a few weeks of float compensation as the payment made its way through the financial labyrinth to the ultimate owner of the mortgage: the security investor.

Freddie Mac's innovation—the reason to break out the champagne— was to shorten this remittance period to 45 days. Freddie hoped that investors would pay a tiny premium to get their money earlier and that this would distinguish us from Fannie, which was still using the longer-dated security. In other words, if a lender did business with us, it would receive— and use—its expected monies earlier in the month, with the same security guarantees and features. Surely that was worth a little premium.

Notwithstanding Freddie's hopes, the Gold PC soon became a sharp thorn in the company's side. Investors balked at paying up for float, and the fact that the security was new meant that it was a lot less liquid than Fannie Mae's. It turned out that liquidity—the ability to easily buy and sell a security—was more valuable to investors than a few hundredths of a percentage point of float. Freddie moved ahead with the new security, hoping it would catch on, but it never did.

The fact that Freddie Mac was slightly underpaid for each security issued was a fatal error in its early life as a public company. Over the next two decades, that little pricing difference would help ensure that we would always be at a competitive disadvantage to Fannie Mae. And so, life at Freddie became defined by trying harder. Price wars would become common and vicious.

Another way Freddie sought to distinguish itself from Fannie was through better risk management. Fannie Mae kept a large supply of mortgages on its own balance sheet and nearly bankrupted itself in the early 1980s, but Freddie was determined to take a different path. As security innovators, we at Freddie prided ourselves on selling all of our securities rather than keeping them, which would have exposed the company to the risk of changing interest rates. We were "steady Freddie," and we were quite proud of it.

Securitization—Good, Bad, and Ugly

The process of securitization has taken just about as much heat for the financial crisis as the GSEs. Many have blamed the "originate to distribute" model, whereby financial institutions originate mortgages with the full intention of selling them to another institution, rather than holding them to maturity. Preferential capital requirements for securities over mortgages, among other considerations, make this a profitable choice in many instances. To ensure that bad loans are not delivered into the mortgage pipelines, securitization requires strong oversight. The weaknesses of securitization would be exposed as the mortgage market started heating up in 2005.

Notwithstanding the timing differences between the two GSE securities, the securitization process they pioneered and perfected was reliable, safe, and efficient. It successfully financed billions of dollars in home mortgages with nary a hiccup. Even amidst the collapse of the housing crisis, GSE mortgage-backed securities held or even increased in value, while their private-label counterparts "declined dramatically," according to the government's inquiry report.[4]

Securitization is the process whereby singular financial assets, such as mortgages, are converted into easily tradable securities. Mortgages, by their nature, are diverse instruments. Each one has a story. For example, borrowers differ in terms of income, occupation, wealth, and credit history, while the collateral differs in terms of the age, condition, and location of the home. These and other idiosyncrasies make up a bank loan file, which in the current era of tight underwriting standards can easily exceed five hundred pages.

That's a lot of details for an investor to wade through just to purchase one loan. Of course, no shrewd investor would do that. Without a way to standardize and pool mortgage assets, we'd have a very illiquid mortgage market, and it would be very tough to buy a home.

To overcome the problem with individual mortgage story bonds, securitization bundles together mortgages with similar features to create an MBS. The GSEs underwrite the underlying mortgages according to their respective risk management policies. Then they stamp the new security with a guarantee: if one (or many) of the underlying loans defaults, it is the GSE's problem. By buying a GSE-backed security, investors were guaranteed to receive their expected interest and principal payments in a timely fashion. In the case of borrower default, principal and interest would continue to be advanced to the investor until it became clear that the borrower could not reinstate. Then the loan was pulled from the pool and put on a path to foreclosure.

With the GSEs playing the role of shock absorber for the system, mortgage investors could sleep at night. The safety and trust of this system enabled mortgage money to trade hands far more quickly and efficiently—and the housing market took off because of it. Foreign investors also placed their trust in Freddie Mac, Fannie Mae, and the US housing market.

At Freddie Mac, we communicators were taught to describe securitization as a super-safe alternative to holding mortgages on balance sheet (like Fannie Mae did) because it diffused risk through the system. Through securitization, the GSEs bore the risk of borrower default; for their part, MBS investors bore the interest-rate or market risk of securities, which fluctuated with interest rate and currency movements. Securitization was an ingenious way to spread mortgage risk among many players over the entire system.

That was true, as far as it goes. What the GSE economists and traders underestimated was that securitization's strength was also its Achilles heel: just because risk was diffused did not mean it had disappeared. The other underappreciated fact was that securitization depends entirely on the quality of the mortgages delivered to the GSEs from the lenders. Before mortgage brokers and their Wall Street enablers came on the scene, GSE securitization was a safe and steady operation. As we will see later, rising home prices led to complacency and the relaxation of lender underwriting standards; new entrants sent mortgages through the securitization pipes that did not live up to their billing or the GSE contracts. Without strong underwriting and with a breakdown in the verification process from broker to lender to GSE, the orderly process of securitization abetted a deadly race to the bottom in terms of the credit quality of the loans.

Securitization's weakness resembles the mishap in the children's book *The Cat in the Hat*, by Dr. Seuss. As the diabolical cat and Things 1 and 2 engage the children in increasingly raucous and forbidden activities, red dye is spilled. In trying to clean up a particularly large stain, the cat gets dye, albeit diluted, all over everything: the carpet, the walls, and even the fish. So it is with mortgage risk.

Securitization does not make risk disappear; rather, it breaks it down into smaller and smaller pieces. But, of course, little pieces add up: The house was shockingly trashed when Mother returned, just like the US mortgage market and its global effects. In the words of former Fed governor Lawrence Lindsey, "Securitization was diversifying the risk, but it wasn't reducing the risk . . . You as an individual can diversify your risk. The system as whole, though, cannot reduce the risk. And that's where the confusion lies."[5]

Rep and Warrant System

While it is understandable to pine for the days when things were simpler and business was based on small-town relationships, there is a problem with idealizing the past. In today's sprawling national mortgage market, there is no way Freddie Mac can be George Bailey, looking each borrower in the eyes to determine if he or she will repay the loan. Even though the GSEs set the standards for the mortgages they buy from lenders, the loans are bought en masse, sight unseen, which means they are often approved for sale weeks before they are actually originated.

The preference for securitization dates back to reforms put in place following the 1980s, when S&Ls found themselves in a severe mismatch between long-term mortgages and short-term demand deposits. Desiring to create a safer system with a tighter asset/liability match, regulators increased the capital requirements for mortgages. In contrast, securitization enabled mortgage risk to be moved off the balance sheet, requiring less capital. Not surprisingly, this difference led to regulatory arbitrage, where lenders had strong financial incentives to securitize their mortgage assets and sell them to long-term investors rather than hold them with higher capital reserves. Quoting again from Kling: "To compensate for the disincentive to invest in mortgages caused by high capital requirements, regulators permitted banks to reduce their capital requirements—but only for mortgages held as securities. This approach had a perverse effect. In addition to lowering the capital requirements for holding safe mortgages in the form of mortgage-backed securities, the reduced capital requirements for securities enabled banks to hold less capital for risky mortgages as well, including subprime loans."[6]

Securitization raises issues of trust. To ensure that lenders deliver the types of loans specified by their contracts with the GSEs, and that the loans are fully compliant with state and local lending laws, lenders make certain commitments to the GSEs. Specifically, lenders represent and warrant that the loans were originated in accordance with published underwriting criteria and/or contract language. If, upon later inspection, it is revealed that the loans were not originated as specified, the GSEs had the right to demand that the lender repurchase the offending loans.

Lenders, of course, do not like this aspect of GSE contracts. Repurchasing a loan long after the fact is costly. But the "rep and warrant" was the essential key to making the entire system work because it gave lenders skin in the game. In economic terms, the lender/guarantor arrangement presents a classic principal/agent problem. This situation arises when one entity works for another (the agent) but their interests are not closely aligned. In the case of a lender sourcing loans for a GSE, it is not hard to imagine situations where the lender might want to unload poor-quality loans on the GSE, which hardly would be aligned with the financial interest of the GSE. The rep and warrant system reduced this risk; lenders would be less likely to sell poor-quality loans to the GSE if they had to make legal assurances that the loans were originated to specifications. They had to "eat" the losses—if they got caught.

As important as the rep and warrant system was, there were a couple of big catches. First, unless a loan defaulted in the first year or two, it was not easy to prove that the default was the result of poor underwriting on the part of the lender. Sometimes borrowers obtain loans that seem appropriate to their circumstances at the time of origination, but things quickly change when there is job loss or divorce, for example.

Second, the system required the GSEs to maintain eternal vigilance over lenders to ensure they were delivering the quality of loans they were under contract to deliver. At Freddie Mac, statistical models were used to determine the appropriate numbers and types of loans to test for such errors. Quality-control sampling is expensive and time-consuming, and concerns about bad loans being pawned off on the GSEs declined as house prices rose and GSE losses fell dramatically. Lulled into a false sense of security, the GSEs reduced the size of the QC samples over time.

Third and most important, the system was susceptible to competitive pressure. When Wall Street entered the mortgage market in the mid-2000s, lenders had an alternative source of liquidity. No longer were they held hostage to GSE underwriting requirements, duopoly pricing, and the rep and warrant system. They could sell to Wall Street banks, which were far less discriminating. Not surprisingly, the GSEs began losing market share. The market guarded by the moat of a cozy duopoly was suddenly breached. With less market power, the GSEs could no longer require lenders to meet their traditionally strong underwriting requirements. Contract terms were increasingly waived. GSE management often opted not to require a lender to repurchase defaulted loans for fear they would take their business elsewhere.

Lenders had their own principal-agent problems because, increasingly, they weren't doing the underwriting or sitting at the closing table either. Rather, a mortgage broker handled the paperwork and then sold the loan to a big mortgage aggregator, who then sold it to one of the GSEs. If Freddie Mac was having trouble holding lenders' feet to the fire, the lenders had the same problem with the Johnny-come-lately of the mortgage market: the brokers.

Often operating on a shoestring of capital and out of a car trunk, mortgage brokers sprung up like weeds in the boom years preceding the crisis. Their presence, and the difficulty of tracking their mortgages from bank to bank, added to the overall risk of the market.

G-Fee Mania

Another weak link in the GSE securitization model was the inability to charge—and sustain—high enough prices to cover the risks and protect against future losses. Downward pressure on GSE guarantee fees when times were good added more instability to the system.

Early in my career, I remember greeting a mortgage banker in the lobby of Freddie Mac's fancy new McLean headquarters, where we moved in 1991. After getting a visitor badge, he gazed around at the granite-floored, chrome-pillared, and azalea-filled atrium and joked, "So this is what it's like being inside a *g-fee!*"

A new employee, I didn't quite know what he meant, but I remember thinking that the company had just been insulted. Welcome to the spongy conduit.

From my first day of employment to my last, people outside Freddie Mac complained about how much the company charged to guarantee a loan against default—in short, the g-fee. Mortgages are inherently risky. Borrowers may intend to repay what often is the largest debt of their entire lives, but bad things do happen. Some people end up not being able to fulfill their commitments. There are many possible reasons why this might happen, ranging from unemployment, divorce, or medical problems to a downturn in local house prices or, in certain instances, to fraud. But whatever the reason, a loan default is bad for the borrower and bad for the creditor who guaranteed the loan in the first place.

In the early 1990s, Freddie and Fannie charged lenders somewhere in the neighborhood of 25 basis points, or 0.25 percent, to guarantee a loan against default. So, on a $100,000 loan, the cost for having a loan guaranteed by Freddie Mac was about $250 a year.

That wasn't very much. A senior leader at the company and later my boss, David Andrukonis, used to say that it took about 50 performing loans to cover the costs of just one loan that went all the way to foreclosure. Said differently, a 25-basis-point fee would be adequate coverage if less than 2 percent of loans defaulted. By contrast, in the subprime mortgage market, which dealt in far riskier loans, 15 to 20 percent of loans eventually defaulted. Given these exceedingly slim margins, the GSEs simply could not bear much additional risk based on the fees they charged. Conservative underwriting standards were thus *de rigeur*.

Charging a fee to cover risk is not rocket science. But you would have thought this was a matter of national security, given the amount of public concern about GSE guarantee fees.

Lenders didn't like g-fees because they made the cost of homeownership slightly more expensive, with little to no apparent benefit to them. Since the creation of the GSEs, there had never been a time when the residential mortgage market hemorrhaged losses as it would starting in 2007. Hence, there was always a suspicion that the fees were unnecessarily high. Smaller lenders also had a bone to pick. Constantly wary of getting pushed (or swallowed up) by the larger banks, small lenders complained that the larger lenders got better pricing. This was probably true, given the economies of scale involved with the delivery of mortgages to the GSEs. To top it off, politicians didn't like the g-fees because the lenders didn't like them, or because the consumer advocacy groups didn't like them. Everyone wanted to keep the American dream of homeownership affordable.

Of course, the 0.25 percent the GSE charged lenders—and ultimately homeowners—to guarantee repayment of the loan for up to 30 years is just one of many costs of obtaining and financing a home. A real estate agent charges the home seller up to 6 percent of the house value, a commission that is essentially baked into the cost of the home and therefore borne by the homebuyer. A mortgage lender charges a minimum fee of 1 percent of the mortgage balance to originate the loan and another point to compensate the guy who filled out the paperwork. Many borrowers don't exactly feel this pain because they roll the lender fees into the mortgage interest rate and pay them over time. States and localities collect their pound of flesh in the form of taxes and recording fees—or, in some areas, indirectly by the imposition of environmental impact fees on new housing.

The fee collection continues long after the loan is originated. The mortgage servicer, acting on behalf of the GSEs and other mortgage investors to collect payments from borrowers each month, charges 0.25 percent, on average, to do that chore. And, if a borrower doesn't have enough money to make a 20 percent down payment, or has an FHA loan, there is the cost of mortgage insurance—another 0.50 percent *at least*.

So it was not that the GSE 0.25 percent guarantee fee was excessive, in and of itself. Rather, it was that the GSEs were the ones collecting it, and for many years the companies made an awful lot of money. It was a common complaint that we were overpricing risk and charging too much in fees.

At times it seemed that way. But in the mortgage business, costs are lumpy. That is, there could be a string of good years when Freddie took in a lot of money from fees and defaults were light. But, in later years, the tables could be reversed, and defaults could significantly outstrip fees. That's exactly what happened.

It was like any other kind of insurance. People pay for health insurance even when they feel healthy; likewise, they buy flood insurance when the ground is dry. In any given year, when claims are light, people complain that the insurance companies have ripped them off. But then there are the years when lightning strikes and claims hit the roof. That's when people rightfully expect their insurance company to be financially strong enough to pay up.

In the mortgage world, today's guarantee-fee revenue might look rich, but it had to cover *tomorrow's* defaults. But figuring all that out was not easy. One challenge was estimating expected losses on different book years of 30-year fixed rate mortgages. Losses were a function of how frequently defaults were expected to happen—and how severe, or costly, each loss would be.

Complicating matters is the fact that most people don't hold their loans for 30 years. In the old days, mortgage rates would have to drop by 2 full percentage points before borrowers went to the trouble and expense of refinancing. When automated underwriting entered the picture in the late 1990s, refinancing became cheaper and faster. Many borrowers would refinance when rates had declined by less than a full percentage point, which made mortgage swapping a lot more common. The shape of the yield curve and the latest Fed moves became common cocktail party conversation. Refinancing was cool.

Another variable in determining the price of guaranteeing a mortgage was the path of local house prices. If house prices rise a little each year, a borrower's equity stake in the property increases, and this tends to make default both less frequent and less severe. Other things being equal, the more equity borrowers have in their homes, the less likely they are to stop making payments and default on the financial obligation. For a mortgage system to be safe, every participant needs to have capital at risk, or what the industry calls skin in the game.

Pressure to Cut Prices

When house prices began rising a lot in 2004—double-digit annual growth in certain fast-growing markets—lenders pressed the GSEs to relax the long-standing down payment requirements as competition heated up. After all, why should a borrower have to make a sizeable down payment if the local housing market was going to build the equity in relatively short order? Borrower equity was growing at impressive rates, driving the risk of mortgage default to minuscule levels. Other aspects of the traditional underwriting equation, the three C's of collateral, capacity, and credit, were under pressure as well. Requirements for borrower credit scores and income relative to debt were gradually relaxed, and appraisals often had a rosy appearance. A truism in the mortgage industry was that rising house prices covered the sins of the underwriters.

Through 2006, house prices climbed still higher, and amnesia set in. The forecast was for full sun in the mortgage market, and just about everybody—from lenders to politicians to consumer groups—stopped worrying about risk and jumped on the pro-homeownership bandwagon. Worse, they were quick to accuse the GSEs of price gouging for charging fees when actual current-year losses were exceedingly low. Attention dangerously turned from risk management to the stark observed differences in homeownership rates. It wasn't long before the GSEs—and their proprietary underwriting algorithms—were viewed as the scrooges responsible for the lull in the upward march of homeownership. No longer valued as the rainy-day fund for the mortgage system, GSE guarantee fees were now seen as unnecessary barriers to homeownership.

The collective thinning of risk coverage—for borrowers, lenders, and GSEs—was largely invisible until 2007, when the 10-year escalation of house prices suddenly went bust. The subsequent crash caused the home equity cushion for many borrowers to evaporate, placing their mortgages underwater. Undoubtedly, some could have weathered the drop in house prices had they not previously monetized the equity windfall in their homes by obtaining cash-out refinances and second liens—or had made sizeable down payments to start with.

As all these factors wreaked havoc on household balance sheets, they devastated Freddie Mac's as well. Thanks to the price wars with Fannie Mae from time to time and then the competitive onslaught from Wall Street, Freddie's financial margins to cover the mounting mortgage losses were driven to unsustainable lows.

Where Things Stand

Following the government takeover of the GSEs in 2008, one of the first actions taken by FHFA, the GSE conservator, was to raise g-fees. Ostensibly the move was to bring GSE pricing in line with actual expected risks of guaranteeing mortgages. Whereas by 2007 average g-fees had been beaten down by cutthroat competition, five years after the crisis fees were at record highs. Testifying before Congress in April 2013, then-Acting FHFA Director Ed DeMarco said that, following two fee increases in 2012, the average fee to guarantee a new mortgage is "around 50 basis points, approximately double what guarantee fees were prior to conservatorship."[7]

In addition to raising fees to be commensurate with risk, DeMarco had another objective in mind: raise fees to make the GSEs uncompetitive by creating an opening for private firms to provide the same type of guarantee at a lower cost. If private companies took the bait and reentered the market, the resulting competition would begin to move mortgage credit risk off taxpayers' shoulders.

Unfortunately, private investors still have their arms crossed, so as of this writing, the price hike has yet to work. Many have opined that price is not the only factor keeping private capital on the sidelines; regulatory uncertainty and the lack of confidence in the ratings on Wall Street–generated securities are but two vexing issues that have yet to be resolved. Also, many providers of private equity capital in the years before the crisis are simply nonexistent today.

DeMarco's tight policies as conservator earned him the scorn of every houser and Democratic policy maker in Washington, and many screamed for his ouster. In addition to raising g-fees, he opposed calls for massive principal reduction on underwater mortgages. To detractors, and there were many, his attempts to stabilize the GSEs and the broader market were hindering economic recovery and raising the cost of homeownership, and that was clearly treasonous. His response was simply to point to the grim duty of a conservator: to conserve GSE assets, which, by then, belonged to the public. And that entailed discipline and vigilance.

DeMarco's last planned g-fee increase was nixed a month later in January 2014 by the new incoming director, Mel Watt, a former Democratic congressman from North Carolina and long-term member of the House Financial Services Committee (HFSC).

The two men could not be more different. DeMarco rose through the ranks in the executive branch, while Watt spent over 20 years in Congress and many of them on the committee with first-hand experience with GSE shenanigans. DeMarco, the former Social Security chief turned GSE conservator, whom a former Freddie colleague termed a true public servant for the flak he endured, was replaced by a pro-homeownership politician. The industry cheered.

In the words of David Stevens, former Freddie Mac SVP of sales, FHA commissioner, and now head of the Mortgage Bankers Association (MBA), "We were surprised by the announcement of the g-fee hikes from (outgoing acting FHFA director) Ed DeMarco . . . The decision by Mel (Watt) was the only decision to be made given the GSEs are making such huge profits."[8]

Tantalizing GSE profits also caught the eye of the US government. Thanks to prolonged conservatorship, higher g-fees are now a revenue source—and a cookie jar for legislators scrambling for cash. In its frantic attempt to fund stimulus measures in 2011, Congress required the GSEs to increase guarantee fees by another 0.10 percentage points to cover the temporary reduction in payroll taxes.[9] The payroll tax reduction has since expired, but the GSE fee premium still rolls into the general fund of the US government, where it counts toward general deficit reduction. The president's 2017 budget estimates the GSEs will remit a combined $40.5 billion in guarantee fee premiums to the government between 2012 and 2026.[10] This amount is above and beyond the dividend repayments.

Using GSE revenues for deficit reduction is an ominous signal that policy inertia has set in, making reform that much more unlikely. In 2013 bipartisan legislation was introduced in the Senate Banking Committee that would prohibit further increases in the g-fees to fund ancillary government programs. The proposal also required congressional approval should Treasury want to sell its considerable stake in the GSEs.[11] According to Senator Bob Corker (R-TN), one of the bill sponsors, "If Treasury were to decide to sell its preferred share investment without Congress having first reformed our housing sector, we would just be returning to a time where gains are for private shareholders and losses are for taxpayers."[12]

After floating around for a few years, the proposal found its way into an omnibus spending bill in November 2015. Today things are truly at a deadlock: Treasury is barred from taking any action to dispose of GSE assets until January 2018 unless Congress enacts legislation directing it to do so—or, even more a remote possibility, enacts the long-awaited reform legislation.[13] No one in Washington is holding his breath.

In the absence of reform, FHFA has embarked on a three-part strategy to "Maintain, Reduce and Build." From ensuring that the GSEs continue assisting borrowers through the HAMP, HARP, and foreclosure mitigation actions to offloading GSE mortgage credit risk to reduce the government's footprint in housing and building a new securitization platform that eventually the whole industry can use, FHFA has taken its conservatorship role admirably seriously.

FHHA worked to repair the weak links in the rep and warrant system and pushed the GSEs to go after lenders who sold them noncompliant mortgages in the years leading up to the crash. Freddie Mac and Fannie Mae have combed through millions of mortgage files looking for defaulted loans that lenders failed to properly underwrite and now are forced to repurchase at an excruciating cost. As of March 31, 2013, Freddie Mac reported having $2.9 billion in outstanding repurchase requests to banks.[14] Banks also are at risk for billions in "put backs" to compensate the FHA for bad loans that government agencies insured. Needless to say, the banks are very unhappy these chickens have come home to roost.

The FHA also has battened the hatches with its lender partners. But it's a delicate dance; both FHFA and HUD have had to balance the need to tighten contract terms with lenders without scaring them off completely. Smaller lenders, in particular, are unable to absorb much repurchase risk, so they will likely make fewer loans, and ultra-safe ones at that.

On the investment side of the GSE business model, FHFA filed 18 lawsuits in 2011 against banks and other securitizers of private-label securities on behalf of the two GSEs. In contrast to the mortgage put backs, these lawsuits deal with shoddy private-label securities purchased by the GSEs from various entities. According to Fannie Mae's SEC filings, "the lawsuits allege that the defendants violated federal and state securities laws and, in some cases, committed fraud by making material misstatements and omissions regarding the characteristics of the loans underlying the securities in the offering documents for the securities that were sold to Fannie Mae and Freddie Mac."[15]

In its *2014 Report to Congress*, FHFA reported combined GSE recoveries of $10 billion from nine investment banks.[16] These large recoveries temporarily boosted GSE performance results. In 2014, settlements with banks over rep and warrant claims and private-label securities litigation totaled $6.4 billion, nearly half of Freddie Mac's pre-tax net income that year.[17] These glowing results were ephemeral, as we shall see.

In short, the GSEs were ripped off coming and going. On the insurance side of their business, they unwittingly guaranteed an awful lot of poorly underwritten loans served up to them by the nation's most revered financial institutions who exploited the originate-to-distribute model. In their investment business, the GSEs bought an awful lot of private-label securities that were riskier than advertised. Simply put, a lot of bad product rolled downhill into waiting government arms—or *implicitly* government arms, that is.

Mortgage Reform

The 2010 Dodd-Frank Act (DFA) contained two provisions governing the origination of residential mortgages: qualified mortgage (QM) and qualified residential mortgage (QRM). (Why the names are confusingly similar is beyond me.) The two provisions had very different objectives. QM was designed to correct the problem of borrowers getting talked into loans they could not understand or afford; it set a minimum underwriting threshold to ensure that borrowers have the ability to repay their loans. QRM was designed to reduce moral hazard in securitization by requiring lenders to hold 5 percent of the risk of the issuance on their balance sheet.[18] QRM was supposed to represent a tougher underwriting threshold to ensure that mortgages going into securities were of good quality. Regulators had the difficult job of deciding where to set the QM and QRM bars.

Under QRM, lenders have to put their money where their mouth is: if a lender sells a high-risk mortgage to a GSE or other investor, it has to put up cash as collateral. In this way, QRM puts lenders in the first-loss position rather than the investor or government. The downside is higher costs for borrowers whose loans were subject to lender capital requirements. Luckily, QRM contained an escape valve: lenders originating lower-risk mortgages are exempt from the 5 percent capital requirement.

In March 2011, in keeping with the statutory objective of a tougher QRM threshold, regulators proposed to exempt mortgages from risk retention if they had down payments between 15 and 20 percent, low debt-to-income ratios, strong borrower credit, and other risk-mitigating factors. Not surprisingly, the proposed criteria (very similar to traditional standards used in the 1990s) met strong industry pushback; in particular, the 20 percent down payment requirement was viewed as overly conservative. Setting the bar too high would choke the nascent housing recovery and was unfair to lower-wealth borrowers, proponents argued.

The debate around QM followed a similar path. QM holds lenders legally accountable for originating mortgages to people who lack the ability to repay the loan and later default. Lenders wanted the QM bar set low so the vast majority of their loans would be out of legal danger.

After months of intense industry lobbying, regulators backed down from their tough stand and implemented weaker versions of both exemptions. In fact, they decided to make QRM and QM the same. The minimum standard—that borrowers merely have the financial wherewithal to repay their loans—is now the standard for sending mortgages through the securitization pipeline. With QM defining the standard for QRM, very few loans will require risk retention.

The two standards were designed to solve different problems and should not have been conflated in this way. Simply being able to repay a mortgage month after month, other things being equal, is a matter of income relative to debt; the size of a borrower's down payment is largely irrelevant in that case. But equity capital—either in the form of meaningful borrower down payments or a 5 percent lender reserve—is critical to preventing loans from going underwater, maintaining skin in the game, reducing losses, and shoring up trust in the securitization process. The mortgage market is possibly in a worse position than if the two standards had not been implemented.

How did this come about? Are memories of the worst crisis since the Great Depression that short?

The tried and true way to argue against tighter underwriting is to claim that down payments keep consumers from becoming homeowners. Citing research showing that many would-be borrowers shoulder even larger housing burdens as renters than they would as homeowners, lenders and consumer advocates argued that mortgage rules should permit lower-income and low-wealth borrowers to (continue to) join the ranks of homeowners. Others claimed that the traditional understanding of down payments as a strong deterrent against default has been overstated.

It is telling that Sheila C. Bair, former head of the Federal Deposit Insurance Corporation, which had to mop up billions in lender losses after the crisis, decried the gutting of the QRM rule, saying such a wide exemption won't impose discipline on Wall Street "when packaging assets such as mortgages into securities." In a letter to her former regulatory colleagues she wrote: "The regulators' proposal would essentially eviscerate risk retention as a tool to reform the securitization market. We should not repeat the mistakes of the recent past when, in the name of credit availability, regulators were far too tolerant of lax lending standards."[19]

In a rare show of bipartisanship, Bair was joined by the author of the legislation himself. Representative Frank also opposed the weakening of the QRM standard, saying that "the single most important part of [DFA] was risk retention."[20]

The appeal to broader homeownership remains a powerful weapon against reform. In the aftermath of the crisis, DeMarco halted GSE purchases of low-down-payment and other higher-risk loans. Since then, not surprisingly, new loans purchased by the GSEs are performing admirably. Of course, the tighter requirements have excluded some borrowers, which puts pressure on policy makers. As before, it looks like the GSEs are creaming the market and not taking enough risk. Just as he reversed his predecessor's course to increase g-fees to entice private capital back to housing, incoming FHFA Director Watt also loosened the underwriting strictures. In 2014, at the MBA's annual conference, Watt announced a loosening of credit standards, hinting that the GSEs would soon lower the down payment requirement from 5 percent to 3 percent to "enable creditworthy borrowers who can afford a mortgage, but lack the resources to pay a substantial down payment plus closing costs."[21] With the government covering the higher risk, banks are more than happy to oblige, and these products are becoming more prevalent in the market once again.

Conclusion

Though we may wish to return to the quaint mortgage market of the past, securitization is here to stay. Along with the securitization of other financial assets, such as credit card receivables, auto loans, and other consumer products, securitization is a highly efficient way to attract funds so that more loans can be made financing all sorts of consumer needs. Since the housing market cannot live without debt, feeding it with abundant liquidity is extremely important.

The problem is that securitization is not a cure-all for reducing risk. Ultimately, a security is only as good as the mortgages that undergird it. The reason why so many losses ended up in the secondary mortgage market was that primary market lenders had little to no skin in the game. Plain vanilla GSE securitization became vulnerable to unanticipated risk when the all-important rep and warrant system buckled under competitive pressure. Many of the worst-performing loans found their way into the GSE system from brokers, which were completely unregulated.

For all the regulatory effort to implement QM and QRM, not much has changed. Perhaps things are even worse today. How can the GSEs set higher underwriting standards than those now ensconced in regulation? How are we to protect securitization from abuse if lenders aren't required to hold capital or borrowers don't have to make meaningful down payments? Rather than private sector companies making business decisions about risk and reward, the government now does it for them.

Although FHFA's repairs to the rep and warrant system are important to reducing moral hazard, the weakening of QM and QRM is hardly a boost to investor confidence. Equity capital is the anchor of the entire system. It benefits everyone from borrowers in the weakest housing markets to overseas creditors buying our mortgage securities sight unseen.

No wonder private investors have little appetite for mortgage securities that are not explicitly guaranteed by the government. But we need private capital to return to the US housing market. Otherwise, it's all on taxpayer shoulders.

CHARTER CONFUSION

The lender rep and warrant system—and searing competitive pressure to lower prices—were not the only weak links of the GSE model of housing finance. The dual nature of the GSE founding charters was an even bigger problem. Not only were the GSEs shareholder-owned corporations, but they were unique, specially protected creatures of Congress. All protestations and public disclosures aside, the congressional GSE charter gave investors the misimpression that the GSEs were tantamount to being agencies of the United States government. They invested in GSEs securities almost as if the GSEs were as safe as the US Treasury itself.

The GSE charters were a classic case of moral hazard—the notion that if there is some sort of underpriced protection against risk, people will take advantage of it and behave in a riskier fashion than they would otherwise.

Neither Fish nor Fowl

In the early 1990s, I helped staff a meeting between our top economists and some visiting officials from Mexico. After a hearty lunch, one of our visitors wiped his moustache and put down his linen napkin. Turning to a Freddie economist, he asked in a thick accent, "So, I am still having trouble understanding what you are saying. Is Freddie Mac part of the United States government or not?"

It was a delicate moment, and I wondered who would answer the question. But the economists were nonplussed. "No, we are not part of the US government," said one firmly. "Rather, we're government-*sponsored*."

Our guests nodded politely but continued to press. They had heard of Ginnie Mae, the government corporation that securitizes mortgages insured by the Federal Housing Administration (FHA) and the Department of Veterans Affairs (VA), both of which are government agencies. What about the GSEs? How were they different?

The discussion went long into the afternoon. Our visitors were impressed with data showing the size and scope of the US housing market, the domestic homeownership rate, and the tight spread between the rates on Freddie-guaranteed mortgage-backed securities and US Treasuries. They just couldn't quite grasp how it all worked. How could Freddie Mac raise funds so cheaply for housing if it was not part of the government?

Foreign banking officials weren't the only ones asking that question. So were a lot of people in Washington, DC.

Government Corporation?

Bestowing governmental benefits on a shareholder-owned company, which gave rise to the notion that Freddie Mac and Fannie Mae were somehow backed by the government, which resulted in a lower cost of capital, which created an uneven competitive playing field—all for the sake of housing— was enough to make any conservative politician want to strangle the GSEs. Take Rep. Jim Leach (R-IA), for example. In 1997, Leach chaired the HFSC when the news hit that Freddie Mac had used its low-cost capital to invest in tobacco bonds, of all things. Apparently the company had borrowed $125 million in the capital markets at 6.99 percent—a comparatively low rate that reflected the implicit guarantee that the government would stand behind the bonds if Freddie couldn't. Using those funds, the firm then bought an identical amount of corporate bonds issued by Philip Morris yielding 7.68 percent.[1]

Freddie Mac—and its shareholders—pocketed the difference. It was what Former Fed Chair Alan Greenspan derisively called "the big, fat gap," according to Bethany McLean and Joe Nocera in their book, *All the Devils Are Here*.[2]

Leach was livid and called for an investigation. After all, Freddie Mac was created to support homeownership, not the tobacco industry. The firm, under a fiduciary obligation to increase shareholder value while creating revenue streams for its own needs, was doing what any shrewd business would do. Freddie reasoned that it needed some nonmortgage investments to diversify its extensive mortgage holdings and hedge the risk. In addition, it would be prudent to have a stash of liquid assets that could be sold in the event of a financial crunch. Holding corporate bonds in other industries obviated the need to sell mortgages, the dumping of which would have dampened mortgage prices and caused rates to rise for borrowers. It is also certain that Freddie did the math and saw a profitable investment opportunity. Aside from the social stigma of investing in the tobacco industry, it was what the corporate finance department of any other corporation would do. But Freddie was not any other corporation.

Social Service Agency?

Republicans weren't the only ones confounded by the things Freddie Mac did. Democrats regularly fulminated that the firm was slacking on *their* top priority, which was to deliver significant social benefits to housing, particularly in so-called underserved areas like central cities and disproportionately minority neighborhoods.

To many Democratic lawmakers and their allies in the affordable housing community, the deep-pocketed GSEs were the hope of the reincarnation of a vibrant US housing policy. Generally seen as a lackluster, if not corrupt, federal agency, the Department of Housing and Urban Development (HUD) experienced significant budget cuts during the 1980s, just as the GSEs were becoming ascendant. In time, it became clear that it would be far easier politically to give the GSEs the job of expanding affordable housing rather than seek increased appropriations through a recalcitrant Congress. Simply put, GSE financing activities were (and still are) off budget and therefore "free" from a public accounting standpoint. So, with nary a concern about the fundamentally dishonest approach to financing the nation's housing needs, Congress began piling on additional social policy chores for the GSEs. In addition to keeping mortgage rates low and serving more and more low- and moderate-income families, the GSEs were expected to preserve decaying and dwindling rural housing, invest in small, higher-risk apartment buildings, buy mortgages on mobile homes (which were high-risk depreciating assets), bring GSE-style finance to Native American reservations (notwithstanding the lack of appropriate legal structure to do so), and "beat the market" in terms of originating loans to minority borrowers, thereby reducing the gap in homeownership rates between minority groups and whites.

It was quite a to-do list. And most of it wasn't in statute or regulation. But it was often spelled out in letters printed on congressional letterhead. Representative Barney Frank (D-MA) was a frequent author of those types of letters.

Not that there wasn't good to be done and improvements to be made. The GSE mortgage purchase activities primarily benefited white, middle-class Americans living in populous suburban areas. Nevertheless, it was hard to meet all those other expectations while managing an increasingly large and risky book and keeping shareholders happy by making a reasonable return. The last thing Freddie Mac wanted was bad press.

The Democrats often complained that a key obstacle to Freddie Mac's ability to buy more mortgages from underserved areas, for example, was the firm's tight underwriting standards. The firms were regularly accused in national newspapers of discriminating against deserving consumers— simply because we didn't buy as many loans from minority homebuyers as Fannie Mae did. Once busloads of consumer advocates came to Freddie Mac's corporate headquarters to protest the firm's mortgage purchase policies. They trooped inside and stood on furniture in the lobby, demanding to speak to the CEO. Another time, a group threatened to stage a boycott of our stock if we didn't accede to its demands. Most groups just complained about us to Congressman Frank, who was influential on GSE issues. After years of dealing with the varied pressures we faced, one CEO complained that "the Rs want to haul us off and shoot us . . . and the Dems want to hug us to death."

And so the GSEs danced with their various partners very, very carefully.

Mission Confusion

Inside the company things were hardly better. We didn't quite know who we were either. All the external confusion about our role played itself out in meetings—often not well.

Freddie's chief economist at the time used to tell me that Freddie had to think about the "greed-head" side of things. Another colleague explained that most risk/return decisions came down to either picking the pocket of the shareholder (who was primarily interested in profitable growth) or the debt holder (who would be stuck holding the bag if things went south). Someone was always going to feel you had cheated them.

Most large businesses are familiar with the tradeoffs between debt and equity. But the GSEs had another layer of complexity to deal with: the unspoken tension between the housing mission and shareholder value. This tension was embodied in Freddie's corporate mission statement, which said: Freddie Mac is a stockholder-owned, government-sponsored enterprise . . . established by Congress to provide a continuous flow of funds for residential mortgages.[3] Without Congress or the two independent GSE regulators helping to balance the conflicting priorities, the GSE mission statement was itself a source of woe.

It got personal at times. One day I witnessed a tense exchange between employees in my division. Some viewed Freddie Mac as a big social welfare agency and expected it to "give away stuff," such as low-cost loans, etc. They were angry with others at the firm, notably the highly compensated employees whose job it was to trade Freddie's mortgage and debt securities. They often opposed just about any good deed the housers wanted to do.

But to Freddie's "Wall Street types" (as they were called), the company existed pretty much for one reason: to make money. Not that the housers didn't also appreciate Freddie's profitability. A number of them had had previous careers at HUD or with nonprofits. They certainly liked the salaries and benefits better at a GSE, even if they desperately wanted to believe that we could both "do well and do good."

The employee bonus system was a case in point. Up until 2002 or so, a few communicators worked in secret each January to create an all-employee letter called "Performance Highlights." It contained the CEO's assessment of company performance relative to its objectives for the year just passed. It was probably the most highly edited and embargoed document the company produced each year.

There were a number of categories of performance measures, and each carried a different weight. One category was financial indicators—Freddie was in business to make money, after all. Within this category were things like market share, the relative price of our security compared to Fannie's, and the stock price. As a category, financial performance was usually generously weighted relative to other categories, like how we did relative to our housing goals or employee-related items like workforce diversity.

Through some strange alchemy, which very few people actually understood, the measures and categories were weighted and combined into an overall measure: above plan, on plan, or below plan.[4] From above-plan ratings flowed rivers of money: Just about everyone with a building pass and a heartbeat was assured of getting an annual performance bonus. I remember my first one. I had only been at the company seven months and had spent three of them at home on maternity leave. It was not exactly my most productive year. Nevertheless, one day, my boss handed me a tiny sticky note and said "Congratulations." It read $2,347, or something similarly random. I was stunned. I had come from OMB, where employee bonuses were small and rare; private-sector perks were privately disdained, particularly for companies that were trading on their government ties like the GSEs.

Bonuses rose to the hundreds of thousands for Freddie Mac's rainmakers: the sales force that contracted with the major lenders to bring in mortgages, and the traders who bought securities for Freddie Mac's profitable retained mortgage portfolio. Activities that contributed to top-line revenue growth were handsomely rewarded. In 2003, following Freddie Mac's accounting scandal, the Office of Federal Housing Enterprise Oversight noted that "hitting on-plan targets for operating earnings per share (EPS) in the profitability portion of the scorecard accounted for a growing portion of the scorecard weight from 1998 to 2002."[5]

By the time the government took the company over in 2008, Freddie's top executives were vying for million-dollar bonuses. For rank-and-file employees, the bonus system's golden handcuffs served as a double vice. It gave employees strong incentives not to bite the hand that fed them and also made it costly to walk away.

Charter Confusion—and Collision

In addition to the company's mission statement, the GSE statutory purposes spelled out in the GSE congressional charter were rife with potential operational conflict. In lay terms, GSE statutory purposes—to provide stability, liquidity, and affordability to the nation's mortgage markets—were ill-defined and gave rise to much confusion. For example, if one interpreted providing stability to mean maintaining conservative underwriting, that could limit the number of mortgage purchases, which would dampen mortgage liquidity and hurt affordability. The trade-offs were patently obvious, and good, sound business judgment was needed to find the golden mean.

Unfortunately, that is not how it worked in practice. Rather than hold the three purposes in balance, business divisions naturally gravitated to the statutory purpose that most suited their business objective. Traders were all about liquidity. Housers screamed for affordability. And the risk managers rallied under the banner of stability. To my knowledge, not one of Freddie's CEOs truly perceived—much less sought to manage—the company's profound existential conflict. A clear set of integrative operating principles was needed but was sadly lacking in most business deliberations.

Family Jewels—and Albatross

As one executive said to me, Freddie's GSE charter was tantamount to the family jewels. It was, indeed, a lucrative piece of parchment, particularly for the market benefits it procured for GSE shareholders. But before describing those princely benefits, it is worth recalling the burdens and duties of the GSE congressional charter.

First, the charter contained numerous restrictions on GSE business that were designed for safety's sake but created negative unintended consequences. For one, the requirement confining the GSEs to the residential mortgage market was designed to ensure a constant GSE focus on housing so there would never again be a shortage of mortgage money. But it also created a corporate pressure cooker with no release valve. If you can only do one thing, you do it and do it and do it.

Unlike other businesses, the GSEs were precluded from horizontally integrating into other related consumer debt markets, such as credit cards or auto loans. This restriction meant that we couldn't diversify our risks across other business lines (like banks) or escape the housing market even when times got bad and no rational private investor would have *anything* to do with US housing.[6] Furthermore, any new mortgage product or program the company wanted to pursue required prior approval from HUD, the GSE mission regulator at the time.

The GSEs also were precluded from vertical integration within residential finance. There were only two activities the GSEs could do: guarantee and invest in mortgages. Everything else related to mortgages (including origination, real estate services, title insurance, and the like) was off limits.

Over time, the division between the two markets became a place of high alert and even open warfare. Fearful of GSE domination, lenders and their trade groups drew what they called a bright line between the GSEs and the primary market mortgage originators. One GSE toe over the line and lenders went complaining to the politicians that the GSEs were out of bounds. At least, that is how it seemed from inside a GSE. But mortgage insurers (MI), the handful of private companies that insure the higher-risk portions of low-down-payment loans, had been burnt by Freddie Mac back in 1998 and would never forgive or forget.

Both GSEs rued the amount of risk (and profits) being handled by the MIs and sought ways to "extract value" from them, which is a polite way of saying stealing back the business.[7] While Fannie Mae took a market approach to getting around the MI requirement, creating new products that skirted the MI requirement ever so slightly, Freddie Mac brazenly went to Congress to get the entire MI requirement expunged from the GSE charter. Freddie lobbyists convinced then-Senate Banking Committee (SBC) Chairman Alphonse D'Amato to insert a technical amendment into a conference report that would allow Freddie Mac to bypass the MI requirement and self-insure the risk instead. Making a bald competitive play, Freddie argued that its capital base was in perfect shape to take on the job of supporting low-down-payment loans. According to Freddie lore, the dastardly deed took place in the dead of night. A death knell to the MI industry, Freddie's technical amendment was anything but; it significantly altered legislation that had already passed both houses of Congress.

Seeing their lives pass in front of their eyes, the MIs went ballistic and applied counter political pressure such that the provision was soon undone. But huge animosity and distrust remained, such that any subsequent GSE innovations, even positive developments such as automated underwriting and standards against predatory lending, were viewed with great suspicion by lenders and others. Their response was to create a GSE watchdog organization known as FM Watch. In later legislative deliberations, the industry successfully fought for a detailed set of "bright line" restrictions and penalties for any GSE that attempted to innovate or otherwise extend itself beyond traditional boundaries.

Other charter restrictions concerned the type and size of the mortgages the GSEs could buy. As a rule, the GSEs were limited to purchasing mortgages with an unpaid principal balance (UPB) up to the conforming loan limit. A complicated formula is used to calculate the so-called GSE loan limit every year; suffice it to say that growth in the limit was expected to mirror the growth in average house prices across the country.[8]

When I started at Freddie in 1990, the conforming loan limit for one-unit properties was around $220,000. When I left it was $417,000 for non-high-cost markets, and it still is. The GSE loan limit was the demarcation between where the GSEs were allowed to play ball and where they were not. Banks and mortgage companies originated higher-value jumbo loans, which were securitized into private-label securities created by Wall Street firms or held in portfolio by banks. Because there was no GSE charter backing these securities, jumbo borrowers paid an additional 25 basis points or more for these loans. This spread would widen dramatically following the 2007 crash in house prices, causing Congress to legislate a temporary increase in the conforming loan limit in areas of the country with particularly high housing costs.[9] In 2016, 39 counties had higher GSE confirming loan limits because they were designated as high cost; California's Napa County topped the high-cost list at $625,500.[10]

As mentioned earlier, by law, GSEs could also only purchase or invest in mortgages that had a 20 percent down payment or carried MI. That seems pretty straightforward, but I recall a leading consumer advocate being shocked and angry when he learned that 20 percent down payments were a charter requirement unless the borrower obtained mortgage insurance or other risk offsets were made.[11] How old fashioned and even discriminatory we were, the advocates would chide. A prevailing view at the time was that because people of lesser means had less money, they would be more committed to their homes and therefore less likely to default on their mortgages.[12] The GSEs were urged to recognize that "fact" in their default models.

Freddie Mac resisted the pressure to change. In light of 30 years of mortgage default data, Freddie maintained its underwriting standards requiring down payments for borrowers of *all* income levels. Freddie Mac considered itself a good risk manager and did not appreciate being cast as anti-poor. In fact, strong underwriting made the system work. Only in that way would investors be willing to invest in GSE-guaranteed mortgages, which helps keep mortgage money available and mortgage interest rates low for consumers.

GSE down payment requirements led to an incessant quest for loopholes on the part of the industry and borrowers. A famous one was the so-called piggyback, or 80/20, mortgage. An ingenious maneuver on the part of banks, the 80/20 enabled lenders (and borrowers) to once again get around the GSE charter requirement for 20 percent down payments or borrower-paid mortgage insurance. Lenders would originate a first mortgage for 80 percent of a property's value and then originate a second loan at a higher interest rate—for a total loan to value (LTV) ratio of 100 percent. In this way, the lender pocketed not one but two origination fees, the GSEs bought the loan without *technically* violating their charter requirements, and the borrower got the house, albeit with 100 percent debt financing. The big losers in the whole gambit—that is, until house prices fell, placing many borrowers deep underwater—was FHA, the traditional source of low-down-payment loans, and the private mortgage insurance industry, which lost thousands of paying customers.

The competitive scramble doesn't end there. Through their lobbying arm, the MI industry successfully got Congress to make the mortgage insurance premium tax deductible along the lines of the mortgage interest tax deduction, the nation's largest tax expenditure. It was an effort to counter the lure of the piggyback loans by lowering the after-tax cost of insurance. And it meant another housing write-off by the government.

Borrowers who took out second liens to dodge GSE down payment requirements experienced high levels of default when house prices collapsed. This is not surprising, since they started with zero equity in their homes and things went south from there. The very loans that made it possible for them to get into homes were the ones throwing them into foreclosure—as first and second lien holders argue over who is going to have to eat the loss. Without a rational settlement between the lien holders, a loan modification is nearly impossible to achieve.

GSE Housing Mission

A final set of charter requirements was designed to ensure that the GSEs served a broad swath of the mortgage market, rather than cherry picking the safe and easy loans. To prevent a repeat of the practice of racial redlining by FHA thirty years earlier, annual affordable housing goals were added to both GSE charters in 1992. Conventional wisdom has it that Fannie Mae, through its formidable lobbying arm, played a key role in getting the housing goals inserted into the legislation. The bet was that housing goals would be a small price to pay to ensure that the firm would forever be linked with US housing policy—and the preferential status and lower borrowing costs that would come with that.

Set each year by HUD, the GSE mission regulator at the time, the housing goals started off requiring that about 30 percent of each GSE's business activities finance housing for low- and moderate-income borrowers and borrowers in so-called underserved areas. Over the years, HUD increased the goals significantly and added additional mortgage purchase subgoals for the GSEs to meet.[13] These requirements set off another round of market distortions, as lenders would often hold off selling goal-qualifying loans to the GSEs until late in the year when the GSEs were desperate for goal-qualifying product.

Taken together, the prohibitions on horizontal and vertical integration, restrictions on the types of mortgages the GSEs could buy, and affordable housing goals meant the GSEs labored under a number of restrictions never encountered by normal corporations. These restrictions caused all sorts of distortions that complicated the running of the company, weakened the regulatory framework, and gave rise to subprime lending on the outskirts of GSE underwriting requirements. The distortions pitted GSEs against their customers and other stakeholders and invited unwanted political intrusion into business affairs.

Wink and Nod: GSE Implicit Guarantee

On paper, the benefits of the GSE charter might seem disproportionate to the prodigious wealth they brought GSE shareholders. However, the value of the GSE charter was not located in the explicit privileges themselves—although they were beneficial—but rather in what the privileges, taken together, signified about the ambiguous relationship of the GSEs with the US government. Despite company protestations to the contrary, that ambiguity made the GSEs appear safer than they really were.

By law, the GSEs were exempt from the registration of their securities with the Securities and Exchange Commission (SEC). Given the job of creating a national secondary mortgage market, the GSEs also were exempt from paying state and local income taxes. Banks also were allowed to hold GSE securities in excess of the so-called 10 percent rule, which gave GSE securities a competitive edge over other bank investments that were limited by law because they were considered higher risk. In addition, the US Treasury was authorized, but not required, to purchase up to $2.25 billion of securities from each company if need be, a provision that would later become euphemistically known as the Treasury line of credit.

Taken together, these and other unusual quirks—like the fact the president could appoint up to five of Freddie and Fannie's board members—were highly symbolic. They contributed to investor impressions that the GSEs were unique among mortgage firms and, thus, very important to the United States government. Thus the GSEs were crowned with the ability to borrow money cheaper than anyone else in the world—except for the US Treasury.

Preferential Capital Treatment

A litany of GSE benefits must also include the issue of capital. As amended in 1992, the charter required Freddie and Fannie to hold capital in the amount of 0.45 percent against the credit risk of mortgages backing our MBSs, which we guaranteed. For mortgages held in investment portfolios, which carried both credit risk and interest rate risk, the GSEs were required to hold 2.5 percent in reserve. At that ratio, the GSEs were hugely leveraged against the risks of the loans on our books, about 40 to 1. This time it was Freddie Mac exerting sway with Congress. Conventional wisdom held that Freddie Mac economists-cum-lobbyists had exerted considerable influence to get that low capital ratio ensconced in law. Small wonder that Hank Paulson, when briefed about the GSEs in 2006 when he become Treasury secretary, took a dim view of both the quality and quantity of GSE buffer stocks, calling it "bullshit capital."[14]

In time, it became clear that what was good for profits was bad for public relations. Because the GSEs' statutory capital levels were low in comparison to banks, detractors of government involvement in housing harped on the GSE capital advantage at every opportunity.[15] Freddie responded to this criticism with an apples-to-apples type of comparison, saying that capital should be commensurate with risk. In other words, the lower GSE capital ratio was appropriate given the relatively higher quality of the conforming mortgages the company traditionally bought. Historically banks engaged in riskier types of mortgage lending than we did, including auto loans and commercial loans, and thus had the higher losses to show for it. In public testimony, Freddie would also defend the lower GSE leverage ratio by pointing to the larger equity stakes conforming borrowers had in their homes compared to jumbo market borrowers and the amount of geographic diversification in our "sold" or guaranteed mortgage portfolio. As for the capital adequacy on the higher-risk mortgage portfolio, Freddie Mac investment gurus used derivatives and investments in callable debt to manage the interest rate risk on the portfolio to near zero. The economists truly believed Freddie Mac had the safest mortgage book around. And for many years it did.

AAA Credit Ratings

Notwithstanding the lower capital ratio Freddie and Fannie had in comparison to banks, the GSEs enjoyed higher credit ratings on their securities. In fact, Freddie and Fannie mortgage securities were rated AAA by the credit rating agencies—the same rating that an investor would see on a Ginnie Mae security or, for that matter, a Treasury security. There was only one difference: Treasuries and Ginnies truly carried the full faith and credit guarantee of the US government. The GSE AAA rating had no such explicit guarantee. Rather, the GSE AAA rating belied a so-called *implicit* guarantee—an artifact derived from the presupposition that the government would stand behind the institutions if one or the other ever got into trouble. The implicit guarantee arose from the unusual quasigovernmental nature of the GSEs—and prevailed even though every member of Congress, the GSE regulator, and every GSE securities offering said otherwise. Shrewd investors remained unconvinced. They believed the government would never let the GSEs fail. And, ultimately, they were right.

An Unfortunate Collusion

Looking back on the decade of heated debates over the implicit guarantee, it is clear that the moral hazard contained in the GSE charter was a recipe for disaster. The highly combustible combination of ambiguity about the government's role, investor shrewdness, and the GSE's own corporate opportunism created a fatal flaw at the core of the US housing finance system.

Public management scholars had long raised alarms about the GSEs' hybrid model, size, and growth. Left unchecked, they warned, the GSEs would "privatize the profits and socialize the losses." (Which they eventually did.) Writing two decades before the crisis, in 1995, Thomas Stanton of Johns Hopkins accurately predicted: "As [the GSEs] expand, the two companies face increasing constraints from the terms of [their] charters. Fannie Mae and Freddie Mac are pushing hard at these limits on their activities, both by increasing the intensity of service to their legally permitted market segments and by weakening the legal constraints on their activities."[16] In 2002, Ronald C. Moe, a specialist in government organization with the Congressional Research Service, published an article entitled, "The Emerging Federal Quasi Government: Issues of Management and Accountability." Moe called the public/private arrangement the GSEs enjoyed a threat to democratic governance. Presciently, he asked, "How well is the public interest being protected against the interests of private parties?"[17]

Official government recognition of this problem dates at least as far back as 1991. A Congressional Budget Office (CBO) report entitled "Controlling the Risks of Government Sponsored Enterprises" recognized the problems with the GSE implicit guarantee but suggested that it would be possible to prevent risks from flowing to the government "if the enterprise is exposed to low levels of risk and is highly capitalized, and if the government has the ability to prevent large increases in risk and declines in capitalization."[18]

Those were big "ifs." As history would show, the GSEs took on risks disproportionate to their capital level while muscling around their admittedly weak regulator. Not surprisingly, when the bust came, the risks (and losses) flowed to the government and the taxpayers.

Still, the implicit guarantee provided significant benefits to a number of powerful stakeholders, including Congress itself. Investors in GSE securities got higher yields, Freddie and Fannie shareholders enjoyed strong stock-price growth, housing market participants—lenders, homebuilders, real estate agents—flourished, and the government got its homeownership on the cheap, with zero budgetary impact. The wink-wink arrangement brought millions in political contributions to members of Congress. It also saved conforming market borrowers billions in mortgage interest over the years. Many wagged their fingers against the system, but since everybody was profiting from it, change was next to impossible.

Not that Republicans didn't try to bring negative light to the implicit guarantee. They regularly reiterated Stanton's warning that by virtue of the implicit guarantee, the GSEs would stick the losses to taxpayers.

For their part, Democrats weren't too bothered by the existence of the implicit guarantee (after all, it was free money), just the issue of how its benefits got distributed. They complained that the GSEs absorbed too much of the subsidy rather than passing it along to conforming market borrowers in terms of lower mortgage-interest rates.

It was an argument only PhD finance economists could love because it seemed contrary to everyday facts. A quick scan of mortgage rates in the real estate section of any newspaper would suggest that the GSEs pass along a benefit of about 25 basis points to borrowers; that was the difference between mortgage interest rates in the conforming and higher-balance jumbo market. That little difference in rates can mean a lot of money over time to most families.

For years, this benefit had been adequate proof of the GSEs' value to society, but in 2004, it was under attack. Former chair of the Council of Economic Advisors and Harvard professor Greg Mankiw said that the GSEs passed through about half the funding advantage, or subsidy, received. A Fed researcher further reduced it to near zero on a net present value basis. Although few lawmakers understood the analysis, the summary point that the GSEs provided little or zero to borrowers made provocative headlines.

Later, in April 2004, CBO issued another report saying that the implicit guarantee gave Freddie Mac and Fannie Mae a combined funding advantage of nearly $20 billion, of which $13.6 billion was passed along to borrowers in lower rates with $6.3 billion retained by GSEs. This size of the funding advantage, or subsidy, was up 70 percent from the CBO's earlier 2001 study due to the large GSE growth in the beginning of the decade.[19]

The funding advantage wasn't actual taxpayer money. It was an economic calculation of the relative financial benefit the GSEs enjoyed over other similarly rated institutions owing to the gold-plated effect of their congressional charters. On the other side of the equation was the borrower benefit of obtaining cheaper financing in the GSE-supported market compared to loans available in the jumbo market, for example.

To rebut the charge that the GSEs only passed along two-thirds of the subsidy, Freddie Mac hired former OMB director (and Republican) Jim Miller, who wrote a report that disputed CBO's methodology and tried to take the argument to a different level by considering a broader set of benefits made possible by the GSEs, such as lower mortgage rates not just in its own market but in the jumbo market as well. Miller concluded that, contrary to CBO, the GSEs actually "passed through" to borrowers more than the size of the advantage, primarily because of their positive impact on other markets that benefited from the liquidity of GSE securities.

For something that no one actually consciously devised—and something that no one could actually destroy—the implicit guarantee was brilliant. Until it blew up.

Where Things Stand

While it seems obvious that policy makers should work to limit the moral hazard in the housing finance system going forward, this is easier said than done. Absolutely everyone in the industry agrees that there should not be another implicit government guarantee, but that's the extent of the agreement. There is much debate about the degree to which the government should—or should not—support any future GSE-type entities or their securities.

Supportive of a hard government guarantee, most Democrats, banks, and consumer groups say that the housing market will not function well (or at all) without whole-hearted government support. Relying solely on the private market will cause either liquidity shortages, significantly higher mortgage interest rates, or the demise of the 30-year fixed-rate mortgage.

A more cynical view is that, even if it could be done, totally shifting the housing market onto a footing of private capital would neither eliminate moral hazard nor insulate taxpayers from risk. The cat is out of the bag, so to speak, now that the government has actually rescued the GSEs after decades of saying it would not. Wharton economist Susan Wachter goes so far as to say that there is no choice but to guarantee the securities since the US housing market, like the massive banks, is simply "too big to fail."[20] Just as with the old GSE implicit guarantee, no investor would believe that the US government would not bail out its mortgage market—again.

On the other hand, moral hazard theoretically could be contained if the government could accurately price for an explicit government guarantee. This is the idea behind legislative proposals that would collapse the GSEs into a single entity like the FDIC, which charges member banks a fee in exchange for government insurance on depository accounts. Of course, over time there would be strong political and competitive pressure to reduce the price of explicit government backing of GSE mortgage securities. This is bound to happen if and when the housing market heats up and consumers start complaining about the high cost of getting a mortgage.

Conservatives are very concerned about the inevitable political pressure to reduce g-fees—that's a big reason why they oppose providing any kind of guarantee to GSE mortgage securities. Whatever the outcome of the reform debate, constant vigilance and political restraint will be needed to keep moral hazard from building up in the housing finance system.

Conclusion

Although well intentioned and generally well functioning for decades, the congressionally designed GSE model of housing finance had a serious fault line. The twin pillars of the market were, at core, two fiercely competitive entities that were neither fully private nor fully public. Their profitability was derived less from talented management, innovative products, and efficient systems than it was from the ambiguity about whether or not the government actually would stand behind their massive obligations.

That fault line seems nakedly obvious now, but before the collapse, most Freddie Mac employees considered the GSE structure a brilliant corner solution, tapping global capital markets to make low-cost mortgage money available for the masses. Perhaps it was brilliant—if the GSEs had resisted the siren's call to enter higher-risk markets that they neither understood nor were adequately capitalized to handle. Like a pleasure boat caught on the high seas, the GSEs were not built for the stresses and strains that gave way to the largest financial crisis in world history.

In testimony before the government's Financial Crisis Inquiry Commission, former Fannie Mae CEO Dan Mudd had this to say: "A monoline GSE structure asked to perform multiple tasks cannot withstand a multiyear 30 percent home price decline on a national scale, even without the accompanying global financial turmoil. The model allowed a balance of business and mission when home prices were rising. When prices crashed far beyond the realm of historical experience, it became 'The Pit and the Pendulum,' a choice between horrible alternatives."[21] Missing in this eloquent summary of the dire situation the GSEs faced is a humble acknowledgment that they, themselves, helped create it.

AFFORDABLE HOUSING

Along with the moral hazard embedded in the GSE charter, conservatives blame the GSE affordable housing goals for driving down underwriting standards, which in turn fueled the ballooning of house prices—and the subsequent crisis. Liberals, on the other hand, categorically deny that government efforts to use the mortgage system to create affordable housing had anything to do with the crisis. As with most things related to the housing crisis, the truth lies somewhere in the middle. The high stakes—and intense Washington, DC, focus—around the GSE affordable housing goals is enough to suggest that they played a far greater role in GSE politics, as well as in running the business, than many are willing to concede.

Dead on Arrival

My personal introduction into the politics of affordable housing came in 2004 when Freddie Mac submitted its response to the startling increases in the goals proposed by the Bush administration a few months earlier. It was my job to direct teams of employees to review the regulatory proposal and write a strong response. After months of feverish work, the market projections were complete, the legal analyses done, and the business assessment succinct. It was several hundred pages long. On the due date, I sent an employee over to the HUD headquarters in a taxi cab with a large envelope. We made it under the four o'clock deadline with just minutes to spare.

But within less than an hour of filing our response, an industry publication published an incredibly negative article highlighting a single sentence that was buried a hundred pages into our response. Following a long assessment of market conditions and forecasts, the offending sentence suggested, in so many words, that HUD's rule should be reformulated. "Scraped" might have been a better word.

Notwithstanding the finer points of Freddie Mac's argument, the trade publication simply was looking for yet another showdown. As the author, I was mortified. My bosses did not like the negative publicity, and within an hour, I found myself in an uncomfortable conversation with the company's general counsel.

The response had taken ten weeks of work. It contained myriad economic and statistical analyses. It made important arguments against overly ambitious goals and the unintended consequences that could result. Our objection was simple: the goals were too high, rose too fast, and would lead to an inordinate dependence on increased purchases of subprime securities. But that was heresy.

Understanding the Goals

Originally established as part of the 1992 legislation that amended the GSE charters, the affordable housing goals stipulate that the GSEs devote specific percentages of their mortgage purchases to support mortgage financing for lower-income and otherwise underserved mortgage consumers.

The GSE affordable housing goals are often compared to requirements placed on banks under the Community Reinvestment Act (CRA) of 1977, which was designed to reduce discriminatory credit practices in lower-income neighborhoods. Both sets of requirements have similar intent, but there are important differences.

CRA does not require specific levels of mortgage lending for depository institutions. Rather, it seeks to ensure that a bank offers credit in all the communities in the area in which it does business. CRA compliance is evaluated using qualitative as well as quantitative measures, taking into account a bank's particular location and context. Finally, CRA emphasizes that a bank's affordable lending activities should not come at the expense of safety and soundness. While there is no annual nail-biting about whether a bank meets its CRA responsibilities as there was for GSE housing goal compliance, issues of bank noncompliance with CRA may emerge when banks seek approval to expand geographically or merge with another institution. The CRA rankings are important to banks, but they are not "pass-fail" like the GSE goals. Plus, there are no specific penalties for noncompliance.

Most people familiar with the issue would agree, however grudgingly, that the GSE housing goals were tougher to meet than CRA. For starters, the GSE housing goals are solely quantitative; they measure how many units of affordable housing (based on different criteria and definitions) were financed by the GSEs in a given year, as a percentage of their overall business. The goals are set years in advance based on estimates of what the mortgage market will do in the future and are not easily adjusted if things don't shape up as expected. So, even if the goals were unrealistic in a particular year, the GSEs would go to extraordinary lengths to meet them, lest they be publicly shamed.

Up until 2008, when GSE regulatory reform was finally enacted, the affordable housing goals were set and administered by HUD, the GSE mission regulator. There was no requirement that the goals take into account safety and soundness concerns, which were the purview of our *other* regulator, the Office of Federal Housing Enterprise Oversight, which was located at least ten city blocks away—and a planetary system away in terms of mission and approach.[1] Failure to achieve a particular goal could result in punitive enforcement actions on the part of the mission regulator. But the safety and soundness regulator would have nothing to say on the matter. The dichotomy was another fault line in the whole structure.

The line widened over time, since no one was really watching out for the consumer. Public policy may have decided that it was a good thing to offer people the opportunity to sign on to massive quantities of debt despite checkered credit records, low income, and little to no down payment. But was it really?

In the early years, the low- and moderate-income goal hovered around 35 percent of Freddie's total mortgage purchase volume. This goal is directed at families whose incomes are at or below 100 percent of the area median income (AMI) where they live, or apartment units that are affordable to such families.

To take one example, for families living in affluent Fairfax County, Virginia, where Freddie Mac is headquartered, the median family income in 2011 was $106,100. On the other hand, the AMI for families living in the vicinity of New Orleans, Louisiana, was $61,100 in the same year. For Freddie to meet a 35 percent low- and moderate-income housing goal would require that 35 percent of the company's purchases or investments in mortgages during a given year would have to fall at or under the AMI levels for each area.

A second goal, known as special affordable, targets very low-income families (with incomes at or below 60 percent of median) and low-income families (those below 80 percent AMI) living in low-income areas as well as those in multifamily units. A third goal, the underserved areas goal, targets families living in central cities, rural regions, and other areas considered by HUD to be underserved in terms of access to mortgage credit.

A rulemaking in 2000 put higher goal levels in place. Freddie began making adjustments in its business to meet the higher goals. In 2004, the low- and moderate-income housing goal hit 50 percent, and Freddie began sucking wind.

Creative Responses

Like any business, Freddie looked for innovative ways to attract new and unconventional customers because that was now part of its mandate. The corporation looked for ways to purchase loans that met the mission, particularly our affordable housing goals, or that provided financing to predominantly minority communities. Of course, Fannie Mae was under the same regulatory imperative, so the two GSEs would beat each other up trying to get access to the same loans. Over time, this meant digging deeper and deeper for qualifying loan purchases, which inevitably placed pressure on underwriting requirements.

High goal levels also pitted the GSEs against the Federal Housing Administration (FHA), the other subsidized government program, which was targeting the same group of borrowers. When the GSEs were on a rampage, they pilfered quality loans away from FHA, a problem known as adverse selection. After a lengthy internal debate, Freddie Mac relaxed its traditional 20 percent down payment requirement to just 3 percent, putting it within spitting distance of FHA's requirements. Adding to the craziness, under the regulatory regime at the time, the FHA commissioner was also the GSE mission regulator on behalf of HUD.

Freddie also got creative and brokered special initiatives with corporations seeking to help their lower-income employees become homeowners.

For example, in 2004 Freddie Mac teamed with Arkansas-based Tyson Food, local lenders, and a credit counselor to provide $50 million in mortgage financing to Tyson team members earning less than $54,500.[2]

Initiatives like this did more for Freddie's branding and reputation—not to mention its political standing in the local congressional district—than they did for its performance under the affordable housing goals. Emphasizing that Freddie would accept flexible mortgage products, a euphemism for lower down payments and more generous underwriting terms, sold well locally but wasn't enough to bring in the big numbers needed to meet the goals.

The GSEs also stepped up their print, radio, and TV advertising—at times angering lenders—in a pitch directly over their heads to consumers. In fact, lenders were doing their own heavy advertising and outreach to minority consumers, in particular.

To meet the tough regulatory requirement, Freddie needed to buy hundreds of thousands of goal-qualifying mortgages year in and year out. Thanks to Fannie's larger size, long history, and influence, it was better at attracting those loans. Freddie's traditional reputation as a tough cookie when it came to credit risk didn't help us in the affordable department.

So Freddie struggled. Most years, Freddie managers would wait until near the end of the calendar year to see how far short the firm was from meeting the annual affordable housing goals. Then there would be an all-out hunt to purchase the loans needed to cover the shortfall. After a few years of this behavior, lenders realized that having the two GSEs competing for the same subset of mortgages would bid up their prices. Lenders noticed that the GSEs started getting desperate for affordable loans by around October. Then they could start calling the shots. There were even suspicions that banks held back goal-rich loans earlier in the year so they could jack up the price in the fourth quarter when they knew Freddie would pay just about anything to keep from missing the goals. One year, I recall talking to a stressed out manager on New Year's Eve who was calling lenders looking for loans to buy.

But in 2003, there simply weren't enough affordable loans to go around. The refinance boom was in full swing, and those mortgages tended to go to higher-income borrowers whose loans didn't count toward the goals. The goal levels had been concocted years before assuming an average refinance share of the market of 15 percent; in 2003, the refi share soared to over 50 percent. There was no way we could make it.

During this period, I attended a meeting with OMB budget examiners—my old stomping ground—but this time I was clearly on the wrong side of the table. In discussing the challenges of meeting the housing goals that year, I suggested that Freddie Mac could simply shrink the denominator in order to get a passing grade. In non-goal speak, this meant we would stop purchasing perfectly good mortgages simply because they did not qualify for the goals. Of course, this approach was inane. While it would do nothing *really* for affordable housing, it would protect the firm against regulatory violation and avoid the unpleasantness of being publicly dragged over the coals for not purchasing loans that did not exist.

The OMB staff reacted negatively. They did not like the idea of a GSE reducing mortgage market liquidity simply to meet the goals, a concept known in goal circles as denominator management. But that is how one little regulatory ratio resulted in all sorts of perverse behavior that might have met the letter of the law but certainly not the spirit.

In short, Freddie Mac's huge refinance business was allowing millions of borrowers to lower their mortgage rates, a welcome jolt to the sluggish post-9/11 economy. And yet Freddie was in danger of failing its mission by not meeting the affordable housing goals as a share of our total business.

Goal failure was costly. Depending on the level of infraction, penalties ranged from having to develop and submit a business plan for reaching the goals in the following year to paying monetary and civil penalties to HUD. However, the real cost of missing a goal was not financial but political. If the goals were, as Fannie Mae had shrewdly foreseen, the price of admission in terms of maintaining congressional support for the GSE charter, then missing a goal threatened to chip away that support.

The HUD regulation did contain an escape clause known among goal watchers as the "infeasibility clause." It said that if, in any year, the goals were economically infeasible to meet, exceptions could be made. But HUD would not provide its absolution for months after the public announcement that a GSE had failed the goals. Since Washington prefers to condemn before hearing all the facts, waiting months for an absolution did little or nothing to minimize the political risk associated with failing to achieve a goal.

In hindsight, it seems eminently defensible that Freddie Mac should have waved a white flag when it appeared that the goals could not be achieved simply because of market dynamics. But since Freddie constantly operated in the shadow of larger, dominant Fannie Mae, the firm could ill afford any unfavorable comparison when it came to serving underserved borrowers. Hence, Freddie Mac chose to soldier on regardless of the impact on the market, itself, or the integrity of the regulatory process.

It's a sad thing to see gifted lawyers working day and night to figure out how to technically satisfy a regulatory requirement while completely violating its spirit. Yet that is exactly what happened when Freddie Mac lawyers crafted the elaborate $6 billion year-end deal with now-defunct Washington Mutual (WAMU).[3]

Late in 2003, Freddie arranged with WAMU, the nation's sixth-largest bank, to purchase 8,000 mortgages on small apartment buildings. These small multifamily mortgages were "goal rich," which made the deal very attractive from an affordable housing goal standpoint. But instead of charging WAMU the typical g-fee to take the loans off their books and guarantee them, Freddie agreed to *pay* WAMU $100 million for the privilege of securitizing their loans and guaranteeing their risk. There was also an escape clause in the contract that allowed WAMU to collapse the security after one year and take the loans back, if it wanted to. It was like renting the mortgages in order to meet the housing goals.

When the details of the deal emerged in early 2004, things got very ugly. HUD was mad. So was Congress. It was clear—to Freddie Mac, anyway—that the affordable goals had become a sham. But HUD kept raising the goal levels anyway.

In 2004, HUD proposed a goal regime for 2005–2008 that was a dizzying staircase for the GSEs to climb. The proposed low- and moderate-income goal started at 52 percent and rose by roughly two percentage points each year to reach 57 percent of business by 2008. Even more challenging was HUD's proposal to raise the special affordable goal from 22 to 28 percent by 2008, nearly a 25 percent increase, which meant that 28 percent of Freddie's book would be required to support very-low-income families or low-income families living in low-income areas. On top of that, HUD created new subgoals under each category that applied to single-family units only. Like the main goals, the subgoals escalated annually and were legally enforceable.

Freddie Mac's regulatory team was incredulous. Even I spoke out publicly about the new levels:

"On first blush there was sort of a gasping going on" when they saw it, Gates said. While she praised some of HUD's work, Gates said that some of the proposed goals may be too challenging and that HUD had "overly optimistic" projections about the mortgage market. "We feel they have estimated the market very high," she said. Gates said Freddie Mac was also concerned about HUD's goal of having low- and moderate-income borrowers account for 57 percent of the homes financed by Fannie Mae and Freddie by 2008. The current 50 percent goal was hard to meet with the explosion in refinancing in 2003, little of which has taken place in those income categories, she said. "Last year was a record year for Freddie Mac . . . in terms of serving low and moderate borrowers in nominal terms," Gates said. "The low and moderate families that we helped last year exceeded the number of all families that we served in 1993, and yet, let me tell you, last year was a squeaker" to meet the 50 percent goal.[4]

My comments fell on deaf ears and were chalked up to whining.

The Surprise Pusher

Why were the new GSE affordable housing goals set so high? The paranoid talk in Freddie Mac's hallways was that the Bush administration had jacked the goals up so high to get us to cry uncle and beg to be privatized. There might be some truth to these allegations.

In the arcane world of government rule-making, an agency is obliged to submit proposed regulations to OMB for review. After that, they tend to disappear for a long, long time.

Up until the government conservatorship in 2008 and Treasury infusion of funds, the GSEs did not appear in the US government budget in the sense that they did not require any appropriations from Congress, nor did their activities contribute to federal outlays or deficit projections. Their obligations did, however, figure in the federal credit budget. There was also a section devoted to GSE financing activities in the President's Economic Report, but it generally wasn't to call out the good things the GSEs did for the economy. Rather, that's where the Bush administration took direct aim at the GSEs' growth, the size of the retained mortgage portfolio, and the debt obligations used to finance it. Within the small, strange world of GSE watchers, it was a ritual every February to read what the administration had written about us and attempt to foresee the coming legislative battles. It was never good; for a number of years, new proposals like charging GSE user fees would be discussed. The GSE stocks would always suffer a downturn the day the president's budget was released.

Something must have happened during OMB's regulatory review process that caused the GSE housing goals to skyrocket. The people at Freddie surmised that party politics were to blame. A little digging in the OMB docket room revealed some telling facts. On January 29, 2004, HUD submitted proposed GSE housing goal levels to OMB, as part of the required rule-making process. But these goal levels were markedly lower than the ones released four months later in May 2004. While this is not startling on its face—OMB has authority to make changes to proposed regulations—it was disconcerting that no new analysis was provided to justify the higher goal levels. They simply increased for no apparent reason.

In its original rule, HUD proposed a one-time, flat increase in the goal levels—not the annual 2 percentage point escalations that were included in the final rule. For example, pre-OMB review, the low- and moderate income goal was raised from 50 to 52 percent for the entire period 2005–2008. Likewise, the special affordable goal was raised from 20 percent to 22 percent for the period. HUD stated that the increases were intended to move the GSEs closer to the projected level of mortgage market originations for 2005–2008.

The post-OMB review goals were far more aggressive than what HUD had originally proposed, based on HUD's own extensive market research. For example, in the OMB version, the low-mod goal rose from 52 percent to 57 percent by 2008. The rationale of the more aggressive goal regime had changed, too: OMB said its higher housing goals were intended to move the GSEs closer to the upper end of the market range projection by 2008. Even more to the point, the OMB goals contained the expectation that the GSEs would lead the market—and we were castigated for our apparent failure to do so in the past. The difference between the projected level and the upper end of the market projections turned out to be quite large.

Another problem was that the goal setting was taking place in 2004. What would happen to the mortgage market by 2008 was anybody's guess. If the market didn't actually produce the anticipated market range of qualifying mortgages, the GSEs still would be obligated to hunt them down and purchase them. It didn't matter whether the predictions were reasonable or not. The outrageous goals were iron clad.

Other Social Expectations

As visible and important as they were, the affordable housing goals were not the only requirements placed on the GSEs. There were other unofficial requirements that posed almost similar amounts of reputation risk. Failing to meet these extra expectations came to be viewed almost as negatively by company leaders as failing to meet the HUD-required goals. They were particularly delicate because they dealt with the racial concentration of Freddie Mac's mortgage purchases.

The first unofficial requirement was to meet or exceed the number of mortgages originated to lower-income borrowers and borrowers of color in the single-family prime mortgage market, as reported under the 1991 Home Mortgage Disclosure Act (HMDA). This measure was used to determine how banks and other entities in the primary market were serving their communities. It was not intended to be a measure of the secondary mortgage market, although it came to be another yardstick to see if the GSEs were supporting all parts of the mortgage market, which would soon come to include subprime lending. Aside from the consumer groups and key Democrats, one of our biggest critics for not leading the market was HUD, the GSE mission regulator.

To help deflect the negative image that clung to the company following its accounting scandal in 2003, incoming Freddie Mac CEO Dick Syron made a voluntary public commitment to "meet or beat HMDA" soon after he arrived in 2004, just before HUD's higher affordable goal levels were proposed. It was a very bold move, considering that Freddie had never come close to even matching the market in terms of purchasing minority loans in the same proportion that they were being originated. Syron's new voluntary goal would mean holding ourselves to yet another standard, one that went beyond the government's existing affordable housing requirement.[5]

Presaging struggles to come, Freddie Mac's wizened risk managers voiced private concern about the CEO's commitment to meeting HMDA while others cheered. Most employees were weary of being pummeled every year for having lower minority and lower-income purchases than Fannie Mae—and many thought Freddie's recommitment to mission was long overdue. On the other hand, striving to meet or exceed HMDA would mean that our book of business was going to look a lot more like the whole mortgage market, of which subprime lending was becoming a larger component. In short, it would mean that we would be expanding the so-called risk envelope. Freddie Mac's old conservatism would have to change.

Every New Year's Day, the *Washington Post* publishes its "in and out" list. The commitment to meet HMDA was such a moment. Heading up the out list was old Freddie, the traditional stodgy approach to risk management and the people who had built their careers on keeping a tight lid on credit losses. On the in list were the new Freddie execs itching for a fresh message: A bold commitment to meet HMDA would steer the headlines away from the firm's accounting travails toward something positive at last.

The tectonic plates of the mortgage industry shifted at that moment. The hairline fracture over the nature of the GSE mission widened jaggedly.

Questionable Research Findings

Mortgage research and policy was another factor that exerted pressure on Freddie Mac to begin loosening its historically strong underwriting standards. Ten years before Freddie Mac's public commitment to meet HMDA, a groundbreaking study found evidence of mortgage discrimination in Boston. Despite intense critique and countercritique, the so-called Boston Fed study had a profound impact on mortgage lending and spawned a decade of analysis into the barriers to obtaining affordable mortgages.[6]

Using newly available HMDA data about mortgage application and denial rates, researchers at the Federal Reserve Bank of Boston (ironically headed at the time by future Freddie Mac CEO Richard F. Syron) found that even after controlling for factors such as income, debt burdens, down payment, and credit history, minority applicants were 60 percent more likely to be denied a mortgage compared to similar white applicants. Quoting from the original study, "this discrepancy means that minority applicants with the same economic and property characteristics as white applicants would experience a denial rate of 17 percent rather than the actual white denial rate of 11 percent. Thus, in the end, a statistically significant gap remains, which is associated with race."[7]

The watershed study was the first of its kind to validate what many consumer activists already knew instinctively: the mortgage market was discriminatory. The study set off an alarm among lenders, GSEs, and Congress. Bank lending practices came under suspicion first, followed by GSE mortgage purchase policies. An easy target was GSE underwriting, which was often derided for having a cookie-cutter approach. Many assailed the GSEs for approving borrowers with predictable, easily verifiable income, to the (assumed) exclusion of borrowers with, say, seasonal or inconsistent employment. Others complained that standard underwriting lacked the flexibility to consider unreported family, rental, or other income, which could cause a mortgage applicant to actually have a stronger cash flow than what might otherwise appear on paper. Many believed it was unfair to not capture that extra cash in the underwriting assessment, assuming it could be documented.[8]

A second dynamic was mortgage research into the relative strength of different underwriting variables in predicting borrower default. Using complex statistical models, mortgage researchers tested different underwriting variables to determine which were most highly correlated with borrower default. They found that borrower income was less robust in explaining why borrowers default on their mortgages than other key underwriting factors, namely, borrower credit history and the size of the down payment. Based on this research, it was thought that mortgage originators could cut some slack on the borrower income requirement, as long as the other two underwriting pillars—down payment and credit history—remained firmly in place.

House prices were taking off in many parts of the country, making homeownership increasingly expensive, just as the conventional wisdom around mortgage underwriting was undergoing a seismic shift. The combination of pressures on lenders to keep volumes high, to fulfill well-intended but ill-advised policy expectations, and to maintain a lender's reputation and market share all contributed to a gradual loosening of underwriting standards.

These attitudinal shifts pre-dated by over a decade the growth of low- and no-documentation and other high-risk mortgages that created so much havoc. Step by step, the collective industry mindset had become unmoored from the anchor of traditional underwriting by the time the dangerous new products hit the market.

Private-Label Securities

From 1998 to 2000, I worked in a newly formed group on Freddie Mac's business side called Credit Risk Oversight. CRO was the first of several internal oversight groups Freddie Mac would create to manage its key risks: credit, interest rate, operational, and reputation risk. Independent risk groups were emerging as a corporate best practice at the time, although it was unclear whether or not they could resist being co-opted by the greater organization. Time would tell.

CEO Leland Brendsel chose Dave Andrukonis to run the new group. Undoubtedly, Brendsel wanted a smart, well-respected leader to keep a firm hand on risk management while the company began exploring higher-risk market segments. Already a 20-year veteran employee, Andrukonis had enjoyed a meteoric rise through company ranks. He did significant tours of duty through Freddie Mac's single-family business line, including security structure, pricing, and risk management. He was the head of the single-family business line when Brendsel tapped him for Freddie's top risk post in 1998.

Commanding great respect with Freddie Mac's board of directors, Andrukonis was deeply skeptical of untested mortgage products, the annual gymnastics to meet the housing goals, and the latest mission fads. Yet he was eminently approachable. He was known around the company for his friendly demeanor, oversized gumball machine, and love for baseball. Years later I was shocked to learn that behind his back some called him "The Boy Scout." It was not a compliment.

One of the main tasks of CRO was to review and approve lender exceptions to the rep and warrants in their mortgage delivery contracts with Freddie Mac. This was painstaking work, and I remember many a day when Andrukonis would sit patiently listening to his staff describe a litany of different underwriting exceptions sought by our customers. Freddie Mac's sales force, of course, always hoped CRO would give blanket approval of the deals. My job was to record the exceptions that had been granted and to whom, as well as key risk indicators, and report them to the board of directors.

Back in 2000, the subprime mortgage market was new and inviting, but Andrukonis was wary; subprime loans had not weathered a business cycle downturn. How would subprime borrowers with blemished credit handle the invariable economic ups and downs? No one knew. To hedge our bets, rather than purchase whole subprime loans directly from the lenders as Fannie Mae would later do, Freddie Mac chose what it thought was a safer path: invest in subprime private-label securities (PLS).

Although the pooling process was similar, subprime PLS were very different from the MBSs guaranteed by Freddie and Fannie. The underlying subprime mortgages carried higher interest rates and weaker borrower credit, and they were often sourced by no-name lenders. But since the securities carried AAA ratings, thanks to S&P and other credit rating agencies who would be later repudiated, a path emerged to begin purchasing PLS consistent with the GSE charter. The mortgage press took notice of the market move, calling it Freddie's "tiptoe" into subprime. (For once we were ahead of Fannie, but that turned out to be a dubious distinction years later.)

The second major difference between PLS and MBS was the source of the guarantee. With its government ties, 30 years of experience, and strong mortgage underwriting (at the time, anyway), Freddie Mac was a trusted guarantor of the securities that bore its name. In contrast, subprime lenders and issuers had no government ties, no implicit guarantee, no experience—and poor-quality loans to boot. How did subprime PLS earn the AAA designation?

Enter Wall Street. Lacking the government indicia needed to provide an external guarantee, Wall Street security issuers created PLS with internal credit enhancements capable of absorbing borrower losses—theoretically, at least. The wizards of Wall Street subprime ingeniously structured PLS to obtain the same top ratings as a GSE security, even though the underlying loans were weak and the originators untested.

Along with my much smarter colleagues in financial research, I attended a seminar in the early 1990s on developments in structured finance. Wall Street quants, as they were known, had come to Virginia to teach our finance types a thing or two. After drowning in mathematical equations for two hours, I recall thinking these guys were wasting their brains. Why weren't they finding the cure to cancer?

Structured finance was in its infancy, and the hubris that came along with fancy calculations would nearly doom us all a decade later. The quants reasoned that by breaking mortgage cash flows into separate pieces, such as interest-only and principal-only strips, mortgage risk could be measured, directed, and even tamed. Investors had different investment objectives and risk appetites, so why not give them what they want? A roasting chicken might cost $5, but cutting the chicken into parts will bring $8.50. So sell parts.

Using elaborate computer modeling techniques, the issuers figured out how to create slices, or tranches, of bundled mortgage cash flows designed to meet investor needs while containing risk. An AAA rating did not mean that the subprime mortgages underlying the tranche were somehow better than others in the pool; rather, AAA simply meant that monies paid by the subprime borrowers each month would flow first to the top-rated tranche.

Risk-averse investors like Freddie Mac were protected from losses not because the loans underlying the PLS pools were safe in and of themselves. Rather, the safety came from having first dibs on borrower cash flows; because the senior-rated tranches were assured of getting paid (unless the models were really wrong or house prices collapsed), they were unlikely to experience serious losses. Yield-hungry investors eschewed the risk and bought higher-risk mezzanine tranches. At the bottom of the cash flow "waterfall" was the residual, the toxin-absorbing appendix of the whole structure. It got whatever cash flows were left after everyone else got paid. Like any junk bond, its low rating came with a tempting yield.

Investors gobbled up the safest tranches, but demand lagged for the riskier junior pieces. So Wall Street issuers took things a step farther and turned unsold chicken parts into hash. Residuals and other junior tranches were sold into even riskier structures called Collateralized Debt Obligations (CDO). By further slicing and dicing the cash flows, the high-risk tranches slated to absorb the brunt of losses on the original PLS were magically turned into senior CDO securities, or sons of CDOs. (It went on and on.) According to FCIC, about 80 percent of CDOs were rated AAA.[9] Credit rating agencies were paid handsomely for putting lipstick on pigs; 90 percent of CDOs were downgraded by the end of 2008 when the bottom fell out of the housing market.[10]

Did investors understand this critical nuance—that subprime PLS ratings had nothing to do with the credit quality of the underlying mortgages or the financial strength of the issuer? Or that BBB PLS tranches could become AAA CDOs? Many did not and suffered huge losses as a result.

In 2009, I was a guest lecturer at a small college in my brother's money and banking class. When I drew a picture of the cascade of mortgage cash flows from PLS to CDO, my brother, with 30 years of experience in teaching economics, was astounded.

Subprime Meets Housing Goals

Investors like Freddie Mac prized safety over yield, so we stayed away from the hard stuff. Instead, Freddie required subprime issuers to structure PLS tranches around GSE charter requirements, a liberalized version of our prime credit standards and the anti–predatory lending measures the company would later put into effect.

The more requirements Freddie stipulated, the less profitable the deal. The securities traders would grumble when they had to do the housers' bidding and ask issuers to exclude mortgages with potentially predatory features, or "stip," for a particular affordable housing goal criteria. Those extra requirements were burdensome and took money off the table.

Freddie's initial foray in subprime securities strove to align with the company's charter and mission. If our research was correct and 30 percent of subprime borrowers actually could qualify for better mortgage terms, why not start by bringing GSE efficiencies to the safer end of that market? Subprime security investment also was a way of meeting the higher affordable housing goals because the profile of subprime borrowers tracked well with the affordable goal definitions. This was implicitly encouraged by the government. In estimating the size of the GSE market, from which goal levels were created, HUD included 50 percent of the subprime market. So, higher goals meant more subprime.

Fast-forward four years. In writing the 2004 regulatory response to HUD's higher housing goals, Freddie Mac argued that the more HUD demanded that the GSEs *meet* the market, as defined by HMDA, the less it would be able to *lead* the market in combating predatory lending. Because the goal levels were so aggressive, it would become less and less possible for Freddie to say no to loans that were legal but had predatory features. In other words, if Freddie was going to be held legally responsible for meeting housing goals that forced the company to mirror what the market was producing, the company would simply salute the flag and buy what the market was producing, notwithstanding reservations to the contrary. Freddie would focus on hitting the goals, rather than trying to purge the market of bad loans. That responsibility fell to the Federal Reserve, which had the regulatory authority to protect borrowers from bad lending under the 1994 Homeowners Equity Protection Act (HOEPA). Former Chairman Greenspan's protestations to the contrary, the Fed utterly failed to do this important job.

In the end, the most risky mortgages purchased by the GSEs, and the ones that contributed to the highest losses, often did not even qualify as a goal purchase. The culprit loans, hungrily sought by Wall Street to fill high-yielding security tranches, were not simply subprime mortgages, as bad as they were. It was the nontraditional mortgages, or NTMs, which Freddie Mac bought in vast quantities after Andrukonis was not-so-politely asked to leave.

Freddie Mac did not buy NTMs to meet the affordable housing goals, since many didn't even qualify for goal credit. Rather, Freddie bought NTMs to boost a sinking market share, to shore up faltering margins, to regain relevance, and to compete with Wall Street.[11] In a word: to make money.

Where Things Stand

What role did the housing goals play in the demise of the GSEs? How risky were these targeted affordable loans, really?

Researchers have concluded that mortgages purchased by the GSEs to meet housing goal requirements have outperformed many of the NTMs created by Wall Street, even the ones on their own books.

Freddie Mac documents obtained by the FCIC confirm that "while the outstanding $60 billion of the [company's] targeted affordable loans [represented] only 4 percent of the total portfolio, these were relatively high-risk loans and were expected to account for 19 percent of total projected losses. In fact, as of late 2008, they had accounted for only 8 percent of losses . . . The company's major losses came from loans acquired in the normal course of business."[12] The new normal was moving Freddie out the risk curve to purchase loans we formerly refused. But times had changed.

Even if affordable loans did not bring down the system, thankfully very few reform proposals call for them going forward.

In February 2013, the Housing Commission of the Bipartisan Policy Center (BPC) released its long-awaited report that included plans for unwinding the GSEs and replacing them with a single public guarantor that would provide an explicit, fully funded guarantee on MBSs. Despite expressing concern for more affordable housing, the report states that "neither the Public Guarantor nor MBS issuers should be subject to numerical housing goals or quotas. Such measures could distort the prudent application of the government guarantee."[13]

Until reform comes, however, the GSEs remain accountable to affordable housing goals set by the conservator. The 2008 Housing and Economic Recovery Act (HERA) reform legislation, enacted within two months of the companies being placed into conservatorship, created three income-based single-family goals and a goal for low-income refinances as well as three income-based multifamily goals. HERA also defined so-called duty to serve requirements for underserved markets (manufactured housing, preservation, and rural areas). In writing the implementing regulations, FHFA built needed flexibility into the system, allowing the GSEs to hit either a benchmark goal level set prospectively or a retrospective market level. Goal compliance was suspended while the GSEs were on their backs, but under the new conservator, Mel Watt, the requirements now apply. The

2017 president's budget notes that Freddie Mac missed three of four goals in 2013 and two goals in 2014. The company is now required to submit a housing plan detailing how it will improve its performance.[14]

HERA also requires the GSEs to make annual financial contributions to three new affordable housing funds based on business volume. The GSEs must set aside an amount equal to 4.2 basis points of the unpaid principal balance (UPB) of mortgage purchases in a given year. The more business the GSEs do, the more money is allocated to affordable housing. Although the monies are not appropriated by Congress, they are administered by federal agencies.[15]

In the first years after the crisis, when the GSEs were struggling to pay sizeable dividends to Treasury, the affordable housing payments were suspended until the GSEs returned to profitability. But the extractions are in force today. Watt reinstated the contributory requirements as of January 2015; according to the president's 2017 budget, $373 million will flow from the GSEs to the affordable housing funds in 2016.[16] In the event the GSEs needed additional taxpayer funds in the form of a Treasury draw, the housing fund commitments would be suspended again.

The requirements don't end there. Indicative of the intense distrust and loathing of the GSEs and their money-making machines, HERA prohibited the GSEs from passing along the costs of the allocations to mortgage originators (and, thereby, to consumers), as any other business laden with government requirements would attempt to do.

Housers cheered this creative approach to sourcing funds for affordable housing. In HERA, lawmakers funded an important social need by taking "rents" from the GSEs while skirting the stingy annual appropriations process and forcing GSE shareholders (not borrowers) to foot the bill. Now those shareholders are taxpayers.

This hat trick has a number of downsides, however. From a governance perspective, it's simply undemocratic (and unwise) to extract a subsidy off a subsidy to fund a public purpose without public involvement while the GSEs remain beholden to taxpayers. It's also pretty roughshod to prohibit shareholder-owned companies (and they truly were in 2008 when HERA was enacted) from managing the costs of government requirements in a competitive fashion. Third, the two companies we're talking about—the ones facing the expropriation of funds—lack adequate capital reserves, broad public support, or a glint of a profitable future. All but a sliver of their profits already go to the Treasury. Is it a good idea to take more money out of these wobbly ATMs for initiatives that HUD rightly should be funding? Or is it another example of being too clever by half?

Last is the issue of inertia. Linking monies for affordable housing to GSE business volume creates powerful incentives for the companies to keep growing, which is inimical to reform. President Obama repeatedly called for the GSEs to be "wound down" if he was going to sign any reform bill that crossed his desk. But after eight years, there has been no such bill, or any viable bill, for that matter. The longer GSE reform is prolonged, the more various constituencies become financially wedded to the status quo and the less likely reform will ever come to pass.

Conclusion

In place for more than 15 years by the time the housing bubble popped in 2007, the GSE affordable housing goals created a cultural openness to loosening time-tested underwriting standards bit by bit, even in the face of mounting evidence that the market was overheating. The goals also created increasingly absurd reactions, such as Freddie Mac's rent-a-mortgage deal with WAMU that clearly was inconsistent with the spirit and intention of the regulation, even though it was technically legal.

Even more dangerously, the goals became a political battering ram. No GSE would dare miss the goals because of the grave reputation risk of looking anticonsumer or, worse, antiminority. Because of the split nature of GSE regulation at the time, the housing goals were not calibrated against the concerns of safety and soundness, exposing the firms to unknown levels of additional credit risk. On top of the quantitative housing goals promulgated by the government, there were other social expectations that the GSEs would be the source of easy money for affordable housing.

As dysfunctional as the goals came to be, however, they were not the *sine qua non* cause of the housing crisis, in contrast to what AEI's Wallison has stated. Many of the very worst loans purchased by Freddie Mac did not even qualify for the goals but were loans to higher-income borrowers in a bid to compete with Wall Street, which was under no such regulatory directive.

Loans made to borrowers of modest means did not, by and large, bring down the US housing finance system. That said, the affordable housing goals did contribute to a sea change in GSEs' and others' views of what constitutes good underwriting, and they eased the transition to even riskier NTMs and subprime mortgages. Interestingly, it was a Republican president who sought the highest affordable housing goal levels in history, levels that proved unattainable and even dangerous, as Freddie Mac's 2004 regulatory response predicted.

While no one in Washington wants to repeat the failed social experiment of numerical housing goals, there remains a stubborn refusal to learn from the past. HERA contains a lot of goals, duties, and funds, and they are operative even though the GSEs are not. To call for a return to traditional underwriting standards is out of favor once again. Bankers are against that. Home builders and real estate agents are against that. Consumer groups are against that, as are an increasing number of lawmakers. The ritual drubbing of anyone who tries to bring up the need for underwriting restraint indicates that disparities of income and wealth, as well as the explosive issues of race and immigration, lie simmering beneath the surface.

SUBPRIME SEMANTICS

Subprime mortgages have rightly earned the disdain of nearly every observer of the 2007 US housing crisis. These loans—infamous for their high, exploding interest rates and punishing features like prepayment penalties—were truly the bad apples in the barrel. Like wildfire, escalating subprime losses quickly engulfed the entire US mortgage market and then systemically infected capital markets around the world.

But getting rid of subprime mortgages is easier said than done. For starters, policy makers, regulators, and even prosecutors have long struggled to define what a subprime mortgage is. In addition, though new DFA regulations seek to prohibit the most egregious features from reemerging, the ingredients for building subprime mortgage bombs remain nascent: continued low interest rates, global capital in search of yield, pent-up demand for homeownership, regulatory loopholes to support underserved borrowers, rampant financial illiteracy, and a forever inventive and profit-seeking US mortgage market.

What Is Subprime Anyway?

Several years after the crisis, I was having a conversation with someone about subprime lending. The person was shocked to learn that the term "subprime" implied a loan of inferior credit quality. Apparently, he had been under the impression that "subprime" meant that the interest rate on the loan was below the prime rate, a common lending benchmark, and therefore a desirable loan. It was another indication of the critical need for financial literacy.

Subprime lending gets its name as the antithesis of prime lending. Traditionally, prime mortgages were analogous to the so-called investment-grade mortgages guaranteed by the GSEs, as specified in their charters.[1] To meet the quality standards of institutional investors like pension and mutual funds, the GSEs established underwriting standards for the mortgages underlying the securities we were selling.

The tighter the underwriting standards, or credit box, the fewer borrowers can obtain a low-cost loan guaranteed by the GSEs. For many years, the only alternative was FHA. As the flagship of government housing policy, the FHA has generally had a looser credit box than the GSEs, acting as a spigot overflow, so to speak. Unfortunately, the FHA program can be cumbersome and more expensive for low-down-payment borrowers. And so a rather lucrative market niche developed just beyond the edge of GSE underwriting standards.

Providing liquidity to this heretofore mortgage wasteland allowed lenders to market their services to borrowers who formerly would have been considered untouchable by the GSEs. These were borrowers with dinged credit, lower income, and lower wealth. Because the mortgages did not qualify for GSE financing, subprime originators like Household Finance, Ameriquest, and New Century had to find other outlets for their subprime mortgages, if that segment of the market was going to grow. Lack of liquidity ensured that subprime remained a small market. Once the GSEs began purchasing subprime mortgages—whether as whole loans or wrapped in risk-protected securities—the newfound source of subprime liquidity was like a vent to fire.

It has been a hot topic in congressional hearings. In a March 2013 hearing of the House Financial Services Committee on the causes of the demise of the GSEs, Joshua Rosner, managing director of Graham Fisher & Co., testified that when the GSEs started buying subprime mortgages, by providing a bid, they "gave comfort" to other PLS investors that it was safe to jump in.[2]

The game was suddenly on. Whether they had intended to or not, simply by virtue of who they were, the GSEs gave a stamp of approval to the subprime market.

Higher Risk and Cost

Before the rise in subprime lending, borrowers with credit scores below 620 out of a possible 800 would have found it difficult to get a GSE-backed mortgage and possibly even an FHA loan. Credit scores are developed by credit repository companies, one of which is Fair Isaac Company, known as FICO. While there are many factors that are statistically amalgamated to create the score, a score could fall to 620 due to a 30-day delinquency or a foreclosure, depending on the borrower's original score before the adverse credit incident. Subprime mortgages were often the only ones available for homebuyers with blemished credit records. In a world where mortgages are evaluated according to a risk/return ratio, the higher the risk presented by the mortgage borrower, the higher the return required by the lender and/ or investor. Hence, subprime borrowers were charged more for their mortgages; many consumer advocates believed that subprime lenders charged above and beyond the risks presented.

The most egregious subprime mortgages were ominously called exploding ARMs. For example, a 2/28 subprime mortgage started with a very low teaser rate that expired just before the two-year anniversary. After that, the interest rate would spike upwards by as much as 5 or 8 percentage points, resulting in a large—and often unaffordable—increase in the monthly mortgage interest payment. To avoid paying the higher rate, many borrowers sought to refinance these loans prior to the mortgage reset. If they did that, however, they were often caught by a prepayment penalty of roughly 2 percent of the loan amount. To resolve the dilemma, albeit expensively, many borrowers simply added the penalty amount onto the back of the loan when they went to refinance. In short, they increased their indebtedness each time they refinanced.

There were other problems as well. Many advocates believed subprime mortgages were unfairly and deceptively marketed. A related problem was known as equity stripping.

Early on, I saw a documentary about a minority woman—a widow— who owned her own home. Along came a salesman who noted that her roof was old and could stand some repairs. She replied that she could not afford the repairs. He asked if she owned her home. She nodded. Well, then, problem solved. To pay for a $3,000 roof repair, the woman took out a high-cost subprime loan. But she lacked the ability to repay and was unaware of the prepayment penalties and adjusting interest rate associated with the loan. It was not long before the lender had stripped all the equity out of the property to cover fees and penalties. On the other side, subprime lenders argued that there was a valid need for their loans. Who else would extend credit to borrowers who simply had fallen down on their luck and needed such loans to get back on their feet? Others argued that subprime loans were fair game, since they were essentially unregulated and legal in all 50 states, according to applicable laws at the time. Consumer choice was often deemed more important than consumer protection.

Freddie Mac Meets the Advocates

"It's like pornography. You know it when you see it," was the classic definition of a predatory loan, according to one of the first judges to rule on cases of predatory lending. The fact that predatory lending was largely undefined and therefore unregulated made it difficult to chart a course for avoiding the purchase of mortgages that many people outside of Washington, DC, were beginning to believe were harmful to borrowers. Perhaps the most vocal critic at the time was Martin Eakes, founder and former head of the Self-Help credit union, based in Durham, NC, and its Washington, DC, policy arm, the Center for Responsible Lending (CRL).

I well remember Freddie's first encounter with Eakes. He had asked for a meeting with Freddie Mac to voice his concerns. Andrukonis, the company's chief credit risk officer, was the one to host it.

The meeting was tense. I was taking notes, glancing between the soured looks of the Freddie Mac execs and Eakes's impassioned face. A Yale-educated lawyer and businessman, Eakes was North Carolina's newly famed consumer advocate. The year was 1999, and he had just championed the first major state anti–predatory lending law in the nation. And right now he was giving Freddie Mac hell.

"Ah'm telling you, Freddie Mac," he chided in a country-boy drawl that belied the fist behind his words. "I am calling for a boycott of your stock if you don't sign up for these restrictions on subprime loans."

Eakes held a piece of paper in the air and looked directly at Andrukonis. "This is my list of the things Freddie Mac needs to stop doing. Now! You have no idea how bad subprime is. It's not like your nice prime market, where people understand the loans they are getting, where rates are competitive." His voice rose and fell like he was preaching on damnation. "Subprime is *predatory*," he intoned. "If you and Fannie start buying a lot of this stuff as is, you will institutionalize all the bad practices."

The Freddie executives stared. Who *was* this guy? Then the pushback began.

"How can you categorically say that all subprime is predatory?" asked one. "A lot of people are in the subprime market because they can't get a loan any other place. GSE involvement in that market is actually improving things."

Eakes shook his head. "Not unless you cut out these predatory features." He waved the list again. "As it is now, people are better off *not* getting any loan at all than getting one in subprime."

That didn't go over well with the people whose job it was to finance homeownership. "Well, that's pretty judgmental on your part."

Eakes conceded nothing. "I'm not judgmental. I am right! There are enough bad things going on in subprime that warrant much tougher restrictions."

The executives looked at each other blankly. "What bad things? Name some."

Eakes looked like he might burst. "Well, let's see. Aggressive marketing. Prepayment penalties. Credit life insurance. Higher interest rates."

Someone murmured from the back of the room. "*Duh*. Rates are higher because the *risk* is higher." Others chuckled quietly.

Another was more willing to engage. "Maybe you are right about the bad practices in subprime, Martin, but what does that have to do with the GSEs? Our job is to buy loans. You need to take your problem to a bank regulator in the primary market. We are the secondary market."

Eakes glared. "You know full well that there is no federal regulation of subprime going on. This is the Wild West of mortgage lending." Visions of shoot-em-ups went through my head.

"OK, so?"

"So that's why I'm asking the GSEs to set the standard. You and Fannie are such a big part of the market that you need to call the shots. If you buy these loans as they are now, you give those damn predatory lenders the seal of approval. And then there will be no telling where it will all end."

The meeting ended with an assignment. As I followed Andrukonis back to his office, he handed me Martin's list. "Are we going to sign up for all these restrictions?" I asked dubiously. I couldn't imagine getting consensus within our conflicted company.

Andrukonis shrugged. "Do some research on prepayment penalties and see if they are as bad as Eakes says."

The results were eye-opening. Compared to about 2 percent of mortgages in the conventional conforming mortgage market—or prime market—nearly 80 percent of subprime mortgages carried prepayment penalties. If a borrower chose to refinance or move before the expiration of the penalty period, a hefty penalty was charged: 2 percent of the UPB or six months' interest. On a $100,000 loan, the penalty could be as high as $2,000. The average penalty period of five years also seemed excessive. In the prime mortgage market, borrowers could be in and out of a couple of mortgages in that time frame for free. But once you committed to a subprime mortgage, you were stuck with it.

The consumer advocates were quick to call the prevalence of prepayment penalty mortgages in subprime discriminatory. The mortgage industry vehemently disagreed. Prepayment penalties were more prevalent in subprime, investors argued, because of the greater difficulty of predicting if and when borrowers were going to refinance their mortgages. In the prime market, people generally refinance when interest rates fall by a certain amount—and that can be modeled based on years of data. Because investors can calculate that risk and include it in the interest rate of the loan, prime borrowers can refinance without penalty. But subprime borrowers tend to refinance for reasons other than just to lower their interest rate. Sometimes borrowers refinance to get into a better loan because their credit position has improved. Other times they refinance to take *more* cash out of their house. So it's impossible for investors to predict and therefore price the prepayment risk—or so the argument went.

Since investors can't figure out what the subprime borrower is going to do next, they just leave it to that borrower to manage his or her own risk of prepaying the loan. For the consumer this means that if you want another loan, for whatever reason, you will have to pay the investor to get out of your current one if the penalty term is still in effect.

A Night with the Focus Group

"How many of you knew that your mortgages contained prepayment penalties?"

I was sitting behind a one-way mirror watching a focus group we had set up to learn about what borrowers really understand about their mortgages. Their responses were distressing.

The group was made up of mostly minority homeowners. No one raised a hand to indicate they knew they had a prepayment penalty when they got the loan. And no hands went up to indicate they knew the interest rate on the mortgage they got.

I remember pausing as I recorded this finding. *Do I know my interest rate?* I wasn't sure. But I did know what kind of loan I had, and it didn't have a prepayment penalty.

In the discussion that followed, the focus group participants said they didn't know they had a penalty on their mortgage until they tried to refinance. That's when the loan officer said, "No problem. We'll just roll the penalty into the new loan."

Just like that, they would get a new mortgage. Of course, it was a larger mortgage than the one they were getting out of; their outstanding debt was 2 percent greater because of the penalty they just paid. And the five-year penalty clock would start all over again. In my mind, five-year penalties had to go.

The Problem with Leading

As in any hierarchical company, decisions have to run up the chain. This one would not be easy. Paring back on lending features that some thought unethical (while others didn't) when we were trying to offset declining margins elsewhere in the business would not be popular with top management.

Carrying briefing books, I followed Andrukonis into the office of his boss, Freddie Mac's president, David Glenn. It was a dry run for the board meeting two weeks hence, and Andrukonis had to sell his anti–predatory lending plan to this group first. Glenn sat at one end of an oblong and highly polished table, the end closest to the floor-to-ceiling windows that gave an expansive view over the front courtyard. On either side of him sat the executive vice presidents, the senior vice presidents, the vice presidents, and then me, the scribe. His assistant sat in the adjoining room. To call the group skeptical was putting it mildly.

"Let me get this straight," said Glenn, flipping to the end of the deck. "You want Freddie to *voluntarily* place restrictions on our investments in subprime because somebody from North Carolina is demanding that we do so?"

A longtime Freddie leader, Glenn was serious and straitlaced. When he did smile, the gesture was slow to warm up his face. "He understands that we're not FHA, that we have to actually *compete* in the market, right?"

Andrukonis took the jibe in stride. "Excellent point. Yes, he knows we're not FHA. His name's Martin Eakes, and he's a charismatic guy all right. But he's a banker, too, and smart."

Mitch Delk, the company's top lobbyist, chimed in. "He's also politically savvy and well connected with House Financial Services. Among consumer groups, he's one of the most reasonable to deal with."

Freddie Mac's president grimaced. It was clear how much he didn't like bringing politics into a business discussion.

Andrukonis continued. "As I was saying, Martin did approach us about making some changes, but I'm not recommending these restrictions to please him." Nodding at me, he said, "We researched some of the products—single premium credit life insurance and prepayment premium mortgages—and they really are bad. If a borrower isn't careful or listening intently at the closing table, he could easily get in way over his head in a high-cost loan."

"I get that," said someone who worked in investments. "But before we consider a pull back from these products, let's remember that these loans are perfectly legal, and borrowers apparently want them. Who are we, God? Our job is to provide liquidity to the market. People have to take responsibility for their own decisions."

"Right," said another. "It's paternalistic to tell people which mortgages they can and cannot have. They are grown-ups. We don't do that in the prime space."

Andrukonis leaned back and crossed his arms. "You're right. We let people make their own choices in prime." He then sat upright, his voice tensing. "We also have 30 years of data on that market. I remind you that we have zero data on subprime. That market has not been through one single business cycle. I highly recommend that we take it slow and *safe*. And we may need to put some borrower protections in place."

Glenn's assistant entered the room and brought him a handwritten note. He glanced at it, eyes widening slightly, then stood up and left the room.

After a moment's pause while everyone wondered what had come up, the conversation resumed, but the gloves came off.

"Dave, I don't like this at all," said one of the mortgage traders, hitting his fist on the table. "It's bad precedent for us to give in to these consumer groups. Remember when that advocacy group sent busloads of people to protest our underwriting policies in the lobby? You give them an inch, and they want everything. Soon we'll be giving away loans for free."

Another executive nodded in agreement. "Besides, why should we make the first move and put ourselves out of the market? What about Fannie? If we do this and they don't follow, we'll be sidelined with the lenders. We'll be out."

"Martin has been talking to Fannie, too," Andrukonis said flatly. "I think they'll come to the same conclusion eventually."

Delk rubbed the back of his neck. "It may be sooner than you think," he said. "All we need to do is make it widely known that Freddie is taking a leadership role in combating subprime. They'll be so mad that they will *have* to follow suit and impose the same restrictions. In no way will they let us win a point on them—especially on the PR front."

Glenn reentered the room and walked back to his place at the table. "I apologize to everyone," he said slowly, "but we'll need to reschedule. I am going down to speak to Leland."

For a moment, no one moved. Then, as if on cue, the executives closed their briefing books, pushed back their chairs, and stood up to go. I sighed quietly. Too many meetings ended like this.

Andrukonis came out last, having been detained by Glenn. I couldn't read his expression.

"What was that all about?" I inquired.

"What?"

"What was so urgent that David had to end the meeting to talk to Leland?"

Andrukonis looked around and then said quietly, "Warren Buffet is dumping the stock."

I knew little about Freddie's shareholders, but I did know this: Warren Buffet was our largest investor.[3]

I walked on, pondering the implications. "Did he say why he was dropping us?"

"It's because of our entry into subprime. He doesn't think we know what we are doing."

"Oh," I said flatly. Trying to lighten the mood, I added, "Well, do we?"

He did not answer but walked on.

I thought how rare—and ironic—it was that both a major consumer advocate and a major shareholder were essentially saying the same thing to us, at the same time, albeit for different reasons: Get out of subprime, Freddie Mac.

A few months later, in March 2000, Freddie Mac became the first mortgage market participant in either the primary and secondary market to set standards on subprime investments. We didn't go so far as to ban prepayment penalties altogether, as Eakes had wanted, but we did reduce the standard five-year penalty period down to three years. Freddie also was the first to ban the purchase of mortgages with single-premium credit life insurance.

It was an important start, but the next few months would be critical. Would Freddie be stuck out on a limb—or would Fannie Mae and the rest of the market follow our lead? As Delk had predicted, Fannie grudgingly followed suit, a pattern that would repeat itself over the next few years.

From Tiptoe to Giant Footprint

Many argue that the seeds of the subprime crisis were sown as far back as 2000, when Freddie Mac and Fannie Mae tiptoed in to see what was going on. The reasons for exploring subprime were both profit-seeking and political—a dense tangle of shrinking margins, outside pressure to reach underserved borrowers, and an altruistic view that the GSEs—with their high standards—could help clean up a market that was known as the Wild West of mortgage lending.

At a time when g-fee income was declining, Freddie eyed the fatter margins in subprime as a potentially profitable expansion of its business. Entering subprime also was consistent with providing liquidity, a statutory purpose, to subprime borrowers who often had no alterative than to purchase the higher-risk (and higher-cost) loans. GSE liquidity would lower the cost of subprime, as it had done in the prime market over many years.

At least that is what the firm said to detractors. To true believers inside the company, it was Freddie's mission to clean up the subprime market. Only the GSEs could enforce the standardization, efficiency, competitive pricing, and market discipline we had brought to the prime market.

Being the Don Quixote of the mortgage market was one thing. Managing subprime credit risk was another.

Under the watchful eye of Andrukonis, a special working group was carved out of the single-family mortgage division to study the vagaries of the subprime market. Freddie's tiptoe into subprime needed to be a controlled experiment with specific risk concentration limits—with the goal of being able to discern good originators from sleazy ones, and good loans from stinkers.

These tests could not be done from the sidelines. They required getting in the game. Mindful of the unknown risks, Credit Risk Oversight (CRO) specified that the special subprime group could only buy untested product from lenders whose business operations Freddie employees had personally inspected and approved. As an added precaution, the bundles of subprime loans were further protected, or wrapped, with bond insurance purchased from a third party. Freddie was slowly and responsibly learning about a segment of the market that lacked liquidity but served a high share of non-white borrowers who were paying exorbitant rates to obtain mortgages that had predatory features. All our safety, soundness, and mission boxes were checked off. What was not to like?

Plenty. Buying whole loans with bond insurance was unprofitable.

Across the way, Freddie Mac's investment group—headed by senior vice president Greg Parseghian, a recent Wall Street hire—didn't appreciate the intradivisional competition for subprime mortgages. In buying subprime mortgages, the single-family group was inadvertently bidding up the prices of the subprime PLSs the traders wanted to buy for the company's retained portfolio. While this competition would theoretically (over time) make sub-prime mortgage rates decline, which would help borrowers, it made things more expensive for Freddie Mac's other business line—and a handsomely profitable one at that.

It was difficult then to see the crack that had just occurred in the foundation of Freddie's mission. Ostensibly Freddie Mac was committed to bringing higher standards (and lower interest rates) to the subprime mortgage market, but the comparably greater profits available in subprime were truly seductive and eventually corrupting.

For subprime borrowers, Freddie's intramural competition would have been beneficial because increased demand would have caused subprime interest rates to decline. But what was good for subprime borrowers was not necessarily good for investors hungry for high yields, like Freddie Mac traders working in the portfolio investment division across the street.

One business line competing against another was an unsustainable situation. And it was not hard to determine which side would win.

After a number of months of heated exchanges between CRO and the investment group, including appeals to top management, the experimental single-family subprime group was closed down. Gone were the on-site inspections. Gone was the careful monitoring of risk at the individual loan level.

The traders had won. Freddie Mac would no longer dabble in subprime whole loans where risks could be monitored and controlled. The company would make a market in subprime securities instead. Freddie Mac's retained portfolio was given the green light by management and the board to buy nearly all the subprime PLSs it wanted. From 2001 to 2005, GSE purchases of PLSs swelled dramatically, rising from $28 billion to $221 billion. Representing as much as 40 percent of the subprime market at its peak, Freddie Mac's purchases of subprime securities were structured to steer clear of predatory features, and many of the loans contained in the securities counted for "goal credit." But profitability remained a key motivation.[4]

As cited in *Regaining the Dream*, "through these purchases, the GSEs added billions of dollars to the already overheated private market and encouraged a fundamental shift from the public to the private sector and, essentially, from the promotion of the public goals to the pursuit of private gains."[5]

Where Things Stand

A lot has changed in the mortgage market since the Wild West days of subprime. From its high point of 20 percent of the market in 2007, the so-called subprime share has fallen to near zero. Gone are the specialty subprime companies. They quickly went bankrupt when their liquidity dried up and losses—and lawsuits—mounted. The subprime shops that were opened up by big banks so they too could partake in the frenzy have been shuttered. The only remaining legacy of that hyped-up era are the losses and the books and movies that tell the sad tale. Bank of America, which swallowed Countrywide Mortgage Company at government behest—itself loaded with subprime loans—spent years paying for those bad risks, as did J. P. Morgan Chase, which subsumed Washington Mutual, and Wells Fargo, which bought Wachovia.

Subprime borrowers, of course, are the biggest losers of all. In 2009, the Pew Hispanic Center looked at homeownership gains—and losses—among racial and ethnic groups. Consistent with other researchers, Pew found that African Americans and Hispanics were 2.5 times more likely than whites to have subprime mortgages, even when controlling for income. According to the study, in 2006, when subprime was at its peak, 17.4 percent of white borrowers obtained subprime loans, compared to 44.9 percent of Hispanics and 52.8 percent of African Americans. When the bottom fell out of the subprime market a year later, minority borrowers and their neighborhoods were the most hurt—and have been the last to recover.[6]

A July 2012 *Washington Post* article described the particularly painful impact of subprime on minority borrowers: "For blacks, the picture since the recession has been particularly grim. They disproportionately held subprime mortgages during the housing boom and are facing foreclosure in outsized numbers. That is raising fears among consumer advocates, academics and federal regulators that the credit scores of black Americans have been systematically damaged, haunting their financial futures."[7]

In 2011, the SEC brought a case against the CEOs of Freddie Mac and Fannie Mae and three top-level employees. One might have thought the case would focus on the actual buying of high-risk loans and the failure to adequately manage the risk. Not so. Doing stupid things is not a criminal offense; failing to disclose your stupidity is.

The GSE executives, former CEO Dick Syron, former chief business officer Patricia Cook, and Donald Bisenius, former senior vice president of credit policy and portfolio management, were charged with misleading investors by failing to properly disclose the quantity and riskiness of the subprime mortgages in their charge. The case against the Freddie execs turned on the fact that internal documents used the word "subprime," while in public disclosures, the pejorative term was not used. Instead, Freddie Mac used specific risk characteristics to illustrate the level of risk in their public disclosures, leaving it up to the investor to determine if the loans were subprime or not.[8]

It was a weak case, but the SEC needed some "pelts," as a former colleague put it. After several years, and perhaps hoping the public's demand for blood had quieted down, in April 2015 the SEC settled with the Freddie Mac executives for a mere hand slap. The executives were barred from signing certain financial reports for a time and were required to pay $310,000 into a fund to compensate defrauded investors—penalties that fell far short of what the SEC was seeking. The core weakness of the case was the lack of a common industry definition of subprime.

Letting investors do their own risk assessments is one thing, but expecting consumers to be able to do it is another. Many consumers had no idea what types of loans—and risks—they were signing up for.

AEI's Pinto has made this argument for several years now, claiming that many of the loans called "A-minus" or "nontraditional" by the GSEs were actually subprime loans. He has also dubbed FHA the government's subprime lender, given the weaker credit background of many FHA borrowers.[9]

Once again, the word "subprime" eludes easy definition. Whereas traditionally it meant mortgages originated to borrowers with poor credit, many have inappropriately broadened it to include low-down-payment loans or loans to first-time homebuyers, a mainstay of FHA's clientele.

DFA curbed the most abusive aspects of subprime lending: exorbitant fees and penalties, deep initial interest rates, and steep rate adjustments. Lenders are now obliged to underwrite ARMs to the fully-indexed rate, not simply the rate in effect for the first one or two years. Pinto remains unconvinced, however. Some of the new DFA regulations are eerily similar to the weak underwriting policies that led to the crisis in the first place, he said in congressional testimony. The only difference is semantic: "loans with 580 FICOs, 50 percent debt-to-income ratios and 3 percent down payments will be called prime loans instead of subprime."[10]

Policy makers who once excoriated PLS investors are now bemoaning the loss of what they now more respectfully call "private capital." Nearly every mortgage originated today has a full government guarantee. Mortgages that are above the GSE and FHA loan limits are tightly underwritten and expensive. So the pressure is on to find a way to bring back private capital without introducing unwanted risk into the system.

Conclusion

How did a high-risk niche market arise and become the darling of the world, only to be spurned and rejected within a matter of years? The answer is complex. There was widespread ambiguity about the definition of subprime, the level of risk, overconfidence in structured finance, lax regulation, and a global market hungry for yield.

The GSE seal of approval added fuel to the previously niche market and brought subprime mortgages into mainstream America. Although Freddie Mac was the first in the industry to set anti–predatory lending standards, those efforts were like screen doors in a tornado. What started as a tiptoe into a potentially lucrative market segment became a nightmare as subprime mortgages defaulted in droves. The subprime contagion spread from Main Street to Wall Street, from PLS to CDO, and from the United States to countries around the world. When borrowers could no longer refinance their way out of the bad mortgages they were saddled with, their losses became not only Freddie Mac's losses but all our losses.

POLITICAL CAPTURE

No book that deals with the GSEs is complete without mention of the steel-knuckled political charades Freddie and Fannie played when they were at the zenith of their powers. The supporting actors and thickening plot have already been introduced: consumers and their politicians falling over themselves to support homeownership; two increasingly large, powerful companies bent on protecting their congressional charters; building social pressure to solve the growing divide between the housing haves and have-nots by loosening mortgage underwriting standards and reforming subprime lending; plus all the industry cheerleaders just trying to keep the easy money—and all the homeownership subsidies—flowing smoothly.

As the larger, more established, and more politically connected GSE, Fannie Mae was the envy of the Freddie lobbyists. As recounted in *All the Devils Are Here*, former CEO Jim Johnson was the chief architect of the company's take-no-prisoners approach to regulators and critics.[1] He left Fannie a decade before the government takeover, so Fannie truly had a head start on Freddie Mac in terms of everything political. However, Freddie's lobbying shop was fast developing a reputation of its own.

A friend and I were eating lunch in Freddie Mac's cafeteria in early 2001 when the CEO Leland Brendsel stopped by. I got flustered when he sat down, took a potato skin off my plate, and ate it. Brendsel asked if I was really leaving Credit Risk Oversight for Government Relations, Freddie's lobbying shop of about 30 people located not far from Capitol Hill.

I said yes, that I had been offered a job as director of public policy. In reality, it was a writing and research job that pretty much kept me chained to the desk, not hobnobbing on the Hill. I was not a registered lobbyist and had no intention of becoming one.

His response startled me. "You're going to DC? That place is a hell hole!"

Freddie Mac behaved like any other corporation seeking to influence the legislative process. But Freddie wasn't any other corporation. Case in point: the top item on my performance appraisal for my new job was "defend the charter." I could only guess what that would entail.

Family Fortunes at Risk

Prior to the government takeover in 2008, entities within the executive and legislative branches of government had certain oversight responsibilities when it came to the GSEs. HUD, an executive branch agency, was the GSE mission regulator responsible for setting the affordable housing goals. The other GSE regulator at the time, the Office of Federal Housing Enterprise Oversight, was located within HUD but had an entirely different mission— that of ensuring GSE safety and soundness. HUD's office of fair housing also kept an eye on the twin firms.

As the GSEs got larger and wielded more power, the White House Office of Domestic Policy and OMB cast a long shadow over the GSEs' activities. In the years leading up to the takeover, OMB would express its disdain for the GSEs in a lengthy paragraph in the president's economic report. From a budgetary standpoint, neither the GSE financing activities nor the implicit taxpayer subsidy appeared in the federal budget. However, given that GSEs were some of the largest corporate income taxpayers, their tax receipts were accounted for in the budget's general revenue account.

On the legislative side, the GSEs were subject to two oversight subcommittees within the powerful Senate Banking and House Financial Services committees, respectively. At least once a year, the GSEs were called to testify in general oversight hearings. They also appeared in Congress to testify on proposed GSE reform legislation and on matters of special concern, such as our accounting travails in 2003 and the growth of the subprime mortgage market in 2007.

Although the GSE charters were forged in a rare moment of bipartisanship, the general atmosphere of the committee hearings was anything but. Representative Barney Frank (D-MA) had a lot to do with that in the House, while Senator Richard Shelby (R-AL) suffered no fools in the Senate.

The committees act as echo chambers for vastly different political perspectives. Democrats continually emphasized the need to broaden access to homeownership for different income and racial/ethnic groups. Up until the takeover, broader access was synonymous with a large, growing GSE financing role, particularly in bankrolling affordable housing and ensuring a role for community banks. On the other hand, Republicans railed against the special advantages of the GSE charters, which created an uneven playing field relative to large banks. The GOP also worried more about risk than the Democrats and sought to limit the GSEs' growing on-balance sheet investments, known as the "retained portfolios." Freddie Mac's had begun to skyrocket in the late 1990s with Greg Parseghian's arrival from Wall Street.

Worrisome Growth of GSE Debt

To finance the purchase of PLSs and other securities (including those issued by Fannie and even Freddie itself), Freddie Mac tapped investors across the globe for funds. The firm issued debt securities in a manner similar to how the Treasury department issues Treasury notes and bonds to finance governmental operations. Because of its special status as a GSE, Freddie could borrow from the rest of the world almost as cheaply as the US government. In the good old days, Freddie pocketed a rich spread between what it paid its debt investors and what it earned on the higher-yielding PLSs. The retained portfolio was a money-making machine; in 2005 it stood around $710 billion.[2]

Under Parseghian, Freddie Mac created a marketing group that sold the GSE debt securities near and far. These were not backed by mortgages but by the company's good name and, to be honest, its murky government ties. Investors read in the prospectus that GSE debt was explicitly not backed by the government, but they bought it anyway—in great quantities. In 2005, the par value of debt securities issued by Freddie Mac that year was nearly $1 trillion, with roughly half of that sold abroad.[3] Some investors undoubtedly believed they were getting an investment just as safe as a US Treasury bond but with a little higher yield. The debt came in a variety of maturities. Freddie Mac was always vigilant to ensure it could roll over its debt, ensuring a continued influx of funds. Investor nervousness would be the kiss of death to the company's growth plans—and to the safety of the entire system.

While the committee members continued to argue, the GSEs and the entire housing industry exploited the political divide for their own ends. Wanting to rein in the GSEs, the banks would appeal to the Republicans about the problems of GSE growth and intrusion into the primary mortgage market. But the banks also would (and still do) make a strong appeal to the Democrats; in the past they had supported higher GSE housing goals and greater leniency in underwriting by stressing that some consumers wouldn't be able to get mortgages if the bar was set too high. Expanding access to traditionally underserved borrowers was not simply altruistic on the part of banks and other mortgage originators; it was seen as a savvy business move (as long as house prices were rising and the GSEs were absorbing the lion's share of the risk). As the largest representation of banks and mortgage companies, the powerful and politically well-connected MBA was particularly adept at making this point.[4]

For their part, the GSEs tended to align with and appeal to the Democrats on the broader access question. If homeownership was good, which was gospel, it stood to reason that expanding homeownership to a broader, more diverse set of borrowers was a good thing as well. Because broader access meant sustained or even greater GSE growth, it was a way of thwarting GOP efforts to trim GSEs' sails by requiring higher capital or shrinking the retained portfolios. Moreover, by purchasing mortgages for the retained portfolio, the GSEs could always say that their mortgage bid increased demand, which raised the price of mortgages and kept mortgage interest rates low. If both sides of the aisle had realized that they were being played by the whole industry, perhaps they could have set aside their differences and charted a path down the middle.

Please Don't Hurt Us!

In March 2000, Representative Richard Baker (R-LA), one of the earliest and most vocal GSE critics, introduced a very strong anti-GSE bill which, among other things, would have stripped the GSEs of the so-called Treasury line of credit, worth $2.25 billion, which the firm considered the absolute diamond of the GSE charter.[5] All of the other benefits in the GSE charters were important, but the Treasury line of credit provided the greatest indicia of government support. Apparently, Representative Baker and many others must have come to the same conclusion—so that's why they took aim at the aorta of the implicit guarantee, the root cause of our phenomenal growth. The bill also would have repealed the exemption that allows banks to invest more than 10 percent of their assets in GSE securities.

Either provision would have been a major blow to Freddie Mac's core business strength. The combination of losing the two provisions was unthinkable if the firm was to remain profitable, or so top management had concluded with the help of some very highly paid business consultants.

Although Freddie Mac's board and management likely shuddered when they learned about Baker's new bill, it was Freddie's lobbyists—with their rather jaundiced view of Congress and the democratic process—who allayed their fears. Just because some legislative provision is inserted into a subcommittee bill it doesn't mean it is going to stay there, they would say, reminding everyone of their high school civics class. Each provision has a long way to go before becoming law.

Representative Baker was easily the most conservative and vocal opponent of Freddie and Fannie. I remember sitting at a few congressional hearings over which he presided, and he would become absolutely livid. Both GSEs could easily arouse his ire, but he had a particular dislike for Fannie's CEO, Franklin Raines. It didn't help matters that prior to coming to Fannie, Raines had been OMB director during the Clinton administration. I vividly remember one hearing when Raines lectured the panel on some aspect of Fannie's business and put huge charts and graphs on the wall to "educate" the members. Humiliate was more like it. Little slights like that are never forgotten in Washington. Years later, the favor was returned when Baker hoisted up a chart of the eye-popping salaries and bonuses of Fannie Mae's top executives and asked Raines to comment on it.

Representative Baker didn't care much for Freddie's CEO, Leland Brendsel, either. He used to call the GSEs government-sponsored hedge funds because of the high degree of leverage supporting an ever-burgeoning retained portfolio. Freddie and Fannie bristled at this adage, as if that were the lowest thing you could say to a financial institution, but the concern was not unfounded.

Freddie Mac lobbyists assured management that Baker's tirades were not representative of the views of the full House Financial Services Committee, which was chaired by Mike Oxley (R-OH). But still, they remained on high alert anytime Freddie's CEO was called to testify.

Ironically the shot heard 'round the world in the GSE battle did not come from a Republican but from a Democrat. In testimony before Baker's subcommittee, the then- undersecretary for domestic finance in the Clinton Treasury department, Gary Gensler, sent shock waves through the markets in early 2000 when he supported Baker's get-tough provisions.

"Congress should seriously consider the best way to repeal such exceptions" to eliminate "the potential for problems at one financial institution to cause instability in the financial markets or at other institutions," Gensler said.[6] The significance of Gensler's comments was so huge at Freddie that employees could remember with absolute clarity where we were and what we were doing when we heard them. Freddie stock skidded noticeably that day.

If that wasn't enough, Gensler repeated his views a few days later after his boss, Treasury Secretary Larry Summers, made it clear that Gensler had not gone off half-cocked but in fact had spoken for the Clinton administration.

Up to this point, the GSEs had always found resonance with the Democrats over the housing mission. In fact, back in 1994, the Clinton administration had set an explicit goal to increase the nation's homeownership rate by several percentage points by implementing a national homeownership strategy. But monetary policy now took precedence over housing. Why the huge reversal?

There had been talk about using GSE securities, which were rated AAA like Treasury securities, as a new global benchmark security, in light of the fact that the supply of US Treasuries was diminishing thanks to the federal budget surplus. The government was using surplus funds to buy back old Treasuries, just at the time that GSE debt issuance was increasing rapidly. As articulated by Gensler, the government was not willing to cede the benchmark role to the GSEs, housing mission or not.

Such a situation seems absolutely inconceivable today. In addition to financing the massive US budget deficit, the government has trillions in mortgage-backed securities riding on its shoulders. But in 2000, it was a very different ballgame. Freddie rather liked its new prominence as debt security of choice. In testimony before Baker's subcommittee in May 2000, CEO Brendsel described the combination of a decline in Treasuries and the rise in GSE debt as a "positive development" for America's families. He said, "mortgage debt has grown in response to the increase in homeownership, and is backed by the safest form of collateral, the equity in people's homes."[7]

Brendsel was right about the equity in people's homes. Equity is the foundation of the strength of the entire housing finance system. It is astounding, therefore, how fast this situation reversed itself in 2008 when millions of homeowners found themselves underwater as house prices plummeted. Today requiring considerable down payments is viewed as old-fashioned. Saving for down payments takes time and will slow the housing recovery. This predominant view either suggests a very short memory or a deep conviction that the government once again will step in to save the system.

A New Boss

In March 2001, I started my new job in Government Relations. I remember being apprehensive that first morning. The commute from Virginia into DC had taken a good hour, and I was unsure where to park. But my nervousness dissipated when I got into the parking garage underneath our downtown office. On the first ramp down, I noticed a few parking spaces were marked, "Reserved for Freddie Mac." I was impressed and pulled into one of the spaces. Not a good move. Thirty minutes after I had hung up my coat, an administrative assistant found me and demanded to know why I had taken Delk's spot.

That may have been the most important thing I could have learned about Freddie's top lobbyist and my new boss, R. Mitchell Delk. Suave with a silken Georgia accent, Delk had headed Freddie Mac's lobbying shop from 1991. Previously, he had been head of legislative affairs for the SEC and counsel to the Senate Banking Committee.

Delk slicked his wavy brown hair back over his forehead into a little ducktail at the nape of his neck. When reading, he would absentmindedly reach back and slide his fingers along the curl. Immaculately dressed, he became somewhat flamboyant after the company went to a business casual dress code. His trademark look was pastel shirts, clogs, and no socks.

As could be imagined, Delk aroused great curiosity among rank-and-file employees. I was often asked, "What's it like to work for him?"

Delk was the consummate politician. Although he was a Republican, he deeply admired President Clinton's political prowess. I once walked into his office while he was watching Clinton give a speech on TV. He was mesmerized.

Delk was prone to doling out intense flattery and lapsing into exaggeration. People seemed to know they were being handled, but for some reason they didn't care. They actually rather liked it. Among the staff, there was a joke where, after a typical interaction with our boss, we'd hit ourselves in the head and say, "Oops, I believed him again!" Delk remained generally aloof from his staff and never worked regular business hours or turned on his computer. His office was littered with magazines and papers. He was fond of good wine, expensive restaurants, and high-stakes political poker.

I think he hired me because I could write. It certainly wasn't because I was a political asset. In fact, he used to tell me, "We are a good team. You do policy. I'll handle the politics."

That division of labor was absolutely fine with me. I wanted nothing to do with lobbying. But I was not as immune from it as I might have liked.

Freddie's outreach to Republicans was an experience I will never forget. The initiative was well underway by the time I reached Government Relations. The main issue facing the GSEs at the turn of the new century was GOP antagonism against their very existence. The firms began a series of strategic steps to get conservatives to drop the sword.

In October 2000, Freddie Mac lobbyists had engineered a major breakthrough with Representative Baker and other Republicans. In an attempt to get our most vocal opponents to bury the hatchet—temporarily, at least—Freddie Mac developed a set of voluntary initiatives known as the Six Commitments that the firm would undertake to improve our financial strength and disclosures. These commitments ranged from releasing a new credit rating that attempted to measure our financial strength while excluding the benefit of the implicit government guarantee (according to us, it only brought us down from AAA to AA-) to the issuance of subordinated debt as another way to get independent views of our actual credit strength. Each voluntary commitment had been carefully researched and crafted to align with state-of-the-art thinking on risk management, as espoused by the Basel Committee on Banking Supervision, the gold standard of risk management and disclosure. The initiatives were so sound that a few years later, the GSE regulator incorporated at least two of Freddie's commitments into its safety and soundness regulation.

In one of my first assignments working in Government Relations, I described Freddie's progress in implementing these Six Commitments in CEO congressional testimony. Brendsel had been called up again to testify before Baker's subcommittee. This time, the air was slightly less charged, and Freddie went on the offensive to demonstrate all the wonderful benefits it brought to consumers, starting with a "safe supply of low-cost mortgage funds," a phrase I would write and rewrite for years to come. Freddie also boasted that our new commitments would "keep us at the vanguard of evolving worldwide practices." "Vanguard" was another favorite Freddie word.

The Six Commitments and the temporary rapprochement they brought with Chairman Baker were huge for the GSEs; these wins told the stock market that GSE political risk was on the wane. The $20-billion bump in market capitalization that followed earned Delk a large end-of-year bonus, and he was not shy about reminding the CEO of the magnitude of his achievement. After the Six Commitments, markets calmed down, and the GSEs went back to making money. With the House GOP somewhat quiescent for the moment, Freddie turned its eye to an even greater challenge: the White House.

Winning Over the "Rs"

At first blush, the "compassionate conservatism" of the newly elected president did not include housing or support for the housing GSEs—Fannie Mae and Freddie Mac. Like Chairman Baker, the George W. Bush administration was not impressed with our size or growth. Like Baker, they did not hide their disdain for Franklin Raines, a former Clinton insider.

Notwithstanding the success of the Six Commitments, Freddie execs were concerned that the administration would signal support for Baker's get-tough provisions on the GSEs and "pull another Gensler." Worse still, many in the Bush White House claimed that the GSEs were no longer needed. Their public rhetoric indicated they would like nothing better than to privatize the GSEs and turn their secondary market functions over to the private market.

Early remarks from former Fed governor and top Bush economic advisor Larry Lindsey suggested that the GSE battle was only getting started. Stock markets returned to high alert any time an administration official said anything negative about the GSEs. In fact, many inside the company believed that Freddie Mac's stock was permanently stuck because of a "political risk premium."

It also didn't help that a major corporate scandal was brewing down in Texas: When Enron blew up in the fall of 2001, every company that used derivatives ran for political cover. The two GSEs relied heavily on derivatives to hedge the risks of our growing mortgage portfolios.

Homeownership Was the Key

The trick to winning over the Bush Administration was to find an ideological space where the Rs could tolerate us. Freddie didn't expect loving kisses, just an armed truce. Freddie was big (and Fannie even bigger), and neither was *really* a private sector company exposed to the buffeting winds of market discipline. This counted as a huge negative for conservatives. Second, the GSEs did housing, and aside from former New York representative and HUD secretary Jack Kemp, conservatives were not into providing public support for private housing.

Multifamily housing was *not* the ticket to play with the Rs. Instead, single-family homeownership aligned perfectly with the ownership society that Bush often talked about. It didn't hurt that a number of academic studies were finding correlations between homeownership and positive family outcomes, such as children's educational achievement. The Washington think-tank crowd had identified housing as a panacea to a number of social ills. Everybody, it seemed, was suddenly talking about the benefits of homeownership.

Even more, a pro-homeownership policy appeared to align with Bush's conservative base. Studies showed that homeowners tend to become more conservative over time because they have a vested financial interest in protecting their property values, which generally entails support for the status quo over progressive values. At least, this was what British prime minister Margaret Thatcher found when she privatized more than a million state-owned units of council housing in the 1980s.[8]

As technology stocks began tanking in the early 2000s, housing also was becoming the preferred investment of the middle class. As house prices started to rise, it became clear that not all groups were sharing in the fruits of increasing property values. Minority homeownership rates lagged the white rate by 25 percentage points, even after controlling for demographic factors such as wealth and income. This gap suggested that something else—something possibly sinister and unfair—was blocking the pathway to a first home. Routinely the GSEs were blamed by the consumer groups and many Dems for contributing to it. GSE underwriting was too tight.

In particular, Freddie was castigated continually for research its economists had done a few years back that found that about 30 percent of subprime borrowers could have qualified for prime loans. When this finding hit the newspapers, Freddie Mac came under attack for relegating borrowers who could have qualified for prime mortgages to the higher-cost subprime market. The fact that a disproportionate share of subprime borrowers happened to be minorities further inflamed the issue. Public pressure from multiple quarters intensified to open the doors to homeownership, as if a new age were dawning. By 2005, Freddie Mac's tag line had changed to "We Make Home Possible."

The 30-percent factoid followed Freddie everywhere. Worse, the number kept getting rounded up by the news media. From 30 percent it grew to one-third. Later reports raised the number to 50 percent of subprime borrowers who had been *forced* into subprime.

So the pressure to expand Freddie's purchases of mortgages originated to minority families intensified to a fevered pitch. By comparison, Fannie seemed largely unscathed by this criticism. With its "Trillion Dollar" homeownership initiatives, Fannie had figured out the reputational and political potency of minority homeownership long before we did.

Minority Homeownership as Political Strategy

The Garbage Can Theory is an inelegant description for the way public policy is made. In contrast to following a linear, rational process, policy outcomes are nothing more than the random and messy confluence of issues, opportunities, problems, and solutions. They all get thrown into a garbled policy process and come out in unpredictable ways. Old solutions get attached to new problems. Important issues like what to do about systemic risk get discarded because they are too hard, while low-hanging fruit, like goosing the homeownership rate in a local congressional district, serve up temptations few politicians can overlook. That's a good way to make sense of the minority homeownership initiative Freddie entered into with the Bush administration.

For Freddie, the hope was that a minority homeownership initiative would help the firm shake off the nagging criticism that it was somehow discriminating by maintaining standard underwriting. However, there was an important side benefit for Freddie: a convergence of Freddie's financial interests with the political interests of the Bush administration. Freddie's top lobbyist and my boss, Mitch Delk, had a hunch that, given Bush's weak showing with the Hispanic vote in the 2000 election, the administration would be willing to work with the firm on a new issue that might resonate with this part of the electorate.

The question was: How important was homeownership to Hispanic voters? To find out, Delk tapped a well-known conservative pollster and ordered up some phone surveys. He asked me to research conservative policy support for homeownership from the early days of the republic, from Reconstruction's 40 acres and a mule to President Nixon's support for a secondary mortgage market in 1970, the year Freddie Mac was created. I also analyzed the benefits of—and barriers to—homeownership and what the secondary mortgage market could do about it. Eventually, a list of 25 things Freddie could do to take down barriers was compiled. Most items were so obvious as to seem quaint today, like printing mortgage documents in Spanish and promoting homebuyer education. Freddie was also a leader in combating predatory lending thanks to the wake-up call we got from Martin Eakes. Consistent with our "own and keep" motto, Freddie argued that it wasn't enough for borrowers merely to get a home—they needed to be able to sustain homeownership in order to build wealth. Freddie's award-winning Don't Borrow Trouble program was being well received in cities across the nation, reaching thousands with its pro-consumer protection message. This and other Freddie initiatives were focused on protecting subprime consumers from the worst excesses, even as the company sought to make a profitable market there.

Delk had grander ambitions, however. If Freddie played its cards right, an administration-led initiative (albeit designed by Freddie) would be a double bonanza: it would help repair Freddie's poor image around affordable lending while helping the White House capture a greater share of the Hispanic vote. If the White House saw that Freddie was important to their chances for reelection in 2004, maybe they would tone down their anti-GSE rhetoric. Best of all, the political premium holding down the stock would shrink—and bonus dollars would flow.

That was the idea, anyway. While I pored over academic studies and history books, Delk was out and about, and that meant a lot of schmoozing with the GOP. It also meant a lot of fundraising dinners at an Italian restaurant named Galileo's, at which Republican Congressman Oxley was often in attendance.

See a Wave, Grab a Surfboard

The results of the Hispanic phone surveys came back glowing. A poll conducted in January 2002 found that Hispanics would strongly favor an

Administration-led effort to increase homeownership. In response to a question asking if the respondent would be more likely to support the president if he made a commitment to increase Hispanic homeownership, 87 percent said yes, followed by a close 75 percent who said homeownership should be a very high national priority.

Delk was pleased. He had Freddie's graphic arts department create a mock newspaper ad with a big picture of Bush and some verbiage about the importance of minority homeownership with subtle mention of the important role played by the GSEs, specifically Freddie Mac. The bait was on the hook.

Later Delk would show the ad to Freddie's various consultants, including former House Speaker Newt Gingrich, to help them envision the political success of a minority homeownership campaign. Delk was confident he would sell the initiative to the administration by claiming that it would garner "significant Hispanic support."

All the consultants said the initiative was brilliant. Two questions left unanswered were, How much of an increase in minority homeownership was feasible? And how much could President Bush reasonably take credit for?

Respected research institutions like Harvard's Joint Center for Housing Studies were projecting that, from 2000 to 2010, minorities would account for over 60 percent of total growth in households and 50 percent of total growth in homeowners. This meant that minorities were going to play a bigger role in the housing market than ever before. In response to this information, Delk was fond of saying: "See a wave, grab a surfboard."

In Washington-ese, this meant that there was an opportunity to take credit for an outcome—or part of an outcome—that would have happened anyway. The minority homeownership rate was projected to rise naturally because the relatively youthful population would simply age over that period, so people in those demographics would be in a better position to own a home. The president thus could lay claim to an observable increase in minority homeownership with just a modest amount of effort on the part of the administration and the industry.

Hence, the goal put forth by Freddie was to increase the minority homeownership rate from 47 to 50 percent over the next five years by putting 3.3 million minority families in homes of their own, including 1.5 million Hispanics. Drawing Fannie Mae into the initiative, it was decided that the GSEs would split the tab along the lines of their relative market share. In dollar terms, Freddie would commit to 40 percent of the increase in additional purchases of minority mortgages, and Fannie would take 60 percent. This was the way the GSEs always split everything.

As I think back on this project, I remember feeling unsure, even uneasy, about the plan as it got underway. I tended to side with the housers in the firm, who wanted Freddie to think more broadly about the different needs and challenges people faced when considering buying a home. On the other hand, I felt uncomfortable with Freddie's broader political agenda that my work was, in fact, supporting.

"Get over it, Susan," one jaded lobbyist griped. "Lobbying is the business of this town." I didn't know if he was trying to make me feel better or worse.

The Golden Ring: State of the Union Address

Armed with the polling data, the homeownership research, and the near-life-sized photograph of Bush, Delk started to test-market his complex strategy. The first stop was to get a buy-in from Freddie Mac's management. Characteristically, the top executives were not happy with the prospect of politics influencing business decisions, even if no material loosening of underwriting was being proposed.

Despite initial skepticism, CEO Brendsel must have given the green light to proceed. Several high-level meetings were hastily arranged, including one with then-HUD Secretary Mel Martinez, who seemed highly receptive to the initiative. Delk was quick to point out a prominent role for the HUD secretary and provided examples of different homeownership events where the president's initiative could be rolled out with great fanfare.

Timing was important. Delk had set his sights on the top prize: He was determined to see President Bush embrace the initiative publicly—and, by extension, the GSEs—by mentioning the minority homeownership initiative in the 2002 State of the Union address, less than a month away. He directed me to draft a few sentences to help White House speechwriters, if needed.

The weeks passed without a word. On the night of the speech, I was perched on the family-room sofa waiting for the president to come on TV when the phone rang. It was Delk. "It's in," he said. Then he hung up. My heart started to race.

A few minutes later, I heard President Bush say the magic words: "Members, we will work together to provide . . . broader homeownership, especially among minorities."

It was just a short sentence, but that hardly diminished the achievement. Delk would later gloat that minority homeownership was one of three domestic policy issues mentioned in Bush's first State of the Union address following the September 11, 2001, attacks on the World Trade Center and the Pentagon.

Six months later, at a church in Atlanta, Georgia, Bush rolled out the administration's minority homeownership initiative. In a brief moment of GSE glory, the president was flanked by the Freddie and Fannie CEOs, Leland Brendsel and Frank Raines. A host of housing and consumer groups applauded vigorously. Freddie ran the huge ad of President Bush in the *Atlanta Constitution*.

At the event, both CEOs publicly committed to expanding minority purchases by a combined $1 trillion over the next five years.

"I want to thank Leland and Frank for that commitment," said Bush. "It's a commitment that conforms to their charters, as well, and also conforms to their hearts."

And to the bottom line, of course. As Air Force One took off with both CEOs on board, GSE political risk evaporated along with the fear of GSE privatization. Freddie stock closed up $2, or 3.19 percent, to $64.68.

"Doing homeownership" with the Bush administration pumped new life into the GSE implicit guarantee. Freddie had become more associated not only with the government but with the political agenda of the White House.

But it was a dangerous liaison. Bush's mention of minority homeownership might have been a mere footnote in a speech otherwise dominated by post-9/11 angst and resolve, but its import was not lost on the US housing finance industry. Perhaps unwittingly, the conservative anti-GSE White House had just given its blessing to a new expansion of mortgage credit.

Protect the Charter

Once the homeownership initiative was launched in June 2002, Freddie Mac lobbyists spotted another dangerous storm brewing on the horizon: congressional threats to the GSEs' prized SEC exemption. The exemption was an extremely important element of the charter because it demonstrated probably more than anything else how unique the GSEs were among US financial companies. And uniqueness was code for favored government corporation and low borrowing costs.

Earlier that year, Representatives Christopher Shays (R-CT) and Ed Markey (D-MA), no friends of the GSEs, had introduced legislation to repeal the SEC exemption, which had been part of the original congressional charter for each company. The purpose of the SEC exemption ostensibly had been to stimulate the development of a liquid secondary mortgage market. But that goal had long ago been accomplished, and now there was growing concern that the GSEs had grown so large that more transparency was needed into their operations.

The exemption had two parts. The first was exemption from the registration of GSE common stock with the SEC. The second exempted the GSEs from having to register each and every security they issued with the SEC. These included both the mortgage-backed securities and the corporate debt securities issued regularly by each company. Compared to the stock registration exemption, the securities exemption was far more encompassing—and valuable—to the companies from both a financial and a perception perspective.

At first Freddie Mac (and the consultants) went on the offensive, arguing that Freddie's financial disclosures already met or exceeded SEC requirements as a result of the Six Commitments.[9] That being the case, removing the exemption would not accomplish much from a transparency standpoint—but could greatly upset the smooth delivery of mortgages into the market if each mortgage security had to be registered.

There was truth to that statement. Part of the efficiency of the GSE-supported mortgage market was that our securities could be sold in the "to-be-announced" market, or TBA. This was shorthand for the uniquely GSE process whereby pools of loans that satisfied average characteristics could be used to create securities. Carrying the GSE guarantee, these TBA securities could be auctioned off before the underlying mortgages had been originated and sold. Inherent in this system was great trust among lender, GSE, and investor, which contributed to a highly efficient system that benefited each entity. But borrowers benefited, too. The TBA market was what enabled borrowers to lock in a particular interest rate before their loan was actually originated. It was the secret ingredient to the high efficiency of the US mortgage market.

Freddie argued that registration of each individual security would upset the smooth functioning of the TBA market, including the rate lock—a prized borrower benefit.

For a time, the lobbying effort seemed to be working. Then came the revelation of WorldCom's derivatives fraud and the eventual passage of sweeping legislation known as Sarbanes-Oxley. That's when OFHEO publicly joined the opposition and called for repeal of the GSEs' SEC exemption.

Not to be outmaneuvered, Freddie decided to throw overboard the registration of the common stock in an effort to save the more valuable part of the exemption: the registration of all debt and mortgage securities. Discussions with Treasury and SEC quickly commenced, and a deal was struck on July 12, 2002. The deal preserved the most valuable aspect of the charter benefit while undercutting the growing momentum to repeal the entire SEC exemption. Luckily, Standard & Poor's had determined that the common stock registration with the SEC would not adversely impact the AAA ratings of GSE securities.

It's a made-for-Washington moment when everybody claims victory. A few weeks later, Treasury Undersecretary Peter Fisher testified in Congress and reversed Treasury's long-standing call for the repeal of the SEC exemption for mortgage and debt securities. Markets responded well to the news of joint announcement with Treasury and the SEC; Freddie stock rose $1.35, or 2.4 percent. A Washington insider reportedly called the agreement brilliant—because we gave nothing up.

Afterwards, there were lots of high fives in the lobbying shop and a trip downstairs to the Caucus Room for a round of drinks on the lobbyists. Of course, the company still had some work to do: getting Freddie's common stock registered with the SEC. But none of the lobbyists gave that a second thought. That was a problem for Freddie's accountants to worry about.

Where Things Stand

Political interference in the housing market did not end when the GSEs were gagged and placed in conservatorship. Nor did the idea of using a State of the Union Address as a checkered flag for the mortgage industry to gun their engines.

In his 2013 SOTU, President Barack Obama said that "too many families with solid credit who want to buy a home are being rejected. Too many families who have never missed a payment and want to refinance are being told no. That's holding our entire economy back. We need to fix it."[10]

The focus of the president's remarks was ostensibly to aid borrowers whose mortgages are underwater but who have solid credit and have not defaulted on their loans. He called for legislation that would make it easier for these borrowers to refinance by waiving requirements on the underlying value of the property.

Obama's SOTU was not the end of the matter. More jimmying of the housing market was soon to come. This one had the fingerprints of the mortgage industry all over it.

Less than two months after the SOTU that focused on borrowers with solid credit, the *Washington Post* reported in April 2013 that the Obama administration was "engaged in a broad push to make more home loans available to people with weaker credit."[11] Within the year, FHFA would loosen GSE underwriting standards, including allowing the GSEs once again to guarantee low-down-payment mortgages. But this time, taxpayers will have to take all the losses.

You could hear the door to homeownership fly off its hinges. Home prices are strengthening in many parts of the country, and mortgage applications are picking up. There are fewer risky products on the market, but nail-biters are already worrying about another bubble.

Other communities have very different concerns—like the distressingly slow recovery in house prices in the very city where President Bush and the GSEs made their historic commitment to minority homeownership. In the communities of south Dekalb County, outside of Atlanta, Georgia, the recovery of home values of African American professionals and other well-to-do residents languishes behind those of white homeowners in north Dekalb, even though the homes are almost identical. According to a May 2016 *Washington Post* analysis of home values in Dekalb County, "in some Zip codes, home values are still 25 percent below what they were [12 years ago]. Families here, who've lost their wealth and had their life plans scrambled, see neighborhoods in the very same county—mostly white neighborhoods—thriving."[12] House-price differences are not new in Dekalb, but since the housing crisis they have only widened.

Conclusion

Many people blame Democrats for goosing up homeownership rates, but Republicans had their hand in the American Dream cookie jar, too. Since homeownership was seemingly a free political good (since the GSEs were off budget), both parties marched in the pro-homeownership hit parade. The fact is that the political divide in Congress over access, safety, and soundness made the political system vulnerable to being picked off—and paralyzed—by special interests including the GSEs, who were some of the most well funded and audacious. The party that holds tightly to the national purse and says no will always be vilified. Yet this type of stewardship is greatly needed today. Financial stewardship and conservatism should be a place of common ground, particularly after the recession of 2008. Down payments, risk retention, and resisting the call to equalize homeownership rates are necessary to rebuilding a safe system. Unfortunately, at the time of this writing, a Democratic administration is falling prey to political pressure to loosen the reins of mortgage underwriting. Barely three years after the passage of the much-maligned Dodd-Frank legislation, the hard regulatory steps to build a safer system were being undone in the name of economic growth and fairness. More broadly, it bears repeating that once the government decides to bestow a benefit on a particular entity, be it a special charter, an exemption, or a nod to producing a desired social end, the beneficiary will fight to the death to keep it. In short order, it will go from being a benefit to a right, from an exception to the rule. And suddenly a lot of corporate and trade association money will be flowing in to keep it that way.

To reduce the prevalence of influence-peddling in Washington, it will be necessary to stop favoring particular sectors and entities over others. It addition, Congress must resist the urge to reward, direct, and social engineer the economy to do the government's bidding. Unfortunately, cronyism is still alive and well in the mortgage market, with its many subsidies, interested parties, and the underlying myth of homeownership providing oxygen. If left unaddressed and unchecked, political pressure to maintain the complex system of rewards and benefits—in the name of expanding access to homeownership—will create another dangerous bubble.

WHO'S ULTIMATELY RESPONSIBLE?

Most Americans' understanding of how public policy is made focuses on the rancorous legislative process in which politicians with diametrically opposed viewpoints duke it out. When the president signs new legislation into law using a commemorative ballpoint pen, we tend to think the issue has at last come to rest. However, that is just the beginning of policy change. The battle quickly resumes in a different gladiatorial arena, one that is much less visible to the everyday citizenry but every bit as contested.

Legislators are like architects. They design the public policy blueprint by deciding the shape, structure, and aesthetics of the house to be built. Then the builders take over. Making sure the roof doesn't leak and the wiring is safe is the job of regulatory experts. Myriads of unelected officials working in government agencies or regulatory shops develop exacting regulations for how the statute will be carried out. Given Washington's penchant for rule-making, there is steady work available for anyone with a mind for detail—and the patience of Job.

Rule-writing bureaucrats are obligated to understand and adhere to the intent of the legislation as much as possible. The fact that the United States had so many financial regulators before the crisis (and still has quite a few today) means there are often jurisdictional battles and disagreements about intent and implementation.

Adding to the complexity, the congressional legislative process is not the only one taking place. In our federal system, states and localities often get frustrated with the long, slow, and generally conservative nature of policy change at the national level—and can move forcefully to take matters into their own hands. To quote former Supreme Court justice Louis Brandeis, states play a needed role as "laboratories of democracy." But sometime those experiments can wreak havoc with federal policy, or lack of policy, as the case may be.

Drafting and finalizing regulations is a tedious and time-consuming process. By law, the public must have an opportunity to comment on the details before officials may finalize and promulgate a new rule, a process that easily adds months, if not years, to the implementation of major regulations. The regulatory comment process provides full employment for another set of lawyers—the ones who work for the interested public, such as major financial institutions and trade groups. These lawyers labor long and hard to write extremely exacting comment letters that must be logged, reviewed, and at least generally addressed by the relevant regulatory staff. Taken together, the patchwork of regulations (and regulators), the policy mismatch between the feds and the states, and the tedium of a bogged-down regulatory process created yet another set of factors contributing to the housing crisis.

When alarms about subprime lending started sounding in the early 2000s, financial regulators were extremely slow to get out of the federal fire station. And there was pitifully little water to put out the flames. So the states jumped into the fray.

Following North Carolina's attempts to slow the growth of subprime lending beginning in 1999, it was Georgia that fired the opening shot. In 2002, the state took aim at mortgage investors, the jugular vein supplying liquidity to the subprime market. As subprime investors, the GSEs were in the crosshairs.

In my new role in Government Relations, I was no longer looking at the issue of predatory lending from a risk perspective but from a political one. And it was just as problematic.

Lax Federal Standards

As the subprime market gained momentum, many housers voiced concerns about hard money lending going mainstream, but Congress was clearly stymied over what do to. Once again lawmakers found themselves caught between the moneyed interests of the mortgage industry and the impassioned jeremiads coming from consumer groups. Consumer advocates were making the rounds in Washington, arguing for greater consumer protection, improved disclosures, and a complete ban of prepayment penalties. On the other hand, the mortgage trade groups, particularly the Mortgage Bankers Association (MBA), were set against any restrictions on lending, whatever the market. A complicating factor was that existing federal legislation could have dealt with the most egregious aspects of subprime lending. Unfortunately, the regulator with authority to implement that law—the Federal Reserve Board—failed to put any teeth into it.

Enacted in 1994, the Home Owners Equity Protection Act (HOEPA) gave the Fed ample authority to regulate the fast-growing submarket rife with high interest rates, hefty points, hidden penalties, and aggressive marketing. HOEPA sought to curtail deceptive and unfair practices in home equity lending by requiring consumer disclosures on so-called high-cost loans, among other provisions.

For example, if the interest rate on a mortgage exceeded a certain level, or if the number of upfront points exceeded another threshold level, then the mortgage loan would be considered a "HOEPA loan." This designation did not make the loan illegal; rather, it required the mortgage originator to disclose to the borrower that the mortgage was "high cost." A HOEPA designation was thus viewed as the scarlet letter of the mortgage industry, warning unsuspecting borrowers of latent risk and costs.

Unfortunately, the Fed set the thresholds so high that very few loans actually received the pejorative distinction. Subprime lenders also performed financial acrobatics to keep the loans a hair below the all-important thresholds. Hence the regulation was too weak to hold back the onslaught of high-cost loans with features unheard of in the prime market dominated by the GSEs. Based on post-crisis interviews with Federal Reserve Chairman Greenspan, despite the Fed's slight tightening of the HOEPA rule in 2005, the nation's only anti–predatory lending law covered 1 percent of subprime loans.[1]

Why did the Fed resist calls to tighten the HOEPA regulation? According to the Federal Reserve's general counsel, "The mind-set was that there should be no regulation; the market should take care of policing, unless there already is an identified problem."[2] Notwithstanding the pleas of consumer advocates for strong Fed action, the HOEPA gate remained wide open.[3]

Enter the States

Frustrated with federal inaction to deal with the growth of subprime, individual states began to take matters into their own hands. North Carolina had been first out of the box in 1999, passing legislation with interest rate and point/fee thresholds tighter than the federal standards of the Federal Reserve. This meant that North Carolina–chartered banks operating within the state were obligated to follow the state's tighter lending standards; in contrast, federally chartered lending institutions operating in the state were not bound by new requirements, which created competitive issues. The mortgage industry fought the new statute, arguing that it would dry up lending in the state. Despite many dire pronouncements, this did not happen.

North Carolina's anti–predatory lending legislation was a prelude to stiffer state laws to come. It tightened the definition of what constituted a bad loan but maintained a long-standing legal doctrine known as "holder in due course," which meant that legal liability remained with the originator and could not flow upstream to the mortgage investor.

Starting with the 2002 Georgia Fair Lending Act (GFLA), that doctrine came under severe challenge. This second-generation anti–predatory lending legislation sought to hold investors liable for the sins of the originators. It was a doctrine known as "strict assignee liability," and it put a bull's-eye on Wall Street investors who heretofore been able to provide liquidity to the subprime market with impunity.

GFLA was the first state law to attempt to hold liable the secondary mortgage market—including any bank, GSE, or Wall Street investor—for the origination of predatory loans in the primary mortgage market in that state. In the past, liability for such loans would have remained with the lender that had originated it. Under the doctrine of holder in due course, unless fraud was committed, any subsequent purchaser of the mortgage would have been largely immune from any legal consequences stemming from the origination of a bad loan or loans. GFLA sought to overturn that precedent and dry up the source of liquidity behind the origination of loans deemed to be predatory. Thus, if any mortgage purchaser, such as a GSE, happened to buy a bad loan originated in Georgia, that purchaser could be exposed to the risk of class-action lawsuits.

Because the mortgage market is extremely well integrated nationally, lenders everywhere were alarmed by the new law and threatened to stop doing business in Georgia. They reasoned that foregoing business from the state was preferable to assuming the risk of inadvertently purchasing or investing in a predatory loan, as defined by Georgia, and the significant legal penalties that could result.

Furthermore, the working definition of predatory lending remained alarmingly vague. Programming a "know it when you see it" standard into an automated underwriting system was deeply problematic.

Georgia lawmakers tried to improve the definition of what constituted a predatory loan, but lenders howled that the law was too broad, bringing even good loans into the predatory fold. Another problem was detecting bad loans before they were swallowed up in the massive secondary mortgage market. Thanks to the efficient TBA market, large mortgage purchasers like the GSEs bought loans sight unseen long after the loans had closed; hence they had no way to control the quality of what eventually was delivered to their doors. The GSEs required that lenders "represent and warrant" that the loans we were buying complied with all applicable state and national laws, but there was no ironclad way to ensure that each and every loan purchased by the GSEs met the definitions put forth by any one state.

"The GSEs are like the whale Monstro in *Pinocchio*," a Freddie Mac lawyer explained to skeptical consumer advocates, including Martin Eakes of North Carolina. "We and Fannie just open our mouths and the loans come in by the thousands every day. That's what keeps the national market working. We tell the lenders what the standards are, but have no practical way to check every loan before we swallow it." Translation: it would be impossible, if not unfair, to hold the secondary market responsible for the quality of loans originated by other entities, which it had agreed to buy before the loans even went to the closing table.

Eakes raised a skeptical eyebrow. He and other consumer advocates emphasized that unless investors, including the GSEs, were held accountable, money would continue to flow to the worst kind of lending because of the promised high returns. GFLA's threat of class-action lawsuits for funding a predatory loan was the big stick designed to starve the state's subprime market of liquidity.

The result was a standoff between the lending industry and the state of Georgia, between consumer groups and primary and secondary markets, and between states and the federal government. It would not end well.

Hardball

Freddie Mac business executives were in a quandary over what to do in Georgia. There was no easy solution.

Delk wanted time to work with state legislators to explain the challenges posed by the new law and to convince them to modify it. But this time Freddie's business execs prevailed and said no way. Georgia simply presented too much risk. On November 1, 2002, Freddie announced that it was suspending the purchase and investment of all Georgia subprime loans for an indefinite period of time. Fannie Mae soon followed suit.

Pulling out of a state was a huge thing to do politically. For years, Freddie Mac had prided itself for staying in markets even when things went south and private investors fled. Staying in was our mission. That was one of the things that made the company unique and worthy of the charter.

Seeking to influence state legislation was a very delicate matter for the GSEs. A few years before, Fannie Mae lobbyists had been spotted in a state legislature, and the firm was pummeled in the mortgage press for meddling in state affairs. Taking a low-profile approach, Freddie began a letter-writing campaign to then–Georgia Governor Roy Barnes explaining the company's decision to leave the state unless technical amendments to the new law were made. Basically, the company wanted a safe harbor: an exception to punitive action if a mortgage purchaser followed a prescribed set of practices and precautions in purchasing loans. The safe harbor would protect the GSEs from class-action lawsuits, even if the firm inadvertently bought a bad loan because it slipped through Freddie's massive purchasing system. If GFLA was modified in this way, the argument went, Georgia could get what it wanted—greater borrower protections—without driving lenders out of the state. A few months later, following the state's gubernatorial upset, Freddie sent a similar letter recommending this modification to Georgia Governor-Elect Sonny Purdue.

Things seemed contained, for a time. But other states were watching the experiment going on in Georgia and considering similar measures.

In an effort to get ahead of the issue, Delk wanted to work proactively to keep such legislation from spreading to other states. It was one thing for Freddie Mac to pull out of a single state like Georgia; it would be quite another if more populous states began to enact the same punitive law. To blunt any bad PR, reputable partners would be needed. To protect vulnerable seniors, the AARP had been working to develop a model anti–predatory lending law that could be transplanted from state to state. In its original form, it looked more like a Georgia-type bill than the North Carolina variety, which was worrisome for the mortgage industry.

Delk reasoned it would be beneficial to alter the AARP model bill before it was introduced in other state legislatures. To accomplish that, something would have to be offered in exchange. The consumer groups were not about to provide a safe harbor without something to show for it. What did they want?

At the time, consumer groups were focused on the elimination of prepayment penalties. Freddie's earlier ban on penalties over three years was passé by 2002. Consumer groups now wanted them banned entirely, but Freddie was not interested in taking another leadership position like that. An easier give would be for Freddie Mac to align with the consumer groups in banning the use of mandatory arbitration (MA) contracts in subprime.

Mandatory arbitration contracts were standard in almost all subprime transactions even though they were not allowed in the prime market. With mandatory arbitration, borrowers were required to forego their constitutional right to a jury trial in the event that a contract dispute arose with the lender. The MA contracts protected subprime lenders from heavy legal costs and class action lawsuits. However, they almost always guaranteed that borrowers got the short end of the stick. The MA requirement helped lenders manage the risks associated with the lender in due course doctrine that held them responsible for the loans they had originated. They arbitrated those risks away.

The consumer advocates wanted MA banned in subprime. A plan was devised to give the groups what they wanted—so Freddie could get what it wanted. In one sense, it wasn't that much of a concession for Freddie Mac to ban MA contracts on mortgages the firm purchased or invested in. Freddie already disallowed MA in its prime market business, so banning them in subprime was a principled position to take. But the irony was not lost on Freddie's customers. In seeking to protect the GSE from the risk of class-action lawsuits, which would arise from laws like GFLA that contained strict assignee liability, Freddie Mac gave away lenders' protection against the same risk.

The lenders were the ones originating the bad loans, Freddie reasoned. They should be the ones held accountable for the risk.

When the MBA, the trade group representing mortgage bankers and many subprime lenders, learned that Freddie had conceded to the consumer groups to ban MA on subprime loans, they went ballistic. I remember the meeting when the then-MBA president turned purple with anger. "How dare you tell *us* what to do!" he raged.

Covering its other bases, Freddie then paid a Wall Street consultant a king's ransom to quietly alert the credit rating agencies about the new legal risks attendant with GFLA. Normally securities investors didn't have to worry about lawsuits involving the underlying loans in a securitized structure. They sailed above that fray. But assignee liability would change all that. Under GFLA, investors further up the chain could be sued in class-action lawsuits—and subprime securities weren't rich enough to cover that kind of bottomless risk. Once the rating agencies understood this, it wasn't long before S&P announced that mortgages originated in Georgia and governed by GFLA would be banned from S&P-rated structured finance transactions because the legal risks could not be quantified.

In a single blow, Freddie Mac had protected itself from GFLA's increased risk while taking away the subprime lenders' mechanism for dealing with the same risk. In addition, Freddie squelched Wall Street competition when the rating agencies gave Georgia private-label securities a black eye. Another good year for Freddie's top lobbyist.

Being shut out of private-label deals would be a huge blow to Georgia's housing and mortgage market. Assuming the other credit rating agencies followed suit, lenders originating mortgages in Georgia would have very few places to sell them. The GSEs already said they would be off limits. Now the rating agencies were essentially saying the same thing, so PLS also was off the table. With nowhere to place its mortgages, the Georgia housing market would likely contract.

For Georgia homebuyers this would mean a serious and sudden mortgage shortage. Lending in the state would dry up—or become very expensive.

The GSEs were not the only ones concerned about the higher risks associated with GFLA; so were federal banking regulators, who oversaw nationally chartered banks operating in the state. It wasn't long before the Office of the Comptroller of the Currency (OCC) and the Office of Thrift Supervision (OTS) issued statements saying that nationally chartered thrifts and banks were not beholden to GFLA on the basis of federal preemption.[4] In other words, by virtue of having a national charter, a bank or thrift could get out from under a more stringent state law.

Much to the chagrin of Georgia state-chartered banks, federal pre-emption of GFLA trumped the state's efforts to govern national lenders operating in the state and created an uneven playing field for the dueling chartered institutions.[5] Only the banks chartered in the state of Georgia would have to abide by GFLA. Georgia's mortgage market had become a battleground—as well as a national mortgage pariah.

Educating or Meddling?

Despite all of Freddie Mac's work with the AARP and the consumer groups to define an acceptable safe harbor for subprime investors, Georgia was not easily persuaded to change its famous law. Freddie Mac's carefully worded letters had implied that if the state did not make the suggested technical amendments to the law, Freddie would change its indefinite ban on Georgia loans to a permanent ban as early as the end of February 2003, just weeks away.

In early February, Georgia's state legislature was set to consider amendments addressing the issue of assignee liability, which Freddie lawyers had helped draft with input from S&P. Hoping for a resolution, Freddie moved its deadline out to March 7, 2003. If a legislative change were not forthcoming, the firm would begin notifying lenders of the decision to make the ban on Georgia loans permanent. On March 6, the Georgia legislature was deadlocked.

Showdown

I was working at Freddie's headquarters in McLean, Virginia, when the phone rang. It was Delk's administrative assistant, calling from Freddie Mac's DC office. "Will you please take a call from Georgia Governor Purdue? He wants to know if Freddie is really going to pull out of the state. He is on hold."

I was aghast. As I would soon learn, my boss was not just out of the office—he was vacationing in Paris.

"I don't know what is going on," I said. "And I will *not* talk to the governor."

What was going on was a heated debate on the floor of the Georgia State Senate. Holding the latest Freddie Mac letter aloft, a Republican senator warned that Freddie Mac would exit the state if the safe harbor was not adopted.

That warning apparently set off a number of frantic phone calls from the well of the Georgia State Senate to Freddie's top lobbyist, who was eating foie gras in a restaurant halfway around the world. When the dust had settled, I learned that a vote had been taken, and Freddie Mac's amendment had passed. The law would permit a safe harbor for investors who adopted anti-predatory policies and implemented standards for checking to see they were being met. The rating agencies would once again rate securities containing Georgia loans. Other states would soon learn about the showdown and adopt similar safe-harbor amendments. And mortgage money would continue to flow to the Peach State.

The struggle over GFLA was not without cost, and the damage to Freddie's reputation was just beginning. The *Atlanta Constitution* vilified Freddie for attempting to "gut" the consumer protections contained in the bill and tamper with state politics.[6]

Remorse

Notwithstanding GSE charter issues, how should a shareholder-owned business engage with its governments? How does federalism square with a national market that thrives on standardization and the diffusion of risk? Freddie had stumbled badly, it seemed to me, although it played its cards up front. I had been the one to draft the company's concerns in letters to the state six months before the showdown, and company lawyers had worked proactively with consumer groups and state officials to find a legislative fix.

However, the hoped-for solution was not won by debate and reason but by double-crossing. Freddie's enemies would not forget.

Nor did the state of Georgia. Five years later, in August 2008, a *Newsweek* article recounted the 2003 episode. In "The Predators' Ball," author Michael Hirsch described how "Fannie Mae and Freddie Mac have helped defang laws that might have prevented the subprime mess."[7]

Preemption also bears some responsibility here, according to a 2010 study by the Center for Community Capital at the University of North Carolina. The study estimates that 28 states had some sort of anti-predatory laws at the end of 2004. Since all 28 were pre-empted by the OCC and other federal regulators, the researchers believe that federal preemption contributed to the decline in underwriting standards on the part of preempted institutions, with broader market effects. Preemption created negative spin-off effects such as increased pressure to weaken state laws (as we saw in Georgia) and "charter shopping," whereby a state-regulated bank would be tempted to trade in its state charter for a more lenient national one.[8]

An empirical analysis of the quality and performance of mortgages originated by preempted institutions—as compared to those originated by non-preempted ones—supports this hypothesis. Using a merged sample of 1.1 million "private securitized loans," researchers found significantly higher default risk for loans originated by OCC-regulated institutions, leading them to conclude that the "2004 OCC ruling did contribute to deterioration in lending standards and a rollback in consumer protection during the subprime crisis."[9]

The OCC, for its part, disputes such a broad-brush indictment. In 2010 testimony before the FCIC, then-OCC Comptroller John Dugan defended strong OCC regulation (even in light of preemption) by pointing out that much of subprime lending was done by non-bank (and, therefore, non-OCC regulated) affiliates of large bank holding companies. By way of example, Dugan stated that "HSBC, Citigroup, Wells Fargo, and Countrywide (when it owned a national bank) conducted most of their subprime mortgage lending in holding company affiliates of national banks that were not subject to OCC supervision, but were subject to Federal Reserve and state supervision."[10] In other words, like a squishy balloon, bad loans kept slipping through the country's many regulatory fingers.

Where Things Stand

In addition to establishing new mortgage lending standards, the Dodd-Frank Act (DFA) created a new regulator, the Consumer Financial Protection Bureau (CFPB), to be a watchdog for consumer interests in financial services. To consolidate responsibility for consumer protection under one roof, DFA transferred a number of responsibilities from the OCC to the CFPB. Before the entity got off the drawing board, conservatives were crying foul and refused to approve the nomination of the Obama administration's nominee, Harvard professor Elizabeth Warren, who had been a vocal critic of banks and now is a US senator and progressive champion. After several years of wrangling, President Obama made a controversial recess appointment of Richard Cordray, former state attorney general (AG) from Ohio.

CFPB supervises banks, credit unions, and other institutions and enforces federal consumer financial laws. Consumers can submit their complaints right on the CFPB website. Getting used to a new overseer has been an adjustment for lending institutions, to say the least.

A third DFA provision limited the ability of federal banking regulators to invoke federal preemption of state laws. As noted by the OCC in a preamble to one of its new regulations, DFA tightens the scope of national entities subject to preemption and sets criteria for invoking it. Generally, state consumer protection laws can only be preempted if they would have a discriminatory effect. The law also requires the OCC to make a preemption decision on a case-by-case basis, taking into account how similar laws have operated in other states and in consultation with the CFPB.[11]

On the broader point about federalism—and the messy jurisdictional issues it creates—the OCC also recognized "the ability of state attorneys general to bring enforcement actions in court to enforce applicable laws against national banks as authorized by such laws."[12] In other words, national banks are no longer immune from legal advances on the part of increasingly active, vocal, and angry state attorneys general.

The National Mortgage Settlement is a case in point. In 2012, following widespread consumer complaints about servicing and foreclosure abuses, a settlement was reached between 49 state attorneys general and the nation's five largest mortgage servicers. The joint state-federal servicer settlement is the largest consumer protection settlement in history; over $50 billion has been paid out to affected borrowers, signing states, and the federal government.

Conclusion

Lax enforcement of HOEPA on the part of the Federal Reserve and the invoking of federal preemption on the part of the OCC was a lethal combination. The ability of nationally chartered banks to sidestep tough state lending laws and originate mortgages to the low-ball national standard was permitted under federal preemption. Many more borrowers got high-risk loans as a result. Time will tell if new regulations—and watchdog organizations—will be sufficient to hold the dual-regulated mortgage market in check. Or if they will overdo it.

The dilemma the GSEs found themselves in is another matter. The need to support a national secondary mortgage market while limiting exposure to GFLA's significant legal liabilities resulted in an ugly showdown. The state of Georgia was forced to weaken its protections for subprime borrowers or lose a pipeline of mortgage money flowing to the state. The fracas over GFLA revealed the conflicting dual nature of the GSE mission and of the secondary mortgage market more broadly. Should the GSEs support the interests of borrowers or of GSE lender customers? Who should ultimately be held responsible, the lender at the closing table or an investor a thousand miles away who is providing the funds? Or both?

The creation of the CFPB, tighter lending regulations, and carefully crafted liabilities should help resolve this dilemma. Time will tell.

SCANDAL(S)

In 2002 and 2003, Freddie Mac executives failed to ask, "What is the right thing to do?" with regard to complex rules pertaining to accounting for derivatives and making political campaign contributions. Instead, they focused on technically meeting, or ever-so-slightly skirting, the exact requirements, according to examinations by their regulator and others.[1] The consequences were tragic for the executives involved and the reputation and integrity of the firm. Freddie Mac traveled along these same fault lines in 2008 to its peril.

Limits of Regulation

The mortgage industry's patchwork of regulations—well-intended, politically motivated, or ideologically unenforced—made indirect but significant contributions to the financial crisis. From OMB's zealous escalation of GSE affordable housing goals to lax enforcement on the part of the Federal Reserve of the Home Owners Equity Protection Act, from lenders shopping for more lenient charters and lower capital requirements, it is clear that rules are not magic wands. Rules are used to govern reality, but they often become reality.

Regulations represent a false precision. Regulations that deal with quantitative requirements, such as capital levels, are inordinately detailed, precise, and complex. The definition of the types of assets that may count as capital, and under what scenarios, are similarly inordinately detailed, precise, and complex. While a highly prescriptive approach may seem logical, trying to meet exact capital ratios or quotas invites game playing to achieve them. Rules are also static; promulgated after months, if not years, of public debate, their utility is weakened when conditions change, as they invariably do. The pace of technological change only makes regulations that much harder to write—and to keep. On the other hand, the lack of regulatory guidance invites mischief as well. The lack of a clear definition of what constituted a subprime mortgage gave rise to borrower confusion and lender opportunism.

Complex regulations result in loopholes, market distortions, and disparities. For example, large, well-heeled firms with the legal and accounting brainpower to make sense of the rules and actually apply and (creatively) adhere to them have an advantage over smaller firms. Notwithstanding efforts on the part of the Consumer Financial Protection Bureau (CFPB) to create regulatory exemptions for small institutions, credit unions and community banks are particularly worried about the sheer volume of regulations on their ability to compete.[2]

Finally, in a society so attuned to rule keeping, overly detailed and punitive regulations can tend to supplant good judgment and stifle innovation. To take an everyday example, if the walk light is on at a busy intersection during rush hour, a pedestrian might venture into the street without looking to the left or the right. The automated light provides a false sense of security, as if it could, in fact, see and interpret the dangers posed by speeding vehicles.

Regulations must be accompanied with good judgment. A reasonable regulation should be viewed as a baseline for performance. If a firm believes that extra capital is necessary given business fundamentals, it should hold more capital than is required. Or, if it believes that the type of capital it is holding, while permitted under a regulation, is of insufficient quality to withstand a downturn, it should invest in higher-quality capital. Shareholders and other stakeholders who are attuned to regulatory requirements may object to these extraregulatory precautions, but they are needed.

If banks only ask, "Can I get away with this under the QM regulation?" they may find themselves back in crisis mode. A better question in times of doubt would be: "Aside from the regulation, what is the right thing to do?" Notwithstanding the ambiguity contained in the word "right," asking ethical questions is needed to navigate an increasingly complex and morally ambiguous marketplace. Simply meeting the letter of the law does not bring about the good society.

Accounting Scandal

While Freddie was fretting that the 2001 Enron scandal would bring unwanted attention to the SEC exemption on the firm's large and growing derivatives portfolio, the CEO and other leaders missed the big Enron domino entirely: the demise of Arthur Andersen.

Arthur Andersen had been Freddie's auditor for years. Indeed, Freddie could tout—and often did—that it had received over 20 years of unqualified financial opinions from the now defunct accounting firm. This was an important indicator that Freddie Mac was financially strong, an absolutely critical point since the GSE was not an SEC registrant.

With Arthur Andersen mortally wounded from having being Enron's auditor, Freddie's board dropped them like a hot potato. That's when Price Waterhouse Coopers (PwC) got the job.

Sometime in the fall of 2002, PwC started raising concerns. The precipitating event occurred in December when Freddie Mac executives received two anonymous letters "alleging three separate accounting, public reporting and internal controls irregularities." While an outside review later concluded that the allegations were false, it did reveal deeper concerns related to possible "smoothing" of financial results.[3]

Not surprisingly, PwC was concerned. A month later, on January 22, 2003, Freddie Mac announced that PwC had not completed its audit of the firm's 2002 financial statement and that a restatement would be necessary.[4] This announcement set the company on a new, tortuous path that would take years of work and billions of dollars to resolve.

Accounting for Derivatives

The issues centered primarily on how Freddie Mac accounted for the derivatives used to hedge the firm's interest-rate risk on the growing number of mortgage securities sitting on the balance sheet. In addition to the mortgage credit risk associated with every loan the firm guaranteed, the mortgages Freddie kept in its retained mortgage portfolio also carried interest-rate risk. Interest-rate risk has two dimensions. First, interest-rate movements could negatively affect the value of the fixed-rate securities held in Freddie Mac's portfolio. Second, borrowers might refinance their mortgages at untimely moments—for the investor, that is. For example, as mortgage interest rates fall, many borrowers terminate their old mortgages and apply for new ones with lower interest rates without having to pay a penalty. While this is a great feature for the prime mortgage borrower, it leaves the investor—who was counting on getting the higher coupon amount—with diminished returns. The borrower's mortgage principal is returned to the investor when rates are low and reinvestment opportunities are less advantageous. Hence, prepayment risk is something mortgage investors care about in the prime market; as we saw earlier, subprime borrowers had to bear that risk themselves.

Investors also find themselves disadvantaged when interest rates start rising. In those environments, borrowers have no desire to part with their low-coupon mortgages, but the institutions holding those loans may find themselves caught in a squeeze when there is not enough revenue generated on the low-coupon book to pay the higher interest rates needed to attract deposits. This asset-liability mismatch contributed to the demise of many S&Ls during the 1980s when interest rates rose to extremely high levels. This mismatch caused Fannie Mae's temporary insolvency in the 1980s as well. Derivatives were a way to avoid that problem.

Super-Sized Mortgage Portfolio

When I joined Freddie Mac in 1990, a common refrain was that the company carried zero interest-rate risk. This statement was entirely true because the firm did not retain any of its mortgages; rather, it securitized and sold virtually all of them to other investors, thus transferring all interest-rate risk out of the firm. But Fannie Mae took a different strategy and held a large number of mortgages in portfolio—and made a lot of money on them.

Freddie eventually realized it wasn't making enough money on securitization alone, so the firm set out to build a mortgage portfolio, too. When Greg Parseghian arrived from Wall Street in 1996 as Freddie's senior vice president and chief of investments, our stodgy (but safe) practice of securitizing just about any mortgage that came our way began to fall by the wayside. That's when Freddie Mac started leveraging the GSE charter to its fullest by buying underpriced mortgage assets.

The first big growth spurt came in 1998 when Freddie's portfolio grew by 50 percent. Of course, the portfolio was starting from a small base, but still the size of the increase got attention. That was the year of the Asian debt crisis, when many investors, including the ill-fated hedge fund Long Term Capital Management, were offloading mortgages. In an aggressive move, Freddie stepped in to buy them on the cheap. The Freddie traders began referring to themselves as "opportunistic" buyers. Buying mortgages when others were dumping them was good business, plus it played an important stabilizing force in the market. Buying huge quantities of mortgages when they were out of favor caused prices to tighten and borrower mortgage rates to fall, thereby enabling me to write in speeches and other public materials, "Freddie Mac provides a stable supply of low-cost mortgage money in good seasons and bad." To deflect criticism of its growing portfolio, Freddie preferred to emphasize the portfolio's positive benefits on mortgage interest rates as being consistent with the GSE liquidity mission.

What about Risk?

Despite the benefits of the growth of Freddie Mac's balance sheet, management knew it would be extremely important to keep close watch on the firm's exposure to interest rates and to manage that risk carefully.

There were several ways to manage portfolio risk, starting with the development of special risk metrics and other indicators that were publicly disclosed monthly. At the time, the nature and frequency of Freddie Mac's disclosures was well ahead of other firms. Freddie also helped develop the callable debt market, which enabled it to better match the duration of assets and liabilities, thus reducing its overall exposure. But, by far, the biggest way the firm managed the interest-rate risk on the burgeoning retained portfolio was through the use of financial instruments known as derivatives to hedge interest-rate risk.

Things seemed to be working well from an economic standpoint, meaning that Freddie Mac was successfully managing the actual risk, but the accounting for it was a whole different story. For starters, the government's accounting rule for derivative accounting, FAS 133, was (at the time) hundreds of pages long and mind-numbing. Freddie chose to interpret and apply it one way, but PwC didn't agree with that. Freddie had to restate the earnings the PwC way, to the tune of $5 billion. Fannie Mae wasn't far behind. In 2006, it was required to restate earnings by $6.3 billion.[5]

While many in Washington went nuts over the GSE restatements, it seems the firms weren't alone in their interpretations of the accounting rules. Numerous other companies found themselves in the same boat, having to restate their earnings to be in compliance with this complex rule.[6]

Grave Litany of Problems

Perhaps PwC was in a get-tough mode following Andersen's demise. In any event, most of the employees I worked with were shocked that it was accounting that cost Freddie's top executives their jobs in 2003. Accounting had been almost an afterthought. The finance people and the economists thought they were a lot smarter (and a lot more important) than the green-eye-shade accountants.

But therein lay the problem. Freddie Mac's accounting systems were outmoded, and the accounting employees were treated like second-class citizens compared to the traders who were busy buying mortgages for the portfolio. The company failed to invest in comprehensive financial report-ing systems needed to track those new investments. In many instances, workstation-based spreadsheets were used to track billions and billions of dollars of transactions.[7]

But it got uglier. Several investigations later, it was revealed that Freddie had engaged in transactions with some big-name Wall Street firms that were clearly noneconomic; that is, they were done purely to improve the accounting.[8]

All told, from 2000 to 2002 the company had shoved $5 billion in outsized profits earned on the retained portfolio into the future. The underreporting of current period earnings was designed to smooth an otherwise lumpy earnings stream, keeping the firm true to its tag line of "Steady Freddie."[9]

In a 2003 report, OFHEO raised a number of concerns with the com-pany's management and disclosure. Not only had Freddie gone to "extraor-dinary lengths to transact around FAS 133 and push the edge of the GAAP envelope,"[10] the company's "tone at the top" had "created an environment that strongly emphasized hitting earnings per share targets." Linking bonus compensation to stock performance created strong incentives to ensure that earnings were managed to meet analyst targets. It also helped ensure very healthy bonuses. As described by the regulator: "The actions by Freddie Mac executives to move 'front loaded' earnings from one quarter to a future quarter had the effect of helping to ensure that the EPS compensation goals would be easily met in future quarters, as well as to possibly bolster the value the stock on which options would presumably be exercised in future quarters."[11]

A third critique concerned how Freddie Mac disclosed the information to investors. According to the 2003 report, Freddie displayed a "disdain for appropriate disclosure standards, despite oft-stated management assertions to the contrary, misled investors and undermined market awareness of the true financial condition of the Enterprise."[12]

Upon reading the regulator's report, one economist I knew exclaimed that he was disgusted and later left the firm. For that one economist who left, Freddie probably hired ten accountants that same month. Clearly a cultural shift was underway.

Management Shake-Up

In January 2003, the month following PwC's revelation about Freddie Mac's need to restate earnings, Freddie's stock dropped by $9 a share, and bonuses were slashed. Hope for a quick solution was fading. Employees were reassigned to the accounting department. But nobody could get their arms around the problems that led to the need to restate earnings.

The word in the hallways was that the board was furious with management.[13] Not long after the March 2003 board meeting, CEO Brendsel disappeared for several weeks, and COO Glenn was given the job of managing the restatement process. Taking a lot of grief publicly about financial mismanagement, Freddie's board hired Baker Botts, an independent law firm, to investigate the underlying causes of the need to restate earnings—and to determine why it was taking the company so long to do it.[14] Parseghian and other executives who dealt with the retained mortgage portfolio spent hours being interviewed about all sorts of complex—and questionable—transactions.

Everywhere there was a feeling of alarm. No piece of paper could be thrown away, and boxes of documents began to stack up in the hallways. The computer servers bogged down in undeleted e-mail. Forensic accountants were even called in to figure out if crucial documents had been changed.

On Monday, June 9, 2003, while driving to work and listening to the radio, I learned that Freddie's whole top management team had been ousted over the previous weekend. Apparently, COO Glenn had not complied with a request for his personal diaries. Later, when he turned over the diaries to Baker Botts, he indicated that they contained alterations and that pages were missing.[15]

Glenn wasn't the only one out of a job. Brendsel was allowed to retire, and CFO Vaughn Clarke was asked to resign. Their offices were sealed with yellow police tape.

Search for a New CEO

Following the dismissal of Freddie Mac's top executives, there was much jostling for position. Soon after the shake-up, the board named Parseghian as CEO and chairman. His appointment sent off shock waves, particularly on the non-quant side of the company.

What was the board thinking? A better question: What had the board been doing all those years? Apparently, not much. According to a 2003 regulator report, Freddie's "Board of Directors was apprised of control weaknesses, the efforts of management to shift income into future periods and other issues that led to the restatement, but did not recognize red flags, failed to make reasonable inquiries of management, or otherwise failed in its duty to follow up on matters brought to its attention."[16]

Being appointed to a GSE board yielded big pay and required little work, particularly for the presidential appointees. As reported by the *Chicago Tribune* in 2009, Rahm Emanuel, who later became President Obama's chief of staff and then Chicago's mayor, had been one such well-compensated board member from 2000 to 2001 when Freddie's political and accounting problems were brewing. How much work do you have to do for $320,000 a year? Appointed to Freddie's board by President Clinton, Emanuel attended six board meetings and escaped the tedium of having to serve on a board committee.[17]

In July 2003, the board released the report of independent counsel. It was damning, not just about the accounting but also the noneconomic transactions. Apparently, the board had second thoughts about Parseghian's fitness for the job.[18] The regulator certainly wasn't pleased, and within two months, the former investment chief and CEO was asked to leave.[19] The regulator also told the board to find another CEO.

By mid-September, Freddie's accounting woes had been the subject of two congressional hearings. As much as the accountants wanted to get the restatement done, it was an overwhelming task. In testimony, Freddie's principal director and acting CEO, George Gould, dropped the bomb that the company wouldn't make the September 30, 2003, date for completing the restatement of the 2002 financials. Congress was very displeased to hear that.

I wasn't happy either. In fact, I was achingly miserable. One evening, while waiting for my daughter's violin lesson, I had driven back to the company just to think—and privately vent. It was getting dark, and the structure's massive, bowed façade, fashioned from pink granite, shone in my headlights. *How ironic. The building looks impregnable.* But inside, I knew, the once proud company was badly defeated. *How could the top executives have been so irresponsible?* I thought bitterly. *How do you work for a company like this?*

In a quiet little prayer group, I groused to another employee. Maybe I would just leave. "Warriors do not leave the battlefield," she intoned sternly.

Political Scandal

Amid all the drama at the top of the company, chief lobbyist Delk positioned himself to lead the company's official response to the crisis. It started with the commandeering of a large conference room at the McLean headquarters, which served as nerve center of the Corporate Action Team, CAT room for short. There was one exceedingly long conference table in the room, and Delk owned the chair at the end. He ordered up a big flat-screen TV—which was a real luxury at the time—so the staff could watch the never-ending coverage of Freddie's "accounting scandal."

TV trucks maintained eternal vigilance over the corporate entrances. If that wasn't enough, Freddie soon had a political scandal on its hands. A reporter was investigating Delk's elaborate fund-raising dinners at Galileo's.

The negative articles started in July 2003 when the Associated Press broke a story about the large number of fund-raising dinners Delk hosted at Washington's trendy Italian restaurant, Galileo's, from 2001 to 2003.[20] More than half of the 50 or so fund-raisers supported Republican members of the House Financial Services Committee. HFSC Chairman Mike Oxley (R-OH) was the featured guest at 19 of the events. The article noted that the fund-raising activity occurred around the time that proposed legislation to strengthen the regulatory regime over the GSEs died in subcommittee.

A few weeks later, Kathleen Day with the *Washington Post* provided tantalizing details about Delk's unusual arrangements with Galileo's: The dinners were offered at a steep discount, and the costs were recorded as in-kind contributions under campaign finance laws.[21] The article made the front page and featured a shot of Delk's invitations wooing various lobbyists and other interested parties to schmooze with HFSC members. The invitations always hinted that Mike Oxley would be attending the dinners as well. The dinners proved popular—spectacular cuisine and good Chianti, all for $25. The contributions poured in.

Delk hosted the dinners, but the corporation's role was obscure. "Freddie Mac spokesman David R. Palombi said Delk hosted the political dinners as a private citizen, not for the company."[22] Even in Washington that was pretty hard to believe. One group decided to find out.

In October 2003, the government watchdog organization Public Citizen filed a complaint with the Federal Election Committee, requesting "an investigation into, and enforcement action against, prior and potentially ongoing violations of the contribution limits, contribution source prohibitions, and reporting of the Federal Election Campaign Act of 1971" on the part of Robert Mitchell Delk, senior vice president of Government Relations at Freddie Mac.[23]

Fool Me Once, but Not Twice

I had a bad feeling that I was going to get dragged into this one. Earlier in the year, Delk had asked me to create a document describing his accomplishments for calendar year 2002, the year just passed, as part of the annual employee performance review (EPM). EPMs represented the opening round in the bonus award cycle. Most years there was a lot of money at stake for the top executives, so those employees took their EPM submissions particularly seriously. But probably no one took them more seriously than Delk.

Looking back, I should have refused to write it for him. But I wasn't the type to do that—yet. The performance summary took two full weeks to write and ended up being 14 pages long, including footnotes. Among other things, Delk had insisted that his political activities be included in the document, despite my and others' protestations to the contrary. He wanted the political fund-raising strategy described as "bold and unprecedented." Great attention was paid to the exact number of Galileo dinners and the millions of dollars raised for members of HFSC, Freddie Mac's congressional oversight subcommittee.

As fate would have it, the bonus process for the top executives was put on hold until the accounting issues could be sorted out. The gloating memo sank into a file.

Then, nearly 10 months later, with the bad publicity heating up about the Galileo dinners, the memo was back like a bad penny. This time Delk called and asked me to delete the section on his fund-raising activities from his 2002 EPM.

I was stunned. But out of timidity came resolve. I refused to delete it.

It was not that I didn't want to delete the section. I recalled how much I despised that particular assignment. But now my boss wanted it stricken from the record. Normally this would have been impossible. EPMs are due from executives in January, and bonuses are paid in March.

But 2003 was different. Things were topsy-turvy because of the accounting scandal, and Brendsel, for whom the EPM document was written, had been ousted in June. During the brief period when Parseghian was installed as CEO—before he too was shoved out for his involvement in the accounting problems—he wanted to review all the pending executive bonuses. Now Delk wanted a *slight* modification in what he had dictated.

I didn't often quibble with my boss when it came to writing; Delk clearly knew what he wanted to say. Often, when I was writing a document, he would read it scrupulously overnight and then leave me three or four long voicemails with detailed edits. I began to dread seeing the message light first thing in the morning. Writing the EPM document had been bad enough. Changing it after the fact would be unthinkable.

So when Delk called to ask me whether I had done as he asked and deleted the political section, I said, "No, I did not. Given the present environment, I would be uncomfortable doing that. Besides, the document was marked as 'final.'"

He tried to talk me out of it, to no avail. I called his administrative assistant and alerted her to the issue. I urged her to not change the document. Two years later, I sat at a table at the Federal Election Commission and recounted this story to an FBI agent with a gun tucked in her belt.

Aftermath

Freddie Mac's accounting and political scandals severely hurt the company's reputation and morale. The movie *The Perfect Storm* had just been released, and employees immediately appropriated the term. The most pressing need was to hire enough accounting expertise to perform the massive and complex financial restatement now looming over us. Every Monday morning, Freddie's great granite lobby was filled with new employees waiting to be escorted up to their new jobs unraveling complex derivatives transactions and then reconstructing them into compliant transactions regulators would approve.

Almost all the new hires were accountants, and there were dozens and dozens of them arriving every week. Many of them were housed at the Ritz Carlton Hotel up the street and bused in each morning for long, grueling days. Freddie staff complained about this, of course, so incentive bonuses were dangled in front of rank-and-file employees in the finance division— employees who had seen their workload double in a matter of months and who did not have a bed or expense account at the Ritz Carlton.

As new faces appeared, Freddie's spacious campus began to feel close. Conference rooms were turned into bull pens of cubicles, and it became hard to find a parking space in the underground garages. File cabinets joined the myriad boxes of retained documents now lining the hallways.

Accounting was only one aspect of the corporate storm. The firm was drowning in the continued flood of withering news articles, congressional hearings and other inquires, and ongoing FBI investigations of both the firm's accounting and lobbying. Job satisfaction plummeted.

Settling Up

On December 10, 2003, Freddie Mac agreed to pay $125 million to settle with OFHEO over the $5 billion understatement of earnings. This was on the heels of the regulator's Report of Special Investigation, which seemed to condemn every aspect of the company's operations, save the cafeteria. In particular, it sharply criticized Freddie Mac's earnings-focused culture. Here is one of many strong conclusions included in the report:

> The intense efforts to manage reported earnings at Freddie Mac drained
> the skills of many of the most talented employees of the Enterprise. Those

efforts compromised the integrity of many employees and damaged the effectiveness of the internal control structure of Freddie Mac. The quest to manage earnings eventually led to the termination of the most senior executives of the Enterprise, and resulted in one of the largest restatements in US corporate history.[24]

As part of Freddie's response to the regulator, I was asked to work with human resources to develop a plan to change our corporate culture. In retrospect, this was an astounding assignment. After all, how could Freddie truly change its shareholder mentality when it was still a shareholder-owned company?

Changing the Tiger's Stripes

The regulator's concerns about Freddie's culture reminded me of the discussions of a small task force I had been on a year before. A long-time economist colleague decided to get some old Freddie types together over lunch to consider exactly who—or what— Freddie Mac was. It wasn't a completely existential exercise; we wanted to develop a new mission statement for the firm. Nobody had asked us to. We just wanted to do it.

After many years at Freddie, I had come to know who in the company was on which side. As we hired more and more fresh faces from Wall Street, our conflicts over who we really were only widened. Once I threatened to bring a peer mediator to our meetings to help work through our different mindsets and expectations.

The fact that our friendly discussions became heated debates is revealing. Almost parallel to the political debates exploding around us, some employees thought Freddie's primary job was about expanding home-ownership, while others thought it was to make the secondary mortgage market more efficient. Yet others said our fundamental purpose was to "maximize shareholder value (subject to not losing the charter)."

That rankled some of us, but here was their point: By maximizing profits, they claimed, we would be the most efficient by definition, and that would be the best way to support homeownership—and society. It was classic business theory for a shareholder-owned company. But we had a problem: Freddie was a GSE. Maximizing profits might have been what the traders thought about every day, but it was not the mission politicians expected us to fulfill.

While the debate over Freddie's identity was energizing, consensus eluded us. My economist friend and I memorialized our thoughts in a memo called "Enduring Greatness" based on the book *Built to Last* by Collins and Porras. Writing primarily to ourselves, we said that Freddie lacked a clear sense of self and that this would hinder our future success. We speculated that the firm's contradictory nature stemmed from a number of factors, including Freddie's tremendous growth in recent years; the move from a private to a public company in 1990; and the creation and dominance of the retained portfolio. We compared how we thought about ourselves before going public and after.

"Looking at annual reports from 1970s, there was no reference to Freddie Mac being a 'shareholder owned company,' nor was there any tension between the retained and [the] single-family [business] during those years when the held portfolio was insignificant," our document read.

The memo went over like English tea at a college beer party. Years later, I found it when cleaning out a file cabinet. I had resigned and was days away from leaving the firm for good.

I stared at it blankly. Any feeling I still had for Freddie had long since left me. If only Freddie had been able to figure out what kind of firm it really was and just be that entity, without apology either to shareholder or politicos. But we didn't have that kind of foresight or courage. Instead, we kept swapping dance partners in a fateful quest to be liked.

In the process of packing everything up, I asked the lawyers if I could keep the old memo, and they agreed. I read from it at my farewell party. One man, a securities trader who had been part of our original group, approached me afterwards. He was in the "maximize shareholder value" crowd.

"Susan, I remember that memo. I did not agree with you," he said kindly. "But I always respected your position."

Fall from Grace

Philosophy aside, most employees didn't think much about Freddie's conflicted soul. Or if they did, it was done privately. More pressing was the need to simply bear up under the recurring body blows. The more bad things that happened to us, the more employees hunkered down, becoming defensive and paranoid. We began to interpret things darkly, through a cynical political lens.

On January 28, 2004, as a prudential regulatory action, OFHEO directed

Freddie to maintain a mandatory 30 percent target capital surplus while the firm worked to fix the issues that had led to the accounting problems two years earlier. OFHEO also made the firm agree to limit the growth of its portfolio to 2 percent a year.[25] Those two actions by our regulator had teeth. The college beer party settled down for a bit.

The 30 percent capital surcharge meant that instead of holding a minimum leverage ratio of 2.5 percent of capital to on-balance-sheet assets, as was required in the charter, both Freddie and Fannie would now have to hold at least 3.25 percent capital. In hindsight, the increase may seem negligible, but in the world of mortgage finance, where profits are computed in hundredths of a percent, it was huge. Holding additional capital necessarily meant purchasing fewer mortgage assets, which meant slower growth and less money. Back in the go-go days, when nobody was really worried about credit risk, this was a problem. If you didn't grow, others would.

Although Freddie Mac hoped to restate its 2002 earnings in a matter of months, it ended up taking a lot longer, as did complying with SEC registration of Freddie's common stock. No one could have dreamed that it would take a full six years and billions of dollars in accounting restatements, fines, and an army of consultants to finally achieve SEC registration of Freddie Mac common stock.

Likewise, no one could have dreamed that within two months following the long-awaited SEC registration in summer 2008, the company would be taken over by the government for being financially unstable. Or that disclosures about the amount of risk the firm was bearing would serve as Exhibit A against top executives in the aftermath of the crisis.[26]

The resolution of Freddie Mac's political scandal was less financially punitive but equally destructive to the firm's reputation and image. At least it felt that way to me; I had worked in the offending department and for the man whose outlandish efforts to protect the charter cost the firm a pretty penny.

In 2006, the Federal Election Commission (FEC) fined Freddie Mac $3.6 million to settle the allegation that it violated the Federal Election Campaign Act and FEC regulations, which prohibit corporations from making or facilitating contributions. At the time, it was the largest fine in FEC history. Here's how the FEC described the chicanery:

Between 2000 and 2003, Freddie Mac used corporate resources to facilitate 85 fundraising events that raised approximately $1.7 million for federal candidates. Freddie Mac documents, prepared by former Senior Vice President of Government Relations R. Mitchell Delk and others and directed to Freddie Mac's Board of Directors and CEO, described the fundraisers as "Political Risk Management" undertaken because Freddie Mac differed from most major corporations which have "a well-funded PAC to buttress their lobbying activities." The fundraisers were organized by Mr. Delk and former Vice-President Clark Camper, and benefited members of the House Financial Services Committee and other members of Congress. Consulting firms were hired to plan and organize the fundraising dinners, many of which were held at the Galileo Restaurant in Washington. Freddie Mac paid monthly retainers to those firms that grew to more than $25,000 per month by the end of 2002.

In addition to conducting fundraising events, Freddie Mac executives used corporate staff and resources to solicit and forward contributions from company employees to federal candidates. The FEC also found that Freddie Mac contributed $150,000 in 2002 to the Republican Governors Association ("RGA"), a contribution the RGA later returned.[27]

Freddie Mac paid the fine without admitting or denying it broke the law.

Conclusion

Freddie Mac's back-to-back scandals provide a cautionary tale for any company, especially where the temptation to seek outsized gains is very strong and regulatory oversight weak. Freddie Mac's misdeeds in both its accounting and political scandals were classic examples of being too clever by half. Arrogance thrives on constantly pushing the envelope.

Sadly, Freddie didn't learn from its mistakes. The same sort of issues cropped up in 2008, as the housing market was collapsing and regulators came to the devastating realization that the GSEs would not be able to save the broader market. Perhaps CFO Buddy Piszel really believed that Freddie Mac's capital was adequate, that the deferred tax assets, a component of capital, weren't overvalued (even though profits were nonexistent for the foreseeable future), and that losses couldn't be that bad. The government certainly didn't agree with that assessment—and it wasn't because of a mathematical error on Freddie's part. Just days before the government takeover, the regulator accused Freddie Mac of "aggressive accounting," as reported by the FCIC: "Despite 'clear signals' that losses on mortgage assets were likely, Freddie waited to record write-downs until the regulator threatened to issue a cease and desist order. Even then, one write-down was reversed 'just prior to the issuance of the second quarter financial statements.' The regulator concluded that rising delinquencies and credit losses would 'result in a substantial dissipation of earnings and capital.'"[28]

In the frantic months preceding the government takeover, when Freddie was under the gun to raise additional capital, I commiserated with another executive about the wobbly state of affairs. He said that Piszel and Cook, the chief business officer, were so convinced that the cup was half full (as opposed to half empty) that "it was spilling all over the place."

Freddie Mac's earlier scandals also are cautionary for those seeking to fix national problems by imposing yet more rules. Rules are critical to the smooth and fair functioning of markets, but they create their own set of problems. Rules cannot anticipate every situation; they are wooden when they should be flexible, and by their very nature, they create the loopholes and temptations firms use to evade them. In the regulatory game of cat and mouse, rules require a significant commitment—and resources—to oversee and enforce them properly. Rules should be seen as minimum requirements. Strong, ethically oriented firms resist the temptation to simply meet the technical requirement. They aim higher by asking, "What is the purpose of this regulation? And does our behavior and reporting line up with that?" These are the companies that are built to last.

However, a lack of regulation also creates problems, particularly in the absence of strong ethical reflection and courageous leadership on the part of top executives.

This would be Freddie Mac's next test, as competition from Wall Street began to seriously cut into its core business and market share. A new mortgage product was beginning to be popular with consumers, and Freddie Mac wanted a piece of the action.

The new loans sounded innocent at first blush. They were anything but.

BATTLE FOR RESPONSIBLE CREDIT LEADERSHIP

While the GSE affordable housing goals set an expansionary tone for the mortgage market, the loans purchased by the GSEs to meet the goals were not nearly as detrimental to their financial solvency as were the newfangled loans called nontraditional mortgages (NTMs). These loans required little to no documentation and permitted different amortization and repayment schedules—features that did not fit well with either the traditional GSE risk posture or operational capabilities.

Another name for this mortgage type was "Alternative A." Alt-A loans had been a niche product for self-employed borrowers and others who couldn't be bothered with paperwork. They were not as high quality as true prime, A-paper loans, but they weren't subprime either. Alt-A borrowers generally passed underwriting muster, but their loans contained less documentation than prime loans. Borrowers had to pay a premium for these types of mortgage shortcuts, which supposedly would cover the higher risks, but it was not hard to envision how the lack of documentation standards could get out of hand.

In years past, loans like these had been called "low doc," and the market's experience with them had not been good. Hence, Freddie Mac traditionally didn't buy a whole lot of Alt-A paper; it was a niche product. But the mortgage world was changing fast, and originations of Alt-A loans were proliferating in the primary market. Another loan type was A-minus. This loan type seemed to fall between the prime and subprime markets; it may have had adequate documentation, but the borrower likely had credit blemishes that posed higher than normal risk.

I remember the first time I heard about the new products. It was a meeting with the account execs from Freddie Mac's sales force, the employees whose job it is to buy mortgages from lenders. The number one goal of the sales force is customer satisfaction. They are paid on commission, which means the more volume they bring in, the better.

As the presentation commenced, one type of loan caught everyone's attention: the NINA. In the acronym-filled world of housing finance, even we longtime policy types weren't sure what the term meant until one of the sales guys explained it.

"It stands for a no-income, no-asset-documentation loan."

A borrower could now get a mortgage without providing any proof of income or of available financial reserves. In fact, for a small increase in rate, a borrower didn't have to put down any income or asset amounts at all. All that would be necessary to originate the mortgage was a property appraisal—and even those were getting pretty dodgy, particularly in strong homebuilding areas, such as California, Nevada, and Florida.

Our customers were urging us to buy other strange products we hadn't heard of. Products like the interest-only loan—where the borrower only pays the interest portion of the loan each month for up to 10 years, in many cases. It was a great loan for borrowers just getting on their feet, we were assured. Young, up-and-coming borrowers could handle the interest payment now; later, when their household income increased, they would be able to start paying down the principal.

And then there was the negatively amortizing mortgage called an Option ARM, where the borrower could decide each month how much of the loan he or she wanted to pay, like a credit card. Payments below the amount needed to fully amortize the loan would simply be added back onto the loan, such that the borrower would be paying interest upon interest for any unmet obligations.

We were told that these loans were really helping people buy homes. Because house prices were rising so fast, borrowers would be able to sell the house for a tidy profit a year or two later. Moreover, the account execs assured us that all the lenders were making these loans and that Freddie would surely lose business to Fannie—or worse, Wall Street—if we didn't buy lenders' NTMs. When the sales force talked about how irate the lenders were that Freddie was turning up its nose at their NTMs, Freddie's top management listened.

After the sales force finished its presentation, everyone was silent for a moment, taking it in. Then a few of us began to joke about having boring 30-year fixed-rate mortgages. I mean, how unsophisticated. I was not the only one thinking maybe I should get one of those NTMs and buy an investment property.

NTMs and Reputation Risk

Prior to the 2003 accounting scandal, Freddie took its stellar reputation for granted. The firm was a Fortune 50 company with a lot of clout in Washington, and the business revolved around a national symbol. In America, motherhood, hot dogs, apple pie, and homeownership go together. It is tempting for politicians to use symbols like these to acquire and retain power. The GSEs knew of lawmakers' weakness for these symbols and exploited it deftly. That's why there was a lot of red, white, and blue on both GSEs' publications as well as dreamy pictures of sweet little homes with wraparound porches and white picket fences.

But after having TV trucks camped out in front of the office and seeing Freddie's headquarters on the evening news, after having our executives expelled like naughty children, and after multiple government investigations, it became clear that a firm's reputation could either be irreparably damaged in a single moment or gradually sullied over time. Either way, it would take years to repair.

Understanding the importance of managing reputation risk was one thing; actually doing it was another, particularly when Freddie Mac had to be so many things to so many people. Most firms place top priority on enhancing their reputation with customers. Beyond Freddie's lender customers, there were other stakeholders whose opinion the firm valued, such as equity and debt investors and regulators—plus advocacy groups and politicians who disagreed bitterly about the firm's role. To manage corporate reputation risk, a small group was created to play devil's advocate among the business leaders. The goal was to envision how an anticipated business decision, action, or statement might be viewed externally. A senior vice president accountable to the board of directors chaired the group; my job was to run the monthly meetings for him. That was no easy task, as the reputation risk group was staffed by people who didn't really like or trust each other: the lobbyists, PR types, lawyers, and business execs.

In 2004, the growing popularity of NTMs came up frequently in reputation risk meetings. Notwithstanding the eagerness of the sales force to jump in with both feet, there were a number of risks associated with NTMs that were beyond the purview of the reputation group. These included the credit, interest-rate, and operational risks of processing these strange ducks correctly. Those primal—and ultimately very dangerous—risks were being debated by the quants elsewhere in the company. The reputation risk group, charged with protecting Freddie's reputation (such as it was after two scandals), had to answer a different question: Would participating in the NTM market be good for the Freddie brand or not?

Surprisingly, the answer to this question was not obvious back then. Everybody and his brother wanted one of these loans. And our job was to serve the market, right?

Understanding NINAs

NINAs represented a huge departure from standard mortgage underwriting. Previously, failure to provide proof of income to support the mortgage was unthinkable. Borrowers had to provide at least three pay stubs as proof of their monthly take-home pay, and self-employed borrowers had to produce several years' tax returns. Lenders also required borrowers to have adequate reserves to cover the inevitable unexpected expenses and repairs and as a cushion against unforeseen events, such as illness or unemployment. Years ago, three months' worth of salary was thought to be a minimal reserve cushion.

But over time, as unemployment fell and credit concerns waned, these and other time-tested precautions were seen as impediments and summarily tossed out the window. Launched as a niche product, NINAs quickly became available en masse.

In one sense, NINAs were a rational response on the part of lenders and borrowers eager to participate in the surging housing market. House prices were rising in communities all across the nation—an extremely rare event—and the price jump was putting homeownership out of reach for many people. On the other hand, the rapid rise in prices meant that borrower equity also was rising, reducing the risk of default for those who did become homeowners. People began clamoring to get into the hot housing market. There were other reasons to take the easy-entry, low-monthly-payment loans. Family incomes hadn't kept up with the pace of house-price inflation, making traditionally amortizing mortgages unaffordable for many people. NINAs were heavily marketed to immigrants, many of whom lacked traditional documentation and the language skills to understand what they were signing up for. Was it a coincidence that the acronym was a girl's name in Spanish?

Adding to the frenzy, mortgage regulation was woefully out of date, and the plethora of financial regulators found themselves pitted against each other. If a bank didn't care for the degree of scrutiny of its primary regulator, it could trade in its bank charter, for example, and apply for a thrift charter, in an attempt to obtain a more lenient regulator. Market watchers would later call this "charter shopping," and it led to increasing amounts of risky business flowing to institutions with the weakest regulator.

As long as house prices kept rising and defaults remained low, scant attention was paid to the actual mortgages that were being originated. With federal regulators once again woefully unprepared for the onslaught about to break upon the market, the GSEs were the unwary, if not de facto, mortgage police. As long as the GSEs could retain market power, that is. Such was the brewing cauldron awaiting Freddie Mac's new CEO, Dick Syron, when he arrived in late 2004.

Mission as Salve

Syron's arrival at Freddie ended a six-month leadership vacuum and brought a needed jolt of energy and verve. Suddenly employees felt hopeful about emerging from accounting and political purgatory. Syron's resume seemed like a dream come true for a GSE with a history of political problems. He had a long career in public service, having been the president of the Federal Reserve Bank of Boston and of the Federal Home Loan Bank of Boston. Earlier, he served as assistant to then-Federal Reserve Chairman Paul Volcker and as deputy assistant secretary of the US Department of Treasury.

Syron also had private-sector experience as CEO of a Fortune 500 company. The fact that his prior firm dealt with scientific instrumentation, rather than mortgages or finance or housing, was largely dismissed at the time—although many think that greater knowledge of credit risk on his part could have averted some very costly decisions down the road.

But no one was thinking about credit risk in early 2004. After Syron's appointment as CEO, Freddie's stock rebounded 22 percent.

Syron had a strong bias for homeownership. In early speeches he would refer to his parents' first home, financed by a VA mortgage, as a way of embracing the GSE mission to help families achieve homeownership. Syron seemed voluble and passionate—and unscripted. He was also a true Bostonian. Employees could barely parse his accent that first day when he held an all-employee town hall meeting in the firm's Virginia headquarters. His inaugural speech was supportive of employee efforts to right the ship following two scandals while bracing to a workforce used to good perks.

Syron's comments and off-color jokes quickly became the stuff of lore. It probably wasn't the best thing to tell five thousand scandal-beleaguered employees that if they don't like working at Freddie Mac they should go work for the Department of Agriculture. He was trying to make the point that employees needed to toughen up. Still, the comment grated on everyone's nerves and was repeated for years to come.

But the most important thing Syron communicated that day was his vision for the future of the firm. In no uncertain terms, he made it clear that Freddie was changing course. There would be no more focus on short-term shareholder gains or political maneuvers, which he claimed had come at the expense of the firm's housing mission. Freddie Mac was going to be pro-mission from now on.

Employees cheered at that, although, as usual, mission was in the eye of the beholder. It was unclear what Syron meant exactly, considering he was so new to the housing industry and had little knowledge of the deep existential conflicts of a GSE. It was further unclear how much more mission-oriented Freddie could be, given its conservative risk posture. Plus, wasn't maintaining the stability of the mortgage market also part of the firm's mission? The risk stalwarts of the company, guys like Andrukonis, heard Syron's mission charge as a bad omen.[1]

On the heels of this speech came Syron's public commitment to "beat HMDA," the measure of primary market originations mentioned earlier. The 1991 Home Mortgage Disclosure Act required banks and other entities in the primary market to report mortgage originations to traditionally underserved groups. Syron was essentially saying that Freddie Mac's mortgage purchases would not only mirror the primary mortgage—we would somehow outdo it. For Freddie Mac, one of the pillars of the secondary mortgage market, to commit to outpace the primary market represented a tectonic shift in the company's legendary tight underwriting policies. Future decisions with regard to NTMs would further reconceptualize Freddie Mac's understanding of mission and widen the breach between the firm it once had been and the firm it was rapidly and dangerously becoming.

The New Freddie

In April 2004, Syron hired Hollis McLoughlin as chief of staff. Freddie's lobbyists had assessed McLoughlin's political leanings before the ink was dry on his executive benefits. Despite all the flak the company had taken over its lobbying activities, the rumor mill the lobbyists relied on to do their jobs was still quite reliable and oblivious to the noxious headlines.

McLoughlin was a "new Freddie" personality: hard-charging, decisive, and impatient. Oblivious to the inside code of passive aggression, the chief of staff was always "breaking china," as he was fond of saying. Easily in a sweat by nine in the morning, McLoughlin would go through the day hitting the table with his fist, pointing fingers, and raising his voice, just as an effective chief of staff is supposed to do. Displayed on his bulletin board was a quotation by General George Patton about valuing decisiveness over perfection. This guy was determined to get things done.

McLoughlin hired me away from Government Relations (thank God). My new title was vice president of public policy, and I had a small team of employees. A little internal think tank, we researched and developed policy arguments in support of legislative positions. We had other assignments, too. In one of our first discussions about Dick's staffing needs, McLoughlin told me that Dick needed someone to worry about "the chattah."

I was puzzled. "The charter? He wants someone to worry about the charter? Well, lots of people do that for a living, starting with the legal department."

Then it was McLoughlin's turn to be confused. "Not *the* charter, Susan. Dick's charter—his charter *plane*. He will head home to the Cape on weekends. He needs help with scheduling." I rolled my eyes—but also had to laugh.

Whatever other attributes McLoughlin brought to the table, the most interesting (from the lobbyists' perspective) was that he was a Republican. This, they speculated, was a move from Syron to keep the *other* side of the aisle happy. Syron and Representative Frank (D-MA) hailed from the same home town and reportedly were good friends. Political balance would be needed.

One of the first things Syron had to do was fill a number of key vacancies on the board of directors and within the firm itself. The accounting scandal had decimated Freddie Mac's top management ranks. Syron needed a new chief operating officer, general counsel, head of investments, and top lobbyist, not to mention some new board members. In fulfillment of an OFHEO order emanating from the 2003 Special Examination, he also needed a compliance officer. In the summer of 2004, the new faces began appearing.

Former president of Bank of America, Eugene "Gene" McQuade soon followed to be our new president and COO. McQuade was ostensibly being groomed to take over the CEO position after Syron relinquished the title, in accordance with an OFHEO directive to split the roles of CEO and chairman.

Patti Cook arrived from J. P. Morgan Chase to be Freddie's executive vice president of investments. My female colleagues were pleasantly surprised with Patti's appointment. Freddie was not known for gender or racial diversity in the ranks of top management.

Cook was smart, petite, and optimistic to a fault. Years later, when she had become chief business officer, a senior vice president told me that "everyone was working on their relationship with Patti." No one felt secure around her.

Dark Shadows

In the enthusiasm of bringing a fresh team of top executives on board, who could have guessed what lay ahead? Within two years, Syron would be so frustrated with the pace of the remediation of our accounting and other issues that he would find a way to get a new chief financial officer.

Within three years, in the summer of 2007, McQuade would abruptly resign—just six months before his expected appointment as CEO—leaving the company unable to fulfill the regulator's order to split the roles of chairman and CEO.

Within four years, Syron himself would be forced out by then–Treasury Secretary Hank Paulson. Just days after that, Cook and Buddy Piszel, Syron's handpicked CFO, would be shown the door as well.

Seven months later, in April 2008, the man selected to take over as CFO after the government placed the firm into conservatorship—16-year Freddie veteran David Kellerman—would be found dead in his home from an apparent suicide.

A Night Out

Early in 2004, my husband and I were invited to an evening soiree celebrating the Barbara Bush Foundation for Family Literacy held at Maryland's Strathmore Music Center. I felt pleased to be invited. Every now and then I would get thrown a crumb off the executives' table, like a seat in Freddie's box at DC's Verizon Center or a dugout view of a Nationals home game—or this. My boss also had invited Cook, Freddie's newest top executive, and her husband.

After listening to former Orioles star Cal Ripken and writers read selections from their works, we were enjoying a light supper. Ever the conversationalist, McLoughlin had elbowed me to jump in. "Susan, tell Patti how you cried after the accounting scandal while sitting in the parking lot."

I stiffened in the chair. Why had I divulged my anger to my new boss? This was not the conversation I wanted to have with the top-ranking woman in the firm. Cook's fork stopped in mid-air as she looked at me inquisitively.

Dutifully I recounted the story of driving back to the office after work hours, staring at the granite building and tearing up, furious that the former executives had been so reckless with the accounting as to engulf the firm in scandal.

The fork went down. "You actually *cried?*"

For a half-second I panicked. Then I found my footing. "Yes, I did." And I thought, *When a business makes poor choices, based on pride, greed, and short-sightedness, that's very sad.*

The conversation trailed off. I would have many angry tears ahead.

Memo Land

"Susan, you need to create a process to get information to and from Dick. There is no control around here," said McLoughlin one morning. "People are just sending him stuff without any context. Like this."

He threw a piece of paper at me. "It needs a cover memo."

Unlike a government agency, Freddie did not have a memo culture. During my years at OMB, I had painfully learned the fine art of memo writing from my branch chief. He would take what I thought was a perfectly fine memo and use a red pen to completely rewrite it. McLoughlin must have had the same experience at Treasury. Not long after he arrived at Freddie, he realized the extent of the information disadvantage he and his new boss now faced. He was also quick to discern the general feuding going on between the business divisions. For starters, Freddie executives weren't used to having to go through a chief of staff to get to the CEO. Both McLoughlin and Syron were smart men, but neither knew anything about the interstices of running a mortgage shop.

In the spirit of fostering open communication, I was asked to create a set of memo templates that everyone in the firm was supposed to use in communicating with the CEO. By far the most comprehensive, the CEO Decision Memo was designed along the lines of an OMB director's Review Issue Paper: lay out the issue, analyze it, propose a solution, and get everyone's views. It was not that everyone had to agree, but executives had to put their cards on the table. That turned out to be hard, if not impossible, for the chronically passive-aggressive corporate culture that defined Freddie Mac.

Some execs avoided the memo process like the plague and tried to deal directly with Syron via e-mail or in meetings. But decision making in meetings was unpredictable. Often staff would work hard to lay out the contours of an issue only to have meetings go haywire. Syron would get prickly about something, then excuse himself to take a phone call from a board member or member of Congress, then call for a cup of Earl Grey, and then wax eloquent on economics. Somehow decisions got made—some fateful. Both the company's memos and e-mails about the pros and cons of purchasing NINAs and other Alt A loans would eventually be made public.

The NINA Memo

The NINA decision memo took the whole summer of 2004 to write, edit, and get approved.[2] There were lots of parts to it, starting with the concern that lenders would walk if we didn't continue to buy their NTMs.

Issues and concerns were smoldering everywhere. For one, the rush to buy those loans, with their different amortization schedules and other quirks, had caught the company off guard from a systems standpoint. Because of the limitations of our mortgage purchasing abilities, which worked well enough for plain vanilla 30-year fixed-rate loans, we had to bring Alt A into the company another way, through bulk transactions. To buy bulk, one price was negotiated for the whole lot of loans based on an analysis of their average credit risk and other factors. The sales force claimed that if Freddie got picky and wouldn't allow NINAs in the bulk packages, some lenders would refuse to sell us the higher-quality loans we did want. If we didn't buy it, they would take the deal to Fannie or to the Street. As a company that *always* played second fiddle to Fannie, Freddie wasn't about to let Wall Street firms steal any more market share.

Elsewhere in the NINA memo, data and analysis on some of the recent bulk portfolios indicated that, in contrast to nontraditional mortgages of yore, where borrowers had strong credit and low down payments, the newer vintage NTMs were looking relatively weak. Plus, there was some concern about lenders coaching borrowers into NINAs, which would put more money in the lenders' pockets.

Then there was Freddie's mission and our new zeal to "beat HMDA." Although purchasing Alt A would help the firm's "minority purchase numbers," which Freddie continued to take flak about, it would not help its performance against the housing goals. Without verifiable borrower income information, the loans could not be counted against two of the three main housing goals.

The memo also considered the reputational aspects of going deeper into nontraditional mortgages. Months before, there had been discussions about taking the Alt-A issue to the consumer advocacy community and asking for "cover" so we could back down and stop buying so many of those untested—and contested—loans. Ken Harney, a syndicated real estate columnist, had just written a scathing piece on NINAs, calling them "liar-liar" loans.[3] Surely the consumer groups would support Freddie on backing out of that market. It was my job to find out.

When the GSEs had strong market power relative to lenders and Wall Street, Freddie and Fannie could pretty much call the shots on underwriting. Lenders usually had to accept our terms because there was no other liquidity game in town. But when the GSEs began to lose market share and relevancy, Freddie Mac needed external support in order to prevail against its own customers, who were holding the firm hostage to take higher-risk loans off their hands.

All the better if Freddie's moral high road—a strategy formulated with the consumer groups—resulted in public pressure on Fannie to take the same position, as had been the case with prepayment penalties a few years before. With both GSEs upholding a conservative underwriting standard, it was a lot easier to tell a lender customer to bug off without a loss of market share. Ditto if the firms could say a member of Congress wouldn't like it, or because they would be publicly pilloried by a consumer advocate group.

But in 2004 the consumer advocates were strangely agnostic about NTMs. Even though privately they told us that they didn't like the new loans, none would take a public stand against them because doing so would threaten their fragile coalition. Latino groups, I was told quietly, viewed NTMs as important to their constituent base, and no one wanted to take that issue on. Besides, the consumer groups were still very focused on fighting subprime abuses. NTMs seemed to be a product for borrowers with higher incomes and higher credit scores, so they were not a hot-button issue. So the groups took a pass and said little to nothing about the most potentially destructive loans pouring into the housing finance system.

Freddie tried to encourage lenders to offer SISA (stated income and assets) loans as an alternative to NINAs. With a SISA, at least the borrower had to fill in the blanks that said "income" and "assets" with actual amounts. But lenders objected. SISA borrowers were obliged to fill out a tax form, which alerted the IRS if the income cited on the mortgage application was not the same as what had been filed on the borrower's annual tax return. Not surprisingly, lenders were not eager to market SISA loans; they knew full well the tax form requirement would not be a strong selling point.

We had reached another dead end. Back and forth the draft memo went.

Some time in the middle of all the jockeying and before the memo was finalized, Andrukonis got frustrated and bucked the bureaucratic process. He sent an e-mail directly to the CEO with copies to several executives, including me.

In the now-famous e-mail, Andrukonis told Syron flat out that NINAs were bad news for Freddie Mac:

Our presence in this market is inconsistent with a mission-centered company and creates too much reputation risk for the firm. An additional problem with this type of loan is that it appears they are disproportionately targeted towards Hispanics. The potential for the perception and reality of predatory lending with this product is great . . .

Exiting the NINA market would be difficult and expensive . . . since NINAs are minority rich, it will make it even more difficult to match the private market level of minority and underserved mortgage production. On the other hand, what better way to highlight our sense of mission than to walk away from profitable business because it hurts the borrowers we are trying to serve. In my judgment, matching the market's production of underserved and minority borrower will require us to engage in market practices that are at odds with our charter if it requires us to make a market in NINAs.[4]

I remember smiling when I read the contents. I especially loved the line "what better way to highlight our sense of mission than to walk away."

My delight was short-lived, however. Upon receipt of the e-mail, McLoughlin blew up. A direct e-mail to the CEO broke protocol. With me in attendance, Andrukonis was hauled into his office and actually scolded for sending the CEO an e-mail that said the loans were *predatory*. How dare he?

Andrukonis calmly replied that it was his job to make an independent assessment of risk. His pithy e-mail had trumped the over-edited, wishy-washy NINA memo. Besides, he had been saying as much to the CEO and board for some time.

There was much table pounding and red-faced expletives. Then came the veiled suggestion that the e-mail should somehow disappear. That was a red flag to a bull. Andrukonis was livid.

A few months later, another memo was slid into a file. At McLoughlin's behest, David Stevens, the senior vice president of sales, wrote a paean to the consumer benefits of NTMs. It would be good for the history books to know there were two sides to the debate, right?

Although he would later be publicly exonerated, Andrukonis's career was over. Syron asked him to leave the firm. It was supposed to look like it was his decision to leave, but employees knew better. Andrukonis was simply an obstacle to the expansionary plans of the Wall Street–styled company Freddie Mac was quickly becoming.

Andrukonis went on to become a middle-school algebra teacher, turning down an overture from the White House to become the next regulator of the firm that had fired him. His silver-bullet e-mail did not disappear but ended up as Exhibit A on congressional websites in the wake of the company's collapse in 2008.

Stevens went on to become the head of the FHA and then the Mortgage Bankers Association (MBA), the nation's largest bank trade group. At an industry event a few years ago at which he was the keynote speaker, a former employee of mine and I locked eyes and winced.

In December 2015, Gretchen Morgenson, a Pulitzer Prize–winning reporter with the *New York Times*, fingered Stevens as one of the key revolving-door interlocutors between the Obama administration and the MBA who favored eliminating the GSEs and replacing them with a bank-centered system. According to Morgenson: "Proponents of eliminating Fannie and Freddie say that allowing them to survive would also mean letting them go back to their abusive ways. The companies were a huge source of capital for reckless loan products, in Mr. Stevens's view. 'We risk going back to that system,' he said, because the public cannot count on regulators 'to protect us going forward and constrain these guys.' "[5] Which guys is he talking about?

The Fissure Widens

As the mortgage market heated up in 2005, Freddie's whole risk management philosophy had came under assault from within and from without. Although conservative risk management had been the firm's stock in trade since its founding in 1970, it was about to be discarded for good.

Market pressures had continued to accelerate, and market share plummeted. As noted in a 2010 study by the Federal Housing Finance Agency, "the Enterprises' share of total loans fell from above 90 percent in 2001 and 2002 to just above 60 percent in 2005."[6] As was typical, Freddie Mac bore the brunt of the competitive pressure and was losing share not only to Wall Street but also to Fannie Mae. Wall Street was issuing as many mortgage securities as the GSEs, which was astounding. The executives were flummoxed by the turn of events and clearly concerned about market share and risk. Political pressures had not abated, nor had any primary market regulators—the Fed or the OCC—taken any action to curb the growth of so-called exploding subprime ARMs, or NTMs. We were on our own to navigate the treacherous waters, and there was no Andrukonis at the helm.

That's when Don Bisenius, a contemporary of Andrukonis's but now a senior vice president under Cook, threw in the towel. He'd had enough of trying to regulate the Wild West of mortgage lending. If you can't beat them, join them was the new philosophy.

Soon after, Freddie Mac launched its fateful strategy called Touch More Loans.[7] I first heard about it in a briefing to Freddie Mac officers, which Cook presented. In a nutshell, the idea was to get the mortgage side of the company (old Freddie) to think about credit risk the same way Cook and her securities traders (new Freddie) thought about interest-rate risk: simply as a commodity that could be traded, hedged, and dynamically managed. It was not, she argued, something to price once and put in a security or a portfolio forever.

Rather, to remain competitive, Freddie would now seek to "touch" the loan when we purchased it, thereby providing liquidity to the market (and, coincidently, getting credit under our affordable housing goals). But if we didn't like the risk associated with that loan, we could choose to sell the unwanted cash flows or to use credit default swaps or other credit derivative to hedge against them.

Cook was convinced that by using these new risk management tools, we would be able to retake our market position, keep lenders happy, and meet our housing goals—all without increasing our credit risk exposure. Cook did not lack for optimism. She was sure of it.

Touch More Loans represented fundamental change for Freddie Mac. Practically, it meant the firm could stop being so picky about the loans it was buying. Because Freddie planned to sell loans it really didn't like "off the back end," it could buy what the market was producing, even if the risk profile of the loans was not to the firm's liking. In other words, we would buy stuff we didn't like because we thought we could pawn it off on someone else.

Even more troublesome, Touch More Loans severed the long-standing alignment of interests between Freddie Mac and our borrowers: the people who, for the most part, had put their entire financial wherewithal on the line to buy a house and with whom the firm shared important financial incentives. If the borrower lost, Freddie, as guarantor, also would lose.

Under Touch More Loans, mortgages lost their essence as a compact with borrowers and were reduced to anonymous cash flows that simply needed to be bought and hedged. The borrower could still lose—perhaps would even lose more frequently or severely because we were looking the other way—but Freddie wouldn't lose because the firm had disposed of the risk.

This is where Freddie lost its conscience. By covering its eyes and buying the market, Freddie chose to abdicate its traditional role as standard bearer and become just another mortgage market player. This major paradigm shift explains why, when the issue of credit leadership surfaced again for the last time in 2005, it was handily rejected by top management.

After Andrukonis's dismissal, neither Bisenius nor the other top executives, all of whom knew better, raised a word in protest. They knew how their bread was buttered.

Touch More Loans would prove good for bonuses, especially Cook's. As recounted in the 2011 SEC complaint:

The Touch More Loans strategy . . . played a role in Cook's compensation. In 2006, Cook's target bonus was $2 million and her target long term equity award for performance was $2.4 million. Cook received a bonus of $2.3 million, or $300,000 in excess of her target, and a long-term equity award equating to $2.763 million, or $363,000 greater than her target, in part due to Cook's Touch More Loans strategy. In 2007, Cook received a bonus of $1.4 million dollars plus a supplemental bonus of $200,000 with a three-year vesting schedule, again in part because of Touch More Loans.

Freddie Succumbs

So with strong competitive pressure to buy whatever the engorged market was producing, without primary market regulators holding back the tide of bad lending, and lacking the political cover to do otherwise, Atlas shrugged. The firm known for its stingy "no" finally said "bring it on." Freddie gave in to the lenders and bought their NTMs, their liar-liar NINAs, their piggybacks, and their Option ARMs.

Unfortunately, Freddie's grandiose plans for using new technologies and instruments to dispose of the unwanted risk lagged far behind the firm's ravenous mortgage purchase appetite. Each year Freddie's management pontificated about the importance of rebuilding the firm's computer systems infrastructure—new mortgage purchase and servicing "platforms"—and big bonuses flowed to the IT execs and their departments to do just that. But to most employees, it seemed that the firm's processing systems never improved; Freddie never reached its goal of being able to handle the new loan terms and repayment schedules. Some said Freddie Mac was so focused on remediating all its financial accounting systems to the regulator's exacting standard that it didn't have the money or bandwidth to rebuild the business processes as well. There is some truth to that contention. For whatever reason, however, the computer systems needed to support Touch More Loans were not adequately built or implemented. Moreover, as the crisis deepened, investors had little interest in buying excess risk being sold by a GSE. As a result, the firm pretty much kept all the bad risk it had bought.

A month following the government takeover of the firms, in October 2008, Eric Stein of the Center for Responsible Lending (CRL)—the policy arm affiliated with Martin Eakes's Self-Help Credit Union—testified before the Senate Banking Committee about the causes of the economic crisis.

Although elsewhere in the testimony Stein noted that more regulations on the GSEs meant more freedom for others to do what they pleased, he chided the GSEs for purchases of Alt-A mortgages, such as NINAs.

The Alt A epidemic was in full flower by the time that the GSEs got into the act . . . In 2004, Angelo Mozilo, then chief executive at Countrywide (mortgage company), reportedly demanded that Fannie Mae buy the lender's riskier loans, or else they couldn't purchase its less risky loans.

"You're becoming irrelevant. You need us more than we need you, and if you don't take these loans, you'll find you can lose much more," Mozilo reportedly said, and at the time, his assertion would have been hard to dispute.

Fannie Mae and Freddie Mac started buying Alt A loans in significant numbers. From 2005 to 2007, Fannie bought three times as many loans without the usual documentation of income or savings as it had in all earlier years combined. By the middle of [2008], Alt A loans account for roughly 10 percent of Fannie and Freddie's risk exposure, but a whopping 50 percent of their combined losses. Losses on Freddie Mac's Alt A loans have accounted for 79 percent of the increase in total credit losses (from $528 million to $810 million) between the first and second quarters of 2008."[8]

As for Freddie Mac's view on what transpired, in a December 2007 *Washington Post* article, Cook and Piszel reflected on the decisions to buy the market. Said Cook, "I don't think we viewed as our role or responsibility to say to the market that [these loans] were inappropriate."[9]

Said Piszel, "I think what happened over time is, we found that our own caution was making us less and less relevant . . . Could we have run for the hills and said we're not going to do any of that? What if things didn't go down? We would basically be just taking our whole future and giving it away."[10] I put the newspaper down in disgust.

Where Things Stand Today

The firm that was once concerned about becoming irrelevant got its wish. Today Freddie Mac and Fannie Mae are so relevant they are scary. Private sources of mortgage finance are few and far between.

As for the exotic, untested mortgage products that led to their undoing, most have been eliminated from the market, thanks to DFA and the

CFPB. It would be naïve, however, to think that NTMs could not rise again in some other form. All it would take is a growing concern that would-be borrowers who don't fit the standard profile of mortgage underwriting are being unfairly blocked from becoming homeowners. They may work seasonally, have hard-to-document income, be new immigrants, or have a weak credit history. Mortgage originators are eager to make mortgages to these applicants as long as the bulk of the risk doesn't fall to them to manage or bear. Politicians are eager to make mortgages to these applicants because homeownership wins votes—whether it is 2002 or 2022. Economists are very eager to see the housing market get humming again—and everyone is blaming tight rules for holding things up.

The temptation is high to begin loosening the rules. But without taming the political promises of homeownership, without expanding the supply of affordable rental housing and developing broad-based financial literacy, and without greater ethical reflection on the part of the housing finance industry, it is likely that loosening the rules is a ticket back to the brink of calamity.

Conclusion

Freddie Mac's nosedive into NTMs followed a power struggle between old and new Freddie. Old Freddie wanted to hew close to its traditional ways, standards, and approaches—at the risk of being pilloried as anti-poor at every turn by liberal politicians, lenders, the cheerleaders of the mortgage industry, and consumer groups, even at the risk of losing market share. New Freddie saw a way to capitalize on these issues and turn risk into gold.

The sad irony is that the company's fateful 2004 reconceptualization of its mission—and the political cover it would soon give to invest deeply and dangerously in high-risk products—did far more damage to Freddie Mac's reputation and its financial well-being.

Freddie Mac's decision to chase the golden ring of market share by purchasing mortgages it knew were not good for borrowers may have seemed rational, assuming the firm could off-load the risks as it had planned.

The tragedy of selling a company's soul speaks loudly of the need for wisdom, restraint, and the ability to say no to powerful interests, even if they are customers and shareholders. Just as tragic were the bevy of regulators who failed to do their job and expected the GSEs to plug fingers in the dike, to their own financial detriment. It was only a matter of time before the dam would break.

ONE TOUGH BILL

Growing concern over GSE performance under the affordable housing goals, accounting and political scandals, and the growing GSE presence in subprime and NTM mortgages lit a fuse in Congress for major reform of the entities that it had created decades before. In prior years, the problems with the GSEs had been largely theoretical. Now they were real. But while both sides of the aisle supported some level of reform, their ideological differences kept them miles apart on key issues.

For many Republicans, the GSEs resembled Frankenstein: abnormally created, socially engineered companies that had outgrown their role and become monsters. To stave off crisis, privatization was the best solution. Short of that, the Rs wanted to severely restrain the GSEs' ability to grow by requiring higher capital, including a surcharge for posing systemic risk, restricting mortgage portfolio investments, and the mind-boggling volume of GSE debt issued to finance them.

Not surprisingly, many Democrats vigorously opposed these reforms. To them, the GSEs were the savior of affordable housing (via underpriced mortgage risk) and small financial institutions such as community banks, which were at risk of being elbowed out of the market by the nation's big banks. To them, GSE growth needed to be carefully monitored rather than curtailed. Shrinkage would mean a smaller share of GSE financing activities devoted to affordable housing (since the goals were stipulated as a percentage of overall mortgage purchases), so they opposed major adjustments in the GSE business model.

Bipartisan reform remained elusive even in the face of mounting evidence that the GSEs were not going to be able to save the mortgage market when the house price bubble burst in 2007. They were, in fact, about to become a very big crisis themselves. Finally, in the summer of 2008, Congress passed the first major GSE reform legislation in sixteen years. But reform came too late. Barely 50 days after that legislation was signed, the GSEs were declared insolvent and placed under government control.

The legislative impasse over GSE reform—and eventual government takeover—raises serious questions about public/private partnerships. It always sounds like a good idea to tap the private sector or the capital markets for social policy purposes. By offloading social responsibilities onto the private sector, government becomes more entrepreneurial, and precious funds can be directed elsewhere. Such was the prevailing mindset since the 1970s, notwithstanding concerns raised by a growing number of scholars, economists, and think tanks.

These party spoilers were the first to recognize that, once out of the bottle, the private-sector genie is hard to control and contain. Oversight of powerful corporate entities is tough and always at risk of being over-run or co-opted. OFHEO, their hamstrung regulator, was simply outgunned by its smart, huge, well heeled, shareholder-owned charges, Fannie Mae and Freddie Mac. Lawmakers also have a poor track record of trying to reform, much less eliminate, popular programs that have grown out of hand. Certainly the GSEs—and a large portion of the housing and mortgage industry—did not side with the lawmakers and other detractors who desperately wanted to write them out of existence.

As quoted in the FCIC report, former HUD Secretary Henry Cisneros said that OFHEO, the GSE regulator until 2008, "was puny compared to what Fannie Mae and Freddie Mac could muster in their intelligence, their Ivy League educations, their rocket scientists in their place, their lobbyists, their ability to work the Hill."[1]

Short of sheer parliamentary force (which did not exist in a divided Congress), the stalemate over GSE reform called for brave leadership on the part of the CEOs and their boards of directors, strong regulatory oversight that earned company respect, creative third-way solutions, and recognition of the deep ideological differences lying just beneath the surface of bitter debates over capital levels and affordable housing. All were sadly lacking.

S. 190

In January 2005, just days into the Republican-controlled 109th Congress, Senator Chuck Hagel (R-NE) introduced a GSE regulatory reform bill that went further than previous GOP attempts to diminish the implicit government guarantee and rein in GSE growth; by 2003, the GSE portfolios weighed in at $1.6 trillion.[2]

To curtail growth in a hurry, S. 190 proposed to slash both companies' retained mortgage portfolios, which for Freddie Mac was about $700 billion at the time. Fannie Mae's had topped $1 trillion. Hagel's bill would give a new regulator the power to force the GSEs to sell off large amounts of mortgage assets and authority to determine what, if any, assets they could buy going forward.

Predictably, the GSEs objected strenuously to the bill, which was the worst of both worlds from our standpoint. First, the near liquidation of the portfolios would reset the GSE capitalistic advance back to 1990, when the primary GSE activity was to package mortgages into securities and sell them to investors. In this way, S. 190 would relegate the GSEs back to the low-margin end of the market, where the only revenue stream was g-fee income. This was a grim prospect, given that g-fees had been driven to depressing lows by brutal price wars, political pressure, rising house prices, and diminished concern about risk. In addition to cutting deep into GSE profits, S. 190 maintained firm regulatory control over GSE operations, dictating new GSE mission requirements, clamping down on innovation, and restricting growth.

Freddie Mac hired McKinsey and other pricey consultants to model the impact of the bill on the current and future viability of the firm. The numbers simply did not add up. By cutting off a major revenue stream, S.190 placed the franchise at risk, and privatization was not a viable exit strategy. Freddie Mac hunkered down and opposed the bill.

Gladiatorial Hearings

In April 2005, the Senate Banking Committee held five days of testimony on S. 190. In a huge show of force, the committee first heard from Federal

Reserve Chairman Alan Greenspan, Treasury Secretary John Snow, and HUD Secretary Alphonso Jackson.

Chairman Greenspan was the first to attack both GSEs' retained mortgage portfolios. He raised the specter of systemic risk arising from their size and growth as well as market misperceptions about the government's backing of GSE debt. Freddie and Fannie had done a good job with securitization in the past, he said. Let that continue, but their retained mortgage portfolios had to go.

Under questioning, Greenspan expressed his view that after taking a few years to reduce the portfolios, the regulator should limit the GSE portfolios to about $100 billion.[3] For Freddie, that would mean a decline of about $600 billion; for Fannie, the drop was even larger.

A second panel of witnesses featured a predictable cast of characters: the mortgage and housing trade groups (homebuilders, realtors, and mortgage bankers) and consumer advocacy groups. Often in league with the large banks, the trade groups predictably supported anything that would reduce the GSE role in the market while insisting that nothing should be done to cause mortgage rates to rise or mortgage liquidity to decline. Of course, since the GSEs—and their huge mortgage portfolios—were largely responsible for those market benefits, it was an impossible ask.

The consumer groups usually came to the defense of the GSEs, mostly because they hated the banks more than they hated Freddie and Fannie. But they continued to complain that the GSEs didn't do enough for affordable housing.

Invoking the Almighty Consumer

Policy advocacy is an art form in Washington, DC. Beyond an unspoken agreement that one should not tell bald-faced lies (a barrier that also has been assailed) there are few rules governing its practice. It is acceptable to push your point—whatever your point is—to the nth degree, if not well into silly abstraction.

Strategic use of language makes the values Americans hold dear—and which deeply resonate with politicians—overly idealized and ultimately devoid of meaning. Real truth gets gagged in this process.

"Consumer" is one such gold-plated word. Invoking this hallowed word in congressional testimony or talking points nearly always succeeds in thwarting any good government initiative. It's the ultimate policy trump card, no matter what issue is being debated. In the housing finance debates, the GSEs would argue against, say, higher capital or the imposition of user fees on portfolio purchases on a number of grounds. Their most potent argument often was that it would raise costs for consumers. If that didn't give a politician pause, its corollary would: the specter of raising the cost of homeownership.

In another example, the real estate trade groups were quick to calculate how many consumers would be denied homeownership for each 0.10 percent increase in mortgage interest rates. Now that's an un-American concept: a denied consumer. A few would find the extra dollars unaffordable. But how many, really? And how long would homeownership be delayed while a borrower accumulated the extra dollars? A few months? A year? Perhaps waiting would be a good thing, all things considered.

Consumers were invoked by subprime mortgage brokers in opposing the imposition of regulatory standards on their risky loans. The brokers moaned that tighter standards would reduce lending to their consumers, who had been pitifully shut out of the primary market and desperately needed their high-cost mortgages. The homebuilders regularly opposed any increase in GSE guarantee fees, which would have made the system safer, because that would raise costs for their consumers—new homebuyers. To their credit, the consumer advocacy groups tried to take the long view and argue for greater protections for underserved consumers—but in the same breath, they also called for unhindered access to low-cost loans for higher-risk borrowers so that more consumers could become homeowners.

In short, everywhere a politician stepped, another consumer land mine would go off. And once the almighty consumer was invoked, it was risky for a politician to attempt to question or deconstruct such assertions. In retrospect, it is ironic that after all the righteous arguments made on their behalf, consumers were the ones to suffer most from the near collapse of the US financial system.

Freddie Mac Testifies

On the fourth day of marathon hearings, Freddie CEO and Chairman Dick Syron was scheduled to testify. And I would write his statement. I viewed the opportunity to write congressional testimony as both a privilege and challenge. I had written speeches and testimony for the previous CEO, Leland Brendsel, and for the interim and acting CEOs following the accounting scandal. During the early days of Freddie's conservatorship in 2008, I wrote my final testimony for CEO David Moffett, who left the firm just six months after he arrived.

The process of drafting testimony would always start with a rumor from one of the lobbyists that there was going to be a hearing around such and such a date and that our CEO would be called up to testify. This was not a rare occurrence. Since 2001, there had been numerous hearings in both the House and Senate on GSE reform. Both parties—and both chambers—were quick to chide each other about the many times they had taken up the issue of GSE regulatory reform, but to no avail.

Then, as predicted, the official letter would arrive summoning Freddie Mac's CEO to testify before the committee on a particular topic. I would get a copy, and the process would begin. Usually it started with a meeting with the CEO, the chief of staff, and a few lobbyists, who gave background information on the hearing: who else would be testifying, what the members were after, and how our CEO should present the views of the company. I would listen and take notes. We'd discuss the particulars of the proposed legislation, but invariably there came a point of frustration, even anger.

"What is Congress trying to do to us?" Syron often would rail.

The Republicans wanted the GSEs smaller or nonexistent. Hadn't private banks and Wall Street firms proven the job could be done without a government guarantee? The Democrats wanted the GSEs to do ever more for affordable housing. The industry groups, like banks and mortgage insurers, wanted the GSEs to stop dictating market terms to them. Consumer groups wanted us to set anti–predatory lending standards since the regulators were asleep and nobody else was doing it. And the homebuilders and realty groups just wanted mortgage rates to stay low so they could keep building and selling.

With a mishmash of ideas and points, I headed back to my office to figure out how to say the same old thing. I would draft, redraft, and edit repeatedly. However much time we had to write the testimony, we would work right up to the very last moment.

The written testimony was Freddie Mac's long program: a comprehensive account, it included data, graphs, and footnotes to support key arguments. Congress required witnesses to deliver the written testimony to the committee electronically 48 hours prior to the hearing. In addition, it was Freddie's responsibility to get 100 hard copies of the document up to the Hill for public consumption just before the hearing began.

The oral testimony was much shorter and designed to be read aloud. Many a witness had been gaveled by the Chairman for droning on past five minutes. Ever the wordsmiths, we would edit the oral statement up until the CEO got in the limousine to go downtown.

The last phase of preparing for a hearing was known as a murder board. The lobbyists would think up hundreds of questions that might come up at the hearing—and the economists and lawyers had to prepare answers to them. Once the CEO was familiar with all the Q&A materials, everyone trooped into Freddie's sophisticated tiger-maple-paneled boardroom to play Congress. Taking seats around a pretend dais, my colleagues would assume the rank and mannerisms of a particular senator, complete with nasal twangs, nasty digs, and windbag opening statements. The CEO would be seated across the room, alone. Then the hardball questions would fly. Political consultants and others were invited to watch and critique the CEO's performance.

It usually took weeks to get testimony structured such that it could thread the needle between internal corporate squabbles and the external maze of interests Freddie Mac regularly dealt with. Because of decorum and party politics, combined with our sense of vulnerability, it was extremely difficult to say *exactly* what we wanted to say.

The CEO began by thanking the legislators for the opportunity to appear before them. (Always show deep gratitude for the chance to be questioned and lectured.) He said the firm was committed to the *process* of passing regulatory reform legislation. (Fair enough, but this really meant we had big issues with the *substance* of the legislation). Then he would express our views delicately, pointing out the risks of unintended consequences and offering suggestions for making the bill more balanced. Freddie hoped for legislation that would find the elusive golden mean between safety and soundness, our mission responsibilities, and give us a way to be profitable in the future. The company was, after all, shareholder-owned, and the shareholders were getting pretty irritated by the demagoguery, denouncements, and threats coming out of Congress. The endless harangue of politicians was hurting the stock price, and the CEO got an earful of complaints.[4]

That was how the company handled public political theater. Our work behind the scenes was different. Freddie Mac strongly disliked that bill and charged its lobbyists to work hard to modify provisions that would weaken the charter and hurt the business franchise. Freddie Mac did what every American corporation has the right to do: speak up for its own interests.

Buying Friends—Including the Former House Speaker

Sometime in 2005, Freddie Mac hired a Republican consulting firm named DCI to help get the company out of the political doghouse. Since 2003 with Freddie's accounting woes—soon followed by Fannie's—Washington had been scorched earth to GSEs. No one listened to anything we had to say. Gone were the days of high-profile fund-raisers at nice restaurants. Under Syron, Freddie had repented of all that and was working hard to reduce the $20 million list of political consultants on the corporate payroll.

In the shadow of the embarrassing FEC fine, Freddie Mac also decided to follow Fannie's lead by starting a political action committee, or PAC. Many employees didn't particularly like the idea of starting a PAC, but it was a way for the company to participate in the political process that was transparent, regulated, and legal.

But building a war chest without the help of fancy Italian dinners was slow going. Starting from zero, FreddiePAC depended on voluntary employee contributions, and there were a lot of restrictions about which employees could be solicited.

Now an officer, I was one of them. I had no desire to part with $2,000, but the company sugar-coated it a bit by giving an equivalent amount to the charity of my choice. So the nonprofit homeless organization of which I was a board member benefited from my political donation. In thanks, Freddie gave me a stuffed animal that was a donkey on one side and an elephant on the other. A perfect metaphor.

But back to DCI. Since it was abundantly clear that no one would listen to—much less believe—anything Freddie said or wrote, we decided we needed help: someone else to say what we wanted to say. It was called third-party advocacy, where a PR firm finds people sympathetic to your cause and assists them in writing an op-ed or speaking publicly on your behalf.[5] The idea was to go outside the DC beltway, where the media air was less charged, and make the case for the GSEs to local homebuilders, realtors, and other opinion leaders with a less-jaundiced view of us.

Sometime around then, former House Speaker Newt Gingrich's name came up as a possible third-party advocate. Years before, Delk had introduced him to me when we were seeking consultant feedback on the minority homeownership initiative. Maybe he could help my staff develop new ways of advocating for a continued strong GSE role.

Gingrich was emphatically not hired to be a historian, as he would later claim during the 2012 presidential primary race.[6] Nor was he hired to lobby for specific pieces of legislation on Freddie Mac's behalf. The fact that he was a conservative Republican at a time when the GSEs were on the GOP's most-wanted list was certainly highly valued. But that was hardly lobbying, right?

The former speaker was hired as an out-of-the-box thinker to help reframe the GSE debate. Perhaps Washington's irrepressible idea man could point out some positive effects brought about by the public-private arrangement known as government-sponsored enterprises.

Gingrich was eager to take Freddie Mac's money ($30K a month) and seemed to enjoy tossing around big ideas, such as how public-private partnerships could help the nation with some really huge and expensive problems like space travel and health care.

As the group overseeing the Gingrich contract, my staff and I would meet once a month or so at his DC office. While the conversation was high-toned and fascinating, I don't recall any specific work products coming out of the relationship. The external environment was fierce, and Syron was not interested in putting out any white papers by the former speaker on the virtues of GSE-hood. Nothing was written that had Gingrich's name on it.

The former speaker's contract was not renewed for 2007. His staff tried hard to convince us to reinstate the contract, but it was over. Perhaps those sour grapes explain why, less than 18 months later when Freddie Mac and Fannie Mae were placed into government receivership just as the 2008 presidential campaign went into high gear, Gingrich publicly denounced Freddie Mac. When he ran for president in 2012, I was called by a number of media outlets to confirm whether Gingrich was hired as a "historian," as he claimed, and if he had urged Freddie Mac to exit the subprime market.

"He said what?" I asked, laughing. On background I denied his boasting claims.

The fact that Gingrich did not lobby for Freddie Mac did not mean lobbying against S. 190 was not going on—or that DCI did not have a hand in it.

On July 28, 2005, the Senate Banking Committee adopted S. 190 by a straight party-line vote, 11-9. Every Republican on the committee supported it, and every Democrat opposed it. Bills passed along party lines have a hard time making it to the Senate floor. That's why Senator Hagel and 25 other Republicans wrote a letter to Senate Majority Leader Bill Frist (R-TN) urging him to allow the legislation to come to the floor for a vote. They were eager for other senators to sign the letter.

I learned about DCI's direct lobbying efforts in the newspaper after the government takeover of the company in 2008. According to documents obtained by the Associated Press, Freddie Mac paid DCI $2 million to undermine support for S. 190 by targeting 17 Senate Republicans in their home states.[7] Payments to DCI supposedly began after July 28, 2005, in effort to keep the bill from being taken up by the full Senate. Reported three years after the fact, the article called the move Freddie Mac's "stealth lobbying campaign."[8]

Critics are quick to blame Freddie and DCI for killing S. 190. The company certainly played a hard game of political cards—but in reality, bitter partisanship had already poisoned the chances for meaningful regulatory reform.

And then another storm broke out. A real one this time.

Shot at Redemption?

The trio of hurricanes that hit during the summer of 2005—Katrina, Rita, and Wilma—easily eclipsed GSE regulatory reform as the top mortgage issue for the remainder of that session of Congress. Affecting a 90,000-square-mile region, the storms left nearly 400,000 homes uninhabitable. More than 1,300 people lost their lives, and 2 million were forced to leave the Gulf Region. Freddie had a lot at stake: it was the guarantor of some 286,000 mortgages in the areas affected by both Katrina and Rita.

After all the criticism that had poured on the GSEs, the hurricanes seemed to unleash an amazing energy inside Freddie. The company and the Freddie Mac Foundation gave $10 million in humanitarian assistance. Employees themselves gave over $300,000, which was generously matched. The firm placed over 2,100 displaced families in temporary or permanent housing. Freddie led the industry in developing new mortgage servicing policies, including one year of blanket forbearance for affected borrowers. The firm helped mortgage servicers affected by the storms to get their operations up and running. We invested $1 billion in mortgage revenue bonds, which provided below-market financing to 10,000 families to repair their home or purchase a new one.

I participated in the twice-daily operations meetings that coordinated all these endeavors. The dedication, smarts, and innovation of my colleagues were impressive, reminding me of old Freddie. Politics had made me cynical about my employer; this was what we did well.

The lobbyists made their own contribution to the effort. Freddie Mac put up the funds to construct wood frames for 100 houses in conjunction with Habitat for Humanity on the Washington Mall—right where members of Congress could see us hammering in our "We Make Home Possible" t-shirts. (There was an R and a D house for each state.) After the photo shoot, the frames were dismantled and put on a semi-trailer bound for New Orleans.

It wasn't long before the legislative battles resumed. This time the Democrats would hold sway.

H.R. 1427

Following the acrimonious midterm elections in 2006, Congress changed hands. In one sense, the Democratic takeover was a relief, as it drove a stake through S. 190. That said, Freddie also feared the Democrats, who, even though they weren't calling for the GSEs to be tarred and feathered, sought to push us into loans and markets that were considered risky or, at a minimum, unprofitable.

Representative Frank now wielded the gavel as chair of the House Financial Services Committee. His counterpart in Senate Banking was Senator Chris Dodd (D-CT), who was more than a little distracted by his ill-fated attempt to get nominated for president.

Early in the 110th Congress, the chair introduced his GSE regulatory reform bill, H.R. 1427. This was largely a re-hash of a bill that passed the House in October 2005 by a broad majority. To broaden the bill's appeal to conservatives, Frank reportedly worked with Bush administration officials to modify some provisions that had become major sticking points in the earlier Democratic bill.

A key point of contention was the financing of the affordable housing fund, which was clearly a top priority for the chairman. Added to the growing list of GSE mission requirements, the fund was envisioned as a way to tax the profits of the GSEs and distribute them to deserving housing and consumer groups. As the chairman explained in his opening comments at a hearing in March 2007, whereas his Republican colleagues were determined to find a way to diminish GSE profitability (by putting restraints on the portfolio and requiring more capital, for example), the Democrats wanted to skim off some profits for unmet housing needs that couldn't be met through the GSEs' affordable housing goals. A direct subsidy would be needed, and the GSEs had deep pockets.

Conservatives complained for two reasons: One, they thought that tying the new housing fund to GSE profits would result in the GSEs further ingratiating themselves with the Democrats, thereby thwarting real reform (true). Two, they believed that the benefiting housing groups would use the proceeds of the fund, estimated to be between $350 and $500 million a year, to enhance Democratic political chances. That is, the funds would simply become political walking-around money for the Democrats. As described earlier, the GSEs have begun directing millions of dollars into these funds.

As a compromise, Chairman Frank kept the affordable housing fund in a new bill, H.R. 1427, but changed the financing to be based on the size of the GSE portfolios, not their profits. The conservatives preferred this mechanism because it supported their objective to deter further growth of the retained mortgage portfolios. If the GSEs insisted on growing, they would have to pay more money into the fund.

A second sticking point was the treatment of capital. The Bush administration was adamant that the new GSE regulator be given authority to require the GSEs to hold more capital, not simply in the case of a safety and soundness issue arising at a particular GSE but to cover systemic risk as well. The administration wanted the regulator to be able to require higher capital to guard against the possibility either that external events could threaten GSE financial stability or because GSE activities were threatening the broader market, even if an individual GSE was otherwise found to be safe and sound.

In hindsight, a systemic risk requirement seems prescient given the events of the past few years, but in 2007, it was unheard of. No other financial regulator had authority to impose such a requirement. Just like the risk-retention requirement in the unpopular qualified residential mortgage (QRM) provision, holding more capital locks up cash, thereby restricting growth. In the extremely competitive and low-margin business of mortgage finance, even a small difference in capital can sideline a firm and make it noncompetitive. Hence, many Democrats viewed proposals for higher capital with suspicion. Conspiracy theories abounded. Was the administration trying to do in the GSEs by giving their regulator greater power to raise capital than any other financial regulator held?

I know the GSEs thought so. Freddie was terribly paranoid by that point.

However, for the Democrats to get a GSE bill passed, administration support was needed. Thus, the bill Chairman Frank introduced contained a systemic risk capital requirement.

Freddie quietly opposed the breadth of the new regulatory powers. In doing so, the firm wasn't saying that the GSEs couldn't be a source of systemic risk—only that the GSEs weren't unique in that regard. Freddie argued that other financial firms, namely big commercial banks that had been growing in both size and scope, could also be viewed as posing systemic risk, as being "too big to fail." If systemic risk was going to be applied to the GSEs, it should be applied to them as well.

By mid-spring 2007, the issue of systemic risk had become a major point of political contention. A bipartisan compromise began to emerge. Rep. Melissa Bean (D-IL) and Rep. Randy Neugebauer (R-TX) drafted an amendment that limited the GSE regulator's power to raise capital to the safety and soundness of the institution per se, as opposed to requiring higher capital for additional risk imposed by the GSEs on the broader system. In other words, GSEs would not be held to a higher capital standard than other large financial firms.

Constrained by his prior agreement with the White House, Chairman Frank personally did not vote for the Bean-Neugebauer amendment when it came up for vote on the House floor on May 22, 2007, but it passed handily nevertheless: 383-36.

The GSEs would not be required to hold additional capital for systemic risk.

Ultimate Anticlimax

A little over one year later, in July 2008, amid the frightening cracks and booms of the tanking US housing market, Congress finally came together to pass GSE regulatory reform known as the Housing and Economic Recovery Act (HERA). But it was hardly a triumphant occasion for Congress or for the GSEs. OFHEO was abolished and renamed the Federal Housing Finance Agency (FHFA).

The weeks leading up to passage were traumatic, and rumors were flying. Foreign governments were skittish about buying GSE debt, which was crucial to both GSEs' ability to raise funds to keep purchasing mortgages. Debt spreads widened dangerously, and mortgage interest rates started to rise, particularly for higher-balance jumbo loans. News reports suggested that the Bush administration was working on contingency plans to take over the GSEs. On these fears and others, Freddie's stock collapsed into the single digits.

In a bid to boost market confidence, Treasury Secretary Hank Paulson had requested so-called "bazooka" language in GSE regulatory reform legislation giving the government unprecedented power to purchase GSE securities and to take other emergency measures. He said the "big gun" was needed to calm everybody down—and not because he actually planned to use it. Privately, Paulson had begun second-guessing FHFA's rather rosy assessments of GSE capital adequacy. Unbeknownst to the rank and file, a high-level plan was taking shape to justify placing the wobbly institutions into conservatorship, a type of Chapter 11 bankruptcy which, according to Paulson, "would provide a stable time-out for the GSEs to avoid defaulting on their debts."[9]

By that time, Freddie Mac employees were shocked by dramatically rising losses and the rapid depletion of the firm's capital base. HERA, the regulatory reform bill that had occupied our minds and passions for at least half a decade, was unceremoniously passed and signed into law.

Not long afterward, Bush, Shelby, and the GSE regulator would all pound their fists and say that the downfall of the GSEs could have been prevented if the Democrats had not weakened key provisions. The Democrats angrily replied that the legislation would have been in place long before if the administration hadn't been so ideologically rigid and unwilling to compromise. In 2010 Rep. Frank said he regretted supporting the GSEs as fervently as he did. According to Morgenson and Rosner, "Frank conceded that not every American should be a homeowner" and that the GSEs should be abolished.[10]

In terms of key provisions, the reform legislation that was enacted in 2008 was very much in keeping with H.R. 1427, introduced in 2006. Ideologically driven perfection had become the enemy of the good.

What-Ifs

Would passage of GSE regulatory reform before 2008 have prevented the financial crisis? If implementation had quickly followed enactment, and regulators and policy makers woke up to the dangers of NTMs, regulatory reform legislation could have lessened GSE losses and perhaps prevented a government takeover. That said, even if the GSEs had been tamed, reform legislation likely would not have prevented the broader crisis because of the other major player out there that was not regulated: Wall Street.

We got a glimpse of this dynamic early on. Under the relatively weak powers of the existing regulatory regime, OFHEO in 2004 moved aggressively to require the GSEs to hold 30 percent additional capital and to limit portfolio growth. An unintended consequence of this was that the GSEs—the relatively more regulated part of the market—lost considerable market share to Wall Street, which was operating with no holds barred. If regulatory reform had been enacted then, and Freddie had been made to hold even more capital and to further shrink the portfolio, GSE losses would have been smaller, and perhaps one or both firms could have avoided being placed into conservatorship in 2008. On the other hand, the shrinking of the GSEs would have made Wall Street's dominance of the market—and the dangerous mortgage products it produced—well nigh complete. In other words, without competition from the GSEs, Wall Street firms would have enjoyed monopoly power, and things could have been even worse.[11]

Another tantalizing question is, in the agonizing years leading up to 2008, why didn't OFHEO use its existing powers to constrain GSE purchases of high-risk mortgages? The root of the crisis for the GSEs was credit risk, the most basic type of mortgage risk and the first responsibility of any prudential regulator to manage. Many believe OFHEO could have required the GSEs to pare back on these purchases but did not. The risks were out there and growing, but so were house prices, so concerns were assuaged. Also, OFHEO seemed to have other issues on its mind: accounting restatements, interest rate risk, and seeking additional regulatory power for itself.

Shutting the spigot at the secondary market is of little avail if the primary market can still produce all the bad loans it pleases—as long as there are alternative buyers, namely Wall Street firms. As it was, primary market regulators were asleep and took no action to restrain the banks' origination of high-risk loans until 2007.

Where Things Stand

Today lawmakers are once again stymied over GSE reform, but the stakes are even higher. Instead of dealing with well-financed, politically savvy companies at the height of their powers, Congress now must deal with two badly tarnished firms upon which the US housing market shakily depends.

The GSEs may appear to be financially stable, but trust in them has been damaged, their management ranks have seen attrition, and the security infrastructure begs for reinvestment.

Even worse for Freddie Mac, the little security pricing difference that has dogged the company for more than two decades has widened alarmingly, threatening the future of Freddie Mac's signature Gold PC. In the legislative vacuum, FHFA is in the process of developing a Common Securitization Platform (CSP) "for use by the Enterprises and adaptable for use by other participants in the secondary market in the future." Another FHFA initiative is to create a single GSE mortgage-backed security, thereby standardizing the two competing securities and assuaging concerns about falling demand for Freddie's.[12] Notwithstanding a host of technical challenges in adoption, a single security would eliminate the inter-GSE security rivalry and ensure no hiccups in the delivery of mortgage money to America's housing consumers.

Like a busy housekeeper, FHFA has also used its conservator powers to drive the GSEs to off-load portfolios of delinquent mortgages and establish credit risk–sharing arrangements with third parties. In the fall of 2015, Watt took the controversial step of proposing to increase CEO compensation levels in an attempt to retain talent; it was met with howls of protest and later barred by legislation. It was the only GSE issue Congress has been able to agree upon in eight years.

While the GSEs have not needed government infusions since 2012, the possibility of needing future draws is not remote. For a couple of years, GSE balance sheets benefited from the return of huge restored tax benefits and litigation settlements, which drugged policy makers into forgetting about the need for reform. The improving financial health of the GSEs caused the credit rating agencies to look more favorably on the national financial health as a whole.[13] In 2015, the threat of the GSEs getting back their mojo—before Congress had weighed in—did not go unnoticed:

- Researchers at the Federal Reserve opined that the continued failure to wind down the failed companies equates to a "colossal missed opportunity" to put US residential housing finance on more stable footing.[14]
- Corporate governance expert Nell Minow called the two entities "duck-billed platypuses from the beginning" and called on Congress to stop quibbling about compensation and do the hard work of deciding "what these organizations are supposed to be."[15]

• The editorial board of the *Washington Post* blasted Watt for slithering back to a new normal by pushing for a big CEO pay raise.[16]

Then, in November 2015, Freddie Mac reported a third-quarter loss of $475 million. That got people's attention. This was on the heels of losses in 2014 of $8.3 billion attributable to accounting losses.[17] Future Treasury draws suddenly seemed a possibility.

In February 2016, in a speech before the Bipartisan Housing Commission, FHFA Director Watt minced no words about the "escalating" risks of conservatorship. Of specific concern are the declining capital buffers that had been put in place by the Treasury Third Amendment and its "net worth sweep." The amendment requires the GSEs to remit an amount equal to their positive net worth, except for a capital reserve amount. The capital buffer was originally set at $3 billion in 2013 and is set to decline by $600 million a year until it is exhausted. "We are now over halfway down a five-year path toward eliminating the buffer completely," Watt said grimly. As of January 1, 2018, the buffers will be gone.[18] In the first quarter of 2016, Freddie Mac reported another quarterly net income loss of $354 million.

What are the implications of depleting the reserve? If the GSEs experience any number of negative factors—from interest rate spikes to a softening in home values and rising defaults—they will be forced to return to the government for support. As of 2016, Fannie Mae has approximately $118 billion of its original commitment left, and Freddie Mac has approximately $141 billion. As these amounts dwindle—and under current arrangements they cannot be replenished—market confidence could be badly shaken. As Watt warned, "Future draws that chip away at the backing available by the Treasury Department . . . could undermine confidence in the housing finance market. It's unclear where investors would draw that line, but certainly before these funds were drawn down in full."[19]

Why is Congress so stuck? GSE reform is a game of chicken, with more to lose than to win. Overhanging every GSE debate is the fear that major reform will damage the uneven recovery of the housing market. As played on the violins of the veteran lobbyists, this latent fear almost sounds like a threat or self-fulfilling prophecy, but it has paralyzed Congress—along with the usual ideological battles.

Although GSEs were already in the government dock before President Obama took office in 2009, his administration showed little verve or leadership on the issue. A commonly heard quip is that only a one-term president could successfully navigate the shark-infested waters of housing finance and get buy-in on replacement structures for the GSEs. The last time the Obama administration put any cards on the table was in February 2011, when Treasury released a white paper on GSE reform. The report suggested that there were three possible paths forward but did not specify which one the administration preferred.

While no one wants to return to the days of the GSE implicit guarantee, the hardest nut to crack is the level of federal involvement in the mortgage market. The main options in the Treasury paper were to privatize the GSEs completely, which essentially would gradually remove all government support from the market; provide a government guarantee on GSE-backed mortgages only when things get rough; or provide a continuous guarantee throughout the business cycle, much like federal deposit insurance for banks. Under Treasury option three, the GSEs would pay an explicit fee for the government backing, which would be passed along to borrowers, of course. Building on these broad categories over 20 separate proposals have been put forward by the industry and its economists. Almost all envision some level of federal guarantee. Once again, the Republican dream of a government-free mortgage market seems unlikely.

In Congress, conservatives have blocked any legislative proposal that does not require the full dissolution of the GSEs and eliminates government support going forward. Democrats have responded by blocking the GOP bills.

Perhaps the most promising of recent attempts was put forth by Senators Bob Corker (R-TN) and Mark Warner (D-VA) in 2013. The bill would terminate the GSEs within five years and replace them with a new entity—the Federal Mortgage Insurance Corporation. Modeled after the FDIC, which insures consumer bank deposits by charging banks an insurance fee, the FMIC would provide federal guaranteed catastrophic reinsurance on MBS. The guarantee fees that today go to the GSEs would be paid to the FMIC; lenders purchasing insurance would have to take a first-loss position in the event of losses.

The bill garnered a fair bit of support; even the Obama administration engaged quietly in shaping the proposal and it advanced through the Senate Banking committee by the spring of 2014. But it was soon tripped up by the usual blame game and never came up for a Senate floor vote. The GOP was unhappy with the continued government role, even if it was limited to covering catastrophic downturn; Dems opposed eliminating the GSEs (even though the president supported the wind-down), and the advocates did not think it did enough for affordable housing.

Not much has changed.

Conclusion

Freddie Mac employed all the standard Washington tools to influence public policy and legislative reform: It formed a PAC, wrote pithy talking points, invoked the consumer at every turn, looked to build coalitions along shared interests, paid millions to consultants (sometimes simply to keep them from working for a political opponent), engaged in third-party advocacy, and even hired a former house speaker to say nice things about its charter and design.

All these things were perfectly legal and permissible. But there is something uncomfortable about it all. Blatant influence peddling is unethical, particularly for GSEs with their dual quality as both congressionally chartered and publicly traded companies.

Yet this is the way the world turns in the nation's capital. Just because the GSEs have been tamed and gagged does not mean that the same tactics are not being used again and again by the banks and trade groups seeking government support for housing and essentially a return to the status quo. On the other hand, if the GSEs are going to be wound down, the bankers will be happy to fill the vacuum.

In Congress, constraining the GSEs became an ideological battle between free market economics and government intervention and subsidies. Instead, lawmakers could have developed a collective awareness and concern about the entire mortgage system, in which the GSEs, Wall Street, homebuilders, realtors, and mortgage bankers all have their parts to play.

Today GSE reform is stalled because of the same forces that dragged the GSEs under in the first place: players, politics, and philosophies. Freddie Mac's story is a cautionary tale involving consumerist passion for homeownership, the problems of moral hazard and political cronyism, and the limits of law and regulation. An ideological breakthrough is urgently needed. But so is a new commercial ethic inspired by a vision of the common good.

Failing to acknowledge—let alone address—these harder issues sets the housing economy up for another earthquake. And sitting squarely in the earthquake zone is the American homeowner.

STAND UP AND SAY

Critiquing public policy and the decisions of policy makers—let alone one's superiors—after the fact can seem mean-spirited and self-righteous. It's a cheap shot to look in the rearview mirror and cast blame. However, the financial crisis, at core, was about people. No matter how inept the regulators, how competitive the market, or how pressing the negative publicity, no one had a gun to their head forcing them to buy bad mortgages. People made their choices freely. Hence, they are responsible for them—regardless of what any judge, jury, shareholder, or regulator says.

The role of individuals is a hard topic to discuss when you are both acting and directing, as I am trying to do in this book. Looking back on a financial marketplace littered with ruined firms, shareholders, investors, and consumers, many have asked, why didn't employees speak out? Was everyone deaf and blind to the dangerous waterfall looming ahead? Did corporate power dynamics mute the dissenting voices? Were we all lured by the siren of greater profits just a little further down the shore?

The truth is that there were individual voices raising concerns and urging a change of course. Not everybody was asleep at the switch. But by 2006, the waters were treacherous, and concerns raised by those laboring at the bottom of the ship were easily drowned out or ignored.

When and how does an employee raise concern about company practices? This question began to haunt me. At Freddie Mac, the first six years of the new century had already been rife with two scandals, huge internal battles over mission, wildly escalating housing goals, and confused messages from HUD, consumer groups, and Democrats about subprime loans and NTMs, not to mention a significant loss of market share and legislation bearing down that seemingly could put the firm out of business. Dave Andrukonis, the one person who had been brave and knowledgeable enough to challenge top management was "pursuing new opportunities." What was the right thing to do?

I found truth at the top of an escalator. I was carrying lunch and heading upstairs one day when I saw the head of Freddie Mac's fraud unit just ahead of me. She was a friend, and I could count on her to tell it straight. I caught up to her and asked what was the worst thing she was seeing in the fraud unit. "NINAs," she answered bluntly. I had my bull's-eye.

Regulators Finally Wake Up

In October 2006 the Federal Financial Institutions Examination Council (FFIEC) issued final guidance with regard to the origination of high-risk NTMs that were gassing up the housing bubble.[1] It had been a long, hard fight—and a long wait. The FFIEC, an interagency group that sets standards to promote uniformity across the patchwork system of federal financial institution regulators, had put out draft guidance the previous December. After 11 months of industry hand-wringing, the regulators finally came out with guidance (as opposed to a hard and fast regulation) to limit the origination of high-risk mortgages. It was too little and too late.

If you are a regulator, you should know there's a problem with your new regulatory advisory when no one screams at you when you put it out. In fact, the October 2006 guidance was so benign that it was hailed by the industry trade groups, notably the MBA, as appropriately narrow. That's because it only dealt with a subset of problem mortgages and sidestepped the subprime market completely, so that the wildly profitable business could proceed as usual.

In the months prior to the October release, newspapers were starting to report problems with hybrid subprime 2/28 and 3/27 subprime ARMs, also known as "exploding ARMs." Accounting for roughly three-quarters of subprime mortgages being originated at the time, these loans were made to borrowers with weak credit histories. Because these loans were higher risk, they carried significantly higher annual percentage rates (APRs). To make them affordable, lenders offered tantalizing upfront teaser rates.

Subprime's significantly higher APRs should have tipped borrowers off about the dangerous waters ahead. However, as described earlier, the amount of the monthly payment tended to be the only consideration for many subprime borrowers.

Subprime originations soared due to consumer ignorance, aggressive lender marketing, and insatiable investor appetite. Given the fat premiums Wall Street was paying, lenders who sold subprime loans to Wall Street found ingenious, if not nefarious, ways to get borrowers into them. The movie blockbuster *The Big Short* recounts the sorry game in which the mortgage market began working backward. Consumers should have been the ones driving demand; instead, it was the investors and their brokers who beat the bushes for loans to fill up CDO tranches. That's why much of the subprime market was predatory; many borrowers were lured into terrible loans they did not need and could not repay.

After the initial teaser period, however, the party was over. Then the interest rate would shoot up by as much as six percentage points. That's where the exploding part came from; few borrowers could handle the sudden payment spike. The only way out of a subprime ARM was to refinance before the interest rate exploded.

As for underwriting, to qualify for low teaser-rate ARMs, borrowers only had to have adequate income to cover the initial rate—not the fully indexed rate that would kick in after two or three years. To avoid paying the higher rate, savvy borrowers would wait until the two-year prepayment penalty expired and then refinance into another teaser-rate loan before the rate jump. Then the process would start all over again.

Despite the substandard underwriting, everything worked as long as house prices kept rising and mortgage rates stayed low. In other words, a borrower could stay above water if the home value rose enough in two years to allow the loan to be refinanced. If some equity had been built up in that time, the borrower could roll the closing costs into the new mortgage and start all over again, this time with a bigger subprime loan on a house that had risen in value probably too fast for its own good.

In the early part of the decade, when the Fed tried to wean the nation off Greenspan's post-9/11 easy credit, the real dangers of these loans became evident. The Fed's stair-step increase in interest rates was wreaking havoc with borrowers who had adjustable-rate mortgages. Many could not afford the new, higher rate when they went to refinance.

Combine that with the slowdown and eventual bust of house-price growth and it is clear why many borrowers found themselves suddenly stuck in bad loans with declining house values. Without the ability to refinance into another low-rate loan at the end of the teaser period, millions of borrowers were at great risk of default.

In December 2006, the Center for Responsible Lending released a gloomy report entitled "Losing Ground," which predicted that 2.2 million households in subprime would eventually lose their homes due to bad mortgages.[2] Exploding ARMs, negative amortization, and prepayment penalties were making it increasingly difficult for borrowers to keep loans current. The report was largely pooh-poohed by the industry as exaggerated.

Unfortunately, the long-awaited FFIEC guidance didn't address the problems of exploding subprime ARMs. The first footnote said it all: "This guidance does not apply to . . . fully amortizing residential loan mortgage products."[3]

In mortgage techno-speak, this meant that the FFIEC's long-overdue guidance only applied to those loans in which a borrower's monthly payments were not designed to fully pay off the loan. Thus, the guidance applied to NTMs like interest-only and payment option ARMs but not to exploding subprime ARMs. These loans were proving to be harmful for borrowers as interest rates rose, but since they were fully amortizing, they were not covered by the guidance. Lenders could continue to originate them at will.

Consumer groups were especially upset with the exclusion. Some pressure must have been applied, because six months later, the FFIEC put out additional guidance that dealt with exploding ARMs. The primary market regulators were the only ones who could rein in the primary mortgage market where the loans were actually being originated. But the horse was galloping out of the barn by then.

Freddie Mac Responds

Starting in 2005, Freddie Mac's decision to stop policing the market was in full sway, and the company was buying huge quantities of NTMs and securities backed by subprime ARMs. The FFIEC had started to curb the bad lending, and I saw an opportunity. "See a wave, grab a surfboard."

I called the new chief credit officer and told him my idea. He was pleased. "I have a board in my car," he said, grinning. So I called a meeting.

It was not easy to get six business-side senior vice presidents together. I worked with their administrative assistants for days to get the meeting scheduled. I also invited the regulatory experts, who were eager to get this issue back on the table. Freddie's growing position in NTMs was beginning to divide employees. The meeting was held in a tiny, windowless conference room. It was cramped and too warm.

"The regulators have started to move," I began. "If we jump on this now and adopt the FFIEC guidance for ourselves, we can start backing off on these loans without losing market share. The banks—the regulated ones, at least—will have to follow."

The six men around the table stared at me.

"Susan, we get where you are coming from," began one in a tone I couldn't quite read—was it sympathetic or patronizing? "But we've been over and over this. Dick, Gene, and Patti made the decision to provide liquidity to the market rather than to choose between loans and ration credit. And as far as I know, that decision still stands."

I tried another tack. "Things are heating up politically. It would be great for Freddie's reputation to say no to NTMs." Reputation always played second fiddle to business, but I was getting nowhere with this crowd.

My final appeal was to conscience, "We simply *should* do it now."

My eyes fixed on the new chief credit officer, but he said nothing. Given the power alliances in the company at that point, I don't think he had much more clout than I did. The executives managing the portfolio and single-family business voiced the all-too-familiar objections to my plan and left.

Later in the day, a lawyer who had attended the meeting called to express his condolences. "You were courageous to try," he said sympathetically.

Two months later, in December 2006, the GSE regulator, OFHEO, issued a directive requiring the GSEs to apply the FFIEC guidance on our own books of business. We were required to have an implementation plan in place by February 28, 2007.

I groaned. So much for trying to get ahead of things. Freddie's core problem was that we had no operating principles to assist us in choosing between mission and shareholder value. There was no principled arbiter, nothing higher to appeal to, and no way to discern our way forward.

Breakthrough?

The next few months passed slowly. Internal discussions on how exactly to apply the FFIEC guidance on NTMs droned on and on. Ours would be a grudging compliance, it seemed. Then, out of the blue, one of Freddie's top portfolio investment executives had a change of heart. We should stop investing in exploding ARM subprime securities as well as NTMs, he said.

I was present at the after-hours meeting when the new initiative was presented. Back and forth the debate went with the usual considerations and tradeoffs. At last, CEO Syron made an impassioned speech on the morality of the issue, and it was settled: Freddie would indeed pull out of the subprime market it had participated heartily in for nearly eight years. Maybe there was hope after all.

On February 27, 2007, with just one day to go before our regulator would have forced the company's hand, Freddie Mac announced its decision to tighten standards for both our subprime and NTM purchases. This went a step further than the FFIEC guidance, which only dealt with NTMs. In addition to curbing NTM purchases, Freddie said it would continue to buy subprime ARMs—and mortgage-related securities backed by these subprime loans—only if borrowers were qualified at the fully indexed and fully amortizing rate. This plan would greatly reduce the likelihood of a borrower defaulting if interest rates rose. Freddie Mac also announced it would limit its purchases of low-documentation mortgages.

It was great news, but there was a catch. The new bans would not take effect until September 1, 2007. This meant we could keep buying and investing in loans we had just labeled as bad for borrowers for six more months.[4]

Cynicism

I should have been more pleased with the announcement, but I was bitter. Between Andrukonis's firing the year before and my own failed attempts to get Freddie out of that market, it was hard to celebrate. And I cringed as Freddie hyped its leadership on this. Let the record show that we really had no choice but to do it—or have the regulator shove it down our throat one day later.

Most galling of all was the six-month implementation delay. Ostensibly, the reason for the implementation delay was "to avoid market disruptions."

In reality, Freddie wanted to wait for everybody else to comply with the FFIEC guidelines so it wouldn't be disadvantaged for pulling out early. We could keep swimming in the subprime cesspool until all our competitors had to towel off as well.

As it would turn out, March 2007 marked the beginning of the "relevant" period in the SEC complaint against Syron, Cook, and Bisenius. From March 2007 to August 2008, the SEC alleged the company was not forthcoming with the amount of subprime risk it was amassing. Not only was Freddie Mac gobbling up vast quantities of untested product, due to a broader decline in underwriting standards, risks on Freddie Mac's regular mortgage business were starting to escalate. According to the SEC, many of these loans resembled subprime loans in terms of credit profile and performance. In failing to disclose a complete picture of subprime-type risk, the three executives were found to have "aided and abetted violations of, the antifraud and reporting provisions of the federal securities laws."[5]

As recounted earlier, the lack of a clear definition of subprime weakened the case. The SEC settled with the executives in 2015.

Called Back to the Hill

A month after Freddie's announcement, on March 12 and 15, 2007, Chairman Frank held hearings on his newly reintroduced GSE regulatory reform bill, H.R. 1427. Syron was called to testify on the second day of hearings.

It would be the last CEO testimony I would write about proposed GSE reform legislation. I outlined the same concerns and same suggestions for finding the elusive balance between safety and soundness and mission. Perhaps I said it a little more urgently, but I am sure it was forgotten all the same.

What I didn't forget was the rueful testimony of our critics from the affordable housing community. In her testimony to the committee, Judy Kennedy, president and CEO of the National Association of Affordable Housing Lenders—who had been the head of Freddie's lobbying shop before Delk—was particularly scornful of Freddie Mac's purchases of subprime securities. In particular, she singled out the GSEs for purchasing "44 percent of the $401 billion in securities backed by subprime loans issued [in 2004], 35 percent of the $507 billion issued in 2005, and 25 percent of the total subprime MBS sold." Consumer advocates believe that the vast majority of these loans are potentially "explosive," she said. Kennedy also noted that a "healthy chunk" of these subprime MBS were used by Fannie Mae and Freddie Mac for affordable housing goals credit.[6]

With comments like that, it was not a surprise to learn a few weeks later that Chairman Frank had again summoned the GSEs back to Capitol Hill. This time the topic was not proposed regulatory reform legislation but the GSE role in the developing subprime crisis. I would nearly lose my job over the writing of this testimony.

Quandary

I could not stop thinking about all the disparagement heaped on the GSEs in congressional testimony the prior month. I was not disputing the data—it was true Freddie had bought a ton of subprime securities—but the accusations and insinuations as to why we had entered that market were overly simplistic and incomplete.

After all, I had been there when Freddie Mac decided to buy subprime securities rather than whole loans to manage the risk of untested subprime mortgages. And I had been there when we succeeded in getting Freddie to ban prepayment penalties through the company so that the firm was first in the industry to do so. I had written the regulatory response to the administration's stiff increases in affordable housing goals in 2004, saying the increase would give Freddie no choice but to go deeper into subprime.

So I believed Syron should tell Freddie's side of the story. In the prep meeting, I urged him to explain why we invested in subprime securities. Against that backdrop, I suggested, our February 27 announcement to pull out of that market would make sense. After all, didn't an announcement that we were pulling out of subprime make it obvious that we had once been in it?

He looked at me doubtfully. I wrote something to that effect in an early draft, but he scratched a line through it. I pushed back—gently. I explained that everyone on the Hill knew Freddie Mac was a major subprime investor. If we didn't tell our side of the story, the testimony of critics would stand uncontested. Syron remained unconvinced, so I cut the paragraph.

Two days before the subprime hearing, on a Sunday morning, I got a call from the president of the company, Gene McQuade. He had read the draft testimony and wanted our role as investor in subprime clarified. "Otherwise, people will think we were the ones originating those loans."

McQuade's careful reading of the testimony surprised me. I had never taken a direct call from him before, nor had he shown any interest in congressional testimony in the past. But he was slated to take over the job as CEO in a few months. Maybe that explained the sudden interest. I thought about my deleted paragraph and determined to get it back in.

Two hours later a group of us were assembled in Freddie Mac's downtown office reviewing the testimony. "What's this doing in here again? Goddamn it, *no!*" said Syron, pounding the large conference table.

I stared down at the page. I replied, "Well, Gene called me this morning and suggested that—"

"What does *Gene* have to do with this?" he thundered. "He's not the one testifying."

Reluctantly, I scratched out the paragraph. Again.

After another hour of wordsmithing and role-playing with the lobbyists, I was dismissed to clean up the edits and get the written testimony up to the Hill. We were already past the 48-hour mark, since the hearing was Tuesday morning.

"Do you want to see the final version?" I asked Syron as I was leaving for my office back in McLean.

"No, it's fine. Thank you."

What Is the Right Thing to Do?

It wasn't supposed to take long. I could easily make the edits Syron wanted. But I was stuck. I just couldn't let it go.

Somewhere in the late-night hours, I knelt on the floor in front of my computer and prayed. I thought back to when I had defied Delk by refusing to cut a paragraph he wanted out. Now I was planning to defy the CEO by inserting a paragraph he didn't want in.

I got back into my chair and stared hard at the computer. I pasted the paragraph back in and e-mailed it to the lobbyist who would distribute it. I was at peace.

The next morning, I walked into McLoughlin's office and said flatly, "I put it back in."

He shook his head. "You didn't."

A few moments later, I was summoned by the CEO. The eyes of his administrative assistant, a dear friend, were wide with fear.

Syron was mad. He yelled. Yes, I had gone against his wishes. But it was a good, strong paragraph—and most important, it was true. He later apologized.

The Collapse Begins

In June 2007, I applied for a six-week program at Wharton business school. After the disaster with Syron's testimony, I was eager to get away.

A little insecure about my business credentials, I wondered if I'd be able to hold my own with the 60 or so top business executives and CEOs from around the world. I was one of just three American women.

One of the most compelling speakers was futurist Jeremy Rifkin. I was mesmerized by his grasp of history, current events, and data. Amid the very international business crowd, there was growing concern about subprime mortgages, and I realized afresh how much was riding on the credit quality of US mortgage-backed securities. S&P had just announced that it was downgrading 100 bonds backed by second-lien subprime mortgages, and Bear Stearns informed investors that it was suspending redemptions from one of its mortgage-related hedge funds. The collapse had just begun, but most of us were still in denial.

Not Rifkin. He made dire pronouncements about the US housing market and predicted that house prices would decline by 20 percent. I was incredulous. At the break, I took him aside and touted a line I'd heard our chief economist say many times: There would be some "bumpy landings" in "some airports." Clearly some localities had experienced house price bubbles that would likely pop, but it was inconceivable that house prices would fall nationally en masse. That hadn't happened since the Great Depression.

At Wharton, we spent time in small groups doing business case studies and the like. Toward the end of the six weeks, we shared career aspirations. I confided in my new friends—six men from around the world, all with big jobs and impressive titles—about how I had changed the CEO's testimony to provide more disclosure. The CEO of a large German firm was stunned. "Susan," he spat out, "I would have fired you on the spot!" The group fell silent, and I nodded morosely.

But then the CFO of a major oil company spoke. "I think Susan was brave," he said quietly.

Months later, I learned that the testimony I had changed in April was being used by company lawyers as a defense against the charge that Freddie had not been forthcoming to the public about our role in subprime.

Where Things Stand

One of the most vociferous postmortem debates about the housing crisis was whether the GSEs' purchases of subprime securities and NTMs were an act in support of the affordable housing goals or just a profit play designed to regain market share.

Peter Wallison with the American Enterprise Institute (AEI) argues strongly that the GSE affordable housing goals were the source of all evil. Quoting from his lengthy dissent from the government's official inquiry report:

> The use of the affordable housing goals to force a reduction in the GSEs' underwriting standards was a major policy error committed by HUD in two successive administrations, and must be recognized as such if we are ever to understand what caused the financial crisis. Ultimately, the AH goals extended the housing bubble, infused it with weak and high-risk NTMs, caused the insolvency of Fannie and Freddie, and—together with other elements of US housing policy—was the principal cause of the financial crisis itself.[7]

On the other hand, most Democrats and housers are loathe to impugn the affordable housing goals and prefer to heap blame on Wall Street. According to the Center for Responsible Lending's Eric Stein, loans bought to meet the affordable housing goals, as strict as they were, were not the source of the GSE downfall. Quoting from his 2008 testimony: "The source of both GSEs' losses, and the reason they are no longer independent, are not these subprime loans to low-wealth borrowers, but rather the Alt A loans that the GSEs purchased that were made to relatively wealthier borrowers. Critiques of Fannie and Freddie tend to conflate the earlier subprime securities purchases and their later jump into purchasing higher-income loans where lenders did not document borrower income."[8]

While the move into Alt-A mortgages was ill advised, it was not driven by pressure to meet affordable housing goals. Alt-A mortgages are generally high-balance, higher-income, high-credit-score loans that are classified as Alt A because they do not document income or assets. Given their income characteristics, they actually dilute the GSEs' affordable housing ratios, yet these are the loans that are causing the GSEs' losses.

To underscore Stein's point that Alt-A loans actually diluted GSE goal performance, consider this example: the infamous NINA—a no-income, no-asset documentation loan—contributed very little to GSE goal performance, as borrower income data were nonexistent with these loans. Because most of the affordable housing goals were based on the income of the borrower, NINAs were not included in the numerator of the GSE housing goal ratio between goal qualifying loans and total mortgage purchases. Rather, NINAs were accounted for in the denominator of the ratio, thereby lowering the percentage of GSE mortgage purchases meeting the goal criteria.

Goal counting rubrics aside, the fact remains that the GSEs bought high-risk loans that, while they have outperformed those purchased by Wall Street, were too risky for the slim margin of capital undergirding the GSE-run secondary mortgage market.

So, who is right in this debate? Was it the housing goals, or was it unregulated Wall Street?

I have argued that both are to blame. Freddie Mac made its business decisions in a muddy delta of motives: political pressure, regulatory pressure, and shareholder pressure.

Conclusion

Analysis of the housing crisis has focused on which policies and regulations—or lack thereof—distorted the competitive landscape, leading to a host of rational responses that were clearly totally irrational (and massively destructive) in the aggregate. While this is an important debate, it obscures the question of how firms and their managers decided to respond to the given pressures. An equally important conversation needs to happen around the role of groups and individuals. Human agents have to make sense of murky, disparate, and conflicting tea leaves in real time.

Eight years later it is easy to see various fateful junctures where different decisions could have possibly directed the runaway mortgage market onto a safer set of rails. Freddie Mac certainly encountered such junctures, but for the most part, it responded timidly, if at all. Why?

First, things were simply not that clear in the first few years leading up to the crisis. When it would have been relatively easy to change course, the few who voiced a contrarian view were not heeded. Some were actually fired. By 2007, the writing was pretty much on the wall, but by then it was too late.

Second, a herd mentality had taken over. Power dynamics are real. Financial incentives are real. Groupthink is real. And denial is real. Individuals who had the knowledge and power to make a difference abdicated.

There will never be perfect policies or regulations. Hence, individual actions matter at every level.

THE UNRAVELING

Within five months of my return from Wharton, bad things were happening at a dizzying rate. Who could have imagined that Freddie Mac had just one year left as a publicly traded company?

Headlines were awful. Lawsuits proliferated. Losses skyrocketed. Under pressure from Treasury, OFHEO, which hitherto had given the firms clean bills of health, now did an about-face and hammered on both GSEs to raise capital. Adding to the strain, it looked like Freddie Mac would fail that year's extremely tough housing goal levels.

Fear had gripped the market, and non-GSE mortgages had started to dry up. Then the sun came out. All was forgiven, and the GSEs moved from ugly and irrelevant to market saviors. OFHEO loosened the purse strings of the hated GSE portfolios, and the GSEs were allowed—even encouraged—to start buying up more mortgages to keep mortgage rates from skyrocketing. This was all part of a last-minute attempt to stave off a broader collapse.

As recounted in the FCIC report, "By the fourth quarter of 2007, the GSEs were purchasing 75 percent of new mortgages, nearly twice the 2006 level. With $5 trillion in mortgages resting on razor-thin capital, the GSEs were doomed if the market did not stabilize."[1]

Then came the bomb: the GSEs were in very bad shape themselves. In late November, Freddie Mac reported a net loss of $2 billion that shredded the company's capital cushion. The market freaked, and the stock price fell 30 percent in one day. Cumulatively, Freddie's stock was down 62 percent on the year.[2]

Within days of the third-quarter earnings release, top executives were taking planes all over the country begging for money from financial institutions and other investors, a deal the buyers would soon come to regret. Having written scores of public documents touting Freddie's capital adequacy, I found the desperate fund raising astounding and shameful.

At last the executives were able to secure the additional capital to keep Freddie a hair above the regulated level—but it came at quite a price. On November 27, 2007, Freddie announced it would issue $6 billion of preferred stock. Freddie also announced that it would reduce its fourth-quarter common stock dividend to $0.25 per share.[3] Steady Freddie was no more.

A Surreal Calm

Other than the terrible financial results and mad scramble for cash, things were going amazingly well for our executives—in a surreal sort of way. A radiantly optimistic Patti Cook graced the cover of *Mortgage Risk* magazine in a cover story entitled "Subprime Winner."[4] The head of communications, David Palombi, threw it across the table at me.

Then there was the sore issue of the executive suite—something akin to a C-suite for big banks. For months it had been under construction. Since moving into the McLean headquarters in 1991, the top business executives had always been located with their respective divisions. The CEO and president had adjoining suites, but everybody else was out in the field.

But McQuade, who would later leave the firm even before the suite was completed, thought we could encourage more synergy if the top people could hang out together. There was concern that our executives weren't getting along so well.

Employees were suspicious as the construction went on. When the lavish area was complete and the door was locked to all but select pass-holders, they got angry. (Eventually the door was opened and a receptionist played gatekeeper.) But we hardly ever saw the executives again. They could leave the building via a private elevator.

The last straw was Syron's amazing bonuses. Employees read about all six of them in the company's November 9, 2007, public disclosure dealing with changes in executive compensation.[5] In addition to a $200,000 increase in base salary, Syron would receive a "special extension bonus" of $3.5 million, an additional equity grant of $800,000 in restricted stock, another equity grant for 2008 valued at $9.4 million, of which $8.8 million was guaranteed, plus a "special cash performance award" of up to $6 million, "depending on the number and strategic value of the performance milestones that have been achieved."[6]

Employees were livid. The company's finances were in tatters. Our bonuses were anything but guaranteed.

Stress Increases

Management also chafed under the regulator's heavy hand. By March 2008, mounting losses placed capital adequacy again in jeopardy. OFHEO was pushing the firm to raise another $5.5 billion in capital, but Freddie Mac resisted. At an investor meeting, Syron reportedly said, "this company will bow to no one." The foot dragging made the eventual capital raise that much more expensive.[7]

Around that time, a few of us were in Syron's conference room discussing legislation. I was the only woman. Dick started swearing. Then he turned to me and asked me to leave the room so he could "continue cursing the regulator."

In awkward confusion, I gathered my things and pushed back my chair. I slammed the door.

Rome was burning, yet the show had to go on. In another incident, I had to attend diversity training with my colleagues. When the instructor said that we were going to play some games to "break the ice," I looked around the room at the lobbyists and decided to bolt. *Our* ice had long been broken.

But the greatest loss of confidence was yet to come. For the previous five years, regulatory lawyers and policy staff had worked laboriously to analyze each and every line of proposed legislation to understand its impact on Freddie Mac's business and its ability to fulfill the mission.

But now that the wheels were falling off the cart, all that analysis was discarded. Self-preservation had set in. Top management decided that if, by chance, some magnanimous member of Congress would let us suggest one or two small changes to the bill, the lobbyists would forego asking for changes that would protect the business franchise and ask, rather, for modifications that would protect top management, such as a reduction in the size of civil money penalties that could be levied against individuals.

After all the years of analysis to find the best solution for the franchise, this was what it came down to?

That day I lost hope. I pulled out of the employee stock purchase fund and the PAC in a small, silent protest against something I could not fight. I no longer knew this company.

Fight or Flight?

What was the point of staying, I wondered over and over. I had stepped into Freddie's management structure too late in the game to make any difference. I could no longer use language to create pretty window treatments to sell a house whose leadership was in such disarray and whose future was so uncertain.

The next morning I was in my boss's office. "Move me to another division."

That's how I got to be the head of corporate strategy, the last job title I would hold at the firm. I had a tiny hope that by taking that job I could have greater influence with the business side, as we called it. Surely there had to be a way out of the tailspin. I believed we'd fare better if we worked with the government to confront the housing crisis rather than continue to fight the regulator at every turn.

Within nine months of my taking the new role, Freddie would be declared essentially insolvent and taken over by the government. The concept of being able to have a strategy at all was soon laughable. Still, I made a last-ditch effort to appeal to the mission, although what that meant at such a time of crisis was anybody's guess.

In spring 2008, corporate strategy facilitated a discussion among top management at a swank Georgetown hotel. I scheduled myself for a policy briefing—my one and only opportunity to address the defensive and cloistered group of executives grappling with the daunting choices before them: pursue the mission or preserve what was left of shareholder value. These were the same choices that had dogged us for years, but now the times were desperate. The company was taking on water, but policy makers expected us to help save homeowners, who were themselves drowning.

Somewhere in the discussion, I quoted an Old Testament prophet: "Beware of fattening ourselves in the day of slaughter." I think my employee who was running the slide show blanched. Either the executives didn't hear me or they didn't understand. They broke for lunch.

Beginning of the End

In July 2008, employees nervously watched the NYSE stock ticker on the TV screens in the hall pantries. Freddie stock had slid dangerously—and precipitously—over the past two weeks. As if $20 a share was not bad enough, Freddie hit $3.89 one afternoon before "rallying" to close at $7.89.

Things looked even worse on the debt side of the equation. As a barometer of investor assessment of risk, the spread to Treasury had risen over 65 percent from its 2007 level; by September the spread was double the level just a year before.[8] Fear of a liquidity crisis set in. As Paulson recounts in his memoir of those harrowed days, "the GSEs were constantly in the markets, borrowing $20 billion a week at times."[9] A Freddie Mac default would have sent shock waves around the world. Would Freddie be able to roll its debt? The stock swooned again.

Another hallway rumor was that major creditors in Russia and China were conspiring to let the GSEs crash. According to Paulson, China said no, and Russia denied asking.[10] Then the rumor started that the White House was preparing a contingency plan to take us over. A stock analyst speculated that a new accounting ruling would require us to move billions of off-balance securities onto the balance sheet, causing a massive shortfall in our capital levels. This meant another stock rout.

Such stories were like blood in the water to the merciless short-sellers who seemed intent on dragging Freddie stock to the ocean floor. From all the negative reporting, I learned a new vocabulary word: parlous. As in, "the GSEs' parlous condition."

To buttress investor confidence, in mid-July the Federal Reserve Board authorized the New York Fed to extend emergency loans to the GSEs "should such lending prove necessary . . . to promote the availability of home mortgage credit during a period of stress in financial markets." Although neither GSE tapped that line of funding, this authorization did result in the GSEs having to open their books to the one agency they knew was smarter than they were: the Federal Reserve.

As recounted in the FCIC report, "the Fed found that the GSEs were significantly 'underreserved,' with huge potential losses, and their operations were 'unsafe and unsound.' " Other problems included poor forecasting, overvaluation of deferred tax assets, understating losses, and postponing write-downs.[11] This critique didn't reflect well on our regulator, who had deemed Freddie Mac "adequately capitalized" just weeks before.[12]

"I Told You So"

At the height of turmoil, in August 2008, I got an unexpected phone call from Andrukonis. He said he was on vacation with his family when a reporter from the *New York Times* reached him on his cell phone. "The guy asked me about Dick," he told me. "I told him about the memo—and let him use my name."

I sat down hard in my chair and read the article. "The chief executive of the mortgage giant Freddie Mac rejected internal warnings that could have protected the company from some of the financial crises now engulfing it, according to more than two dozen current and former high-ranking executives and others. That chief executive, Richard F. Syron, in 2004 received a memo from Freddie Mac's chief risk officer warning him that the firm was financing questionable loans that threatened its financial health."[13]

The *Times* article was a long piece that quoted Andrukonis and other former employees about how they had counseled Syron time and time again to back out of the subprime market. Syron had been interviewed for the article as well, and the juxtaposition of comments and defenses did not paint a flattering picture of our CEO.

Within minutes, Palombi was in my office asking if I knew what memo Andrukonis was talking about. I had a hunch it was the 2004 e-mail to Syron about NINAs being predatory.

"But Dave is quoted as saying it was a memo," he screeched.

And so we yanked out old files. Sure enough, Andrukonis's NINA missive was not a memo but an e-mail, but the discrepancy was irrelevant. Andrukonis had made his objections clearly known in numerous formats—risk measures, presentations to the board, memos, and e-mails to the CEO. Everyone knew where Andrukonis stood on high-risk mortgages.

Down the hall, in the executive suite, Syron was furious with the article. According to Palombi, the interview with the *Times* reporter had gone well until Syron made a jarring statement as the reporter was leaving. It was one of those throw-away lines our CEO would inexplicably add at the end of an otherwise well-managed interview: "'I've had four other jobs as CEO, and I came out of them all pretty well,' Mr. Syron said. 'What I'm working for right now is my reputation.'"[14]

The reporter must have smiled to get such a quote without even trying and gladly reopened his spiral notebook to jot it down. It was akin to a bomb in Freddie Mac's hallways.

Syron's reputation—with employees at least—was already in shambles. The next day Freddie Mac put out a press release with Syron's harsh rebuttal of the *Times* story and a personal attack on Andrukonis.

Andrukonis had always been well regarded. Now, in the eyes of many Freddie employees—old and new—he was a hero. The Boy Scout had won.

Rumors of Takeover

By late August 2008, Freddie Mac stock had fallen to $3.25. The short-sellers were having a field day, swatting us like a cat. Many were saying that the company was at an end and that the government soon would be forced to step in.

After some intergovernmental wrangling, in early September, FHFA changed its assessment that the GSEs were adequately capitalized and agreed with the Fed and Treasury assessment that both were insolvent. FHFA sent harsh midyear reports listing each GSE's specific sins.

In FHFA's view, "after being told by the regulator in 2006 that its purchases of subprime PLS had outpaced its risk management abilities, Freddie bought $22 billion of subprime securities in each subsequent quarter."[15] Freddie Mac also was taken to task for "aggressive accounting" on earnings and capital and a "series of ill-advised and poorly executed decisions and other serious misjudgments."[16]

Shortly thereafter, late Friday afternoon before the fateful weekend in September, one of my employees let me know she'd heard a rumor that the regulator was going to place one GSE in conservatorship over the weekend.

I stared at her across the room. No one said anything.

We all assumed, of course, that it would be Freddie—not that Fannie was in much better shape. We had such an inferiority complex relative to Fannie. Unbeknownst to us, our competitor had received its own "dear John" letter.

Game's Up

On Sunday, September 6, 2008, the government placed Freddie Mac in conservatorship, which was akin to bankruptcy reorganization.[17] FHFA was now both regulator and conservator. Within one week, the government fired CEO Syron, CFO Piszel, and Chief Business Officer Cook.

That first week of conservatorship dragged miserably. Employees were almost completely idle and in varying degrees of emotional distress, rage, and denial.

While employees were consumed with Freddie's dire straits, Congress had other fish to fry. On the heels of the GSEs, Treasury was dealing with Lehman Brothers and AIG and maneuvering the passage of bailout legislation known as the Troubled Asset Relief Program.

The 2008 presidential election heated up like missile fuel. Senator McCain (R-AZ) stumped on Freddie's supposed "venality," and a Democrat later introduced a bill calling for a year-long investigation of Freddie Mac officers and board members. Everyone wanted a scapegoat, and Freddie and Fannie were top picks.

Scolding the GSEs at every turn, Senator McCain soon got caught in his own hypocrisy. Within the housing industry, it was common knowledge that Rick Davis, his top political advisor, had been paid $2 million over the years by Fannie and Freddie as head of a pro-homeownership organization started by the GSEs to curry favor with Congress.[18]

On the other hand, the GSEs had a few tepid defenders. Testifying in October 2008, the Center for Responsible Lending's Eric Stein illuminated the complex interplay of factors that contributed to the financial crisis. According to Stein, placing more requirements on the GSEs meant more freedom for others to do what they pleased. We were understandably gratified when he testified, saying:

> Unfortunately, those who have been calling for greater regulation of the GSEs have not been calling for the reining in of abusive lending practices, or the securitization practices that enable them. This is because for the most part, these advocates are themselves frequently industry players who want a bigger share of this market for themselves. For this reason, they urge the abolition of these practices for the GSEs alone, while urging that the rest of the industry have free reign to continue them.[19]

In December 2008, former CEOs of Freddie and Fannie were called to testify in Congress. Brendsel seemed almost contrite at points. Syron was feisty and came out swinging.[20] The common refrain was that there was nothing the GSEs could have done to avoid hitting the iceberg. The truth was, they had steered right into it.

Where Things Stand

Why do bad things happen to good people? Why do organizations admonish truth tellers and punish whistleblowers, often the best employees with the most integrity? The very things they suffer to bring to light will often be fatal to the institution if not identified and stopped.

Reflecting back, Andrukonis acknowledges that if Syron had followed his advice and pulled out of subprime, it would have cost the firm millions, drawn criticism from shareholders, and further eroded market share. But Freddie Mac would have emerged in one piece, likely obviating the need for billions in capital injections, not to mention a taxpayer bailout. And Freddie's tattered reputation might have been restored. Steady Freddie might have survived—and been vindicated.

No good deed goes unpunished. Andrukonis was not treated well by Freddie Mac following his public statements to the press. There were misstatements about his character and performance. Family members were aggrieved, and there were threats of reprisal. He had broken the cardinal corporate rule and revealed "confidential information." It didn't matter that his confession was about the reckless pursuit of a business strategy that has cost the nation billions.

On December 16, 2011, the Securities and Exchange Commission (SEC) charged former top executives of Fannie Mae and Freddie Mac with securities fraud. The three former Freddie Mac executives charged were former Chairman of the Board and CEO Richard F. Syron, former Executive Vice President and Chief Business Officer Patricia L. Cook, and former Executive Vice President for the Single Family Guarantee Business Donald J. Bisenius. According to Robert Khuzami, Director of the SEC's Enforcement Division:

> Fannie Mae and Freddie Mac executives told the world that their subprime exposure was substantially smaller than it really was. These material misstatements occurred during a time of acute investor interest in financial institutions' exposure to subprime loans, and misled the market about the amount of risk on the company's books. All individuals, regardless of their rank or position, will be held accountable for perpetuating half-truths or misrepresentations about matters materially important to the interest of our country's investors.[21]

Four long years later, in April 2015, the SEC settled with the former Freddie Mac executives. Whereas the SEC had sought stiff financial penalties and disbarment, it settled for temporary restrictions on the careers of the accused and a total contribution of $310,000 to compensate defrauded investors. Even more galling for many, that small amount would not come from the executives' pockets; rather, it would be paid from indemnity insurance.

Nor would there be any remorse. Don Bisenius, former Freddie Mac senior vice president of credit policy and portfolio management, gloated: "The undertakings to which I have agreed in order to put this case behind me do not limit me in any practical way."[22]

The drawn-out case against the former executives and minimal finding of fault suggests that to appease an angry public, the Obama administration needed to get tough on the GSEs, but in the end, the case was weak. No one would ultimately be held responsible. It also suggests that this could easily happen again.

Conclusion

During most of my 19-year tenure at Freddie Mac, I focused on the ins and outs of housing finance policy. Learning the details of Freddie Mac's business took longer, but that was because I was better with words than numbers. Compliance with laws and regulations came up frequently, almost incessantly. But rarely did Freddie's leaders openly consider questions of ethics, although ethically complex questions could emerge without warning. What was the right thing to do? Or to say? Or to write?

The company's bifurcated mission, regulation, allegiances, and culture had a lot to do with that lack of clarity. How could there be a single right answer?

Not long after the government takeover, I sought out a colleague in Freddie Mac's compliance division. I closed his office door as I entered. "Isn't it ironic," I mused, "that while you compliance guys were busy checking individual employees' compliance with Freddie Mac's Code of Conduct (for instance, did you accept baseball tickets from a customer?), Freddie's management was throwing dice?" There was simply no mechanism for asking the harder ethical questions.

Interestingly, the SEC case against the GSE executives did not accuse them of bad business decisions, poor management, or political interference, although, as has been reported, these things did occur and contributed to the debacle. Rather, the SEC case focused on the narrow question of whether or not the company disclosed what it knew about its risks to investors. In short, it was a problem of half-truths. And even that indictment didn't stick.

This accusation probably doesn't seem very satisfying to the average consumer, policy maker, economist, or homeowner. But it's actually huge. At its core, a capitalist system feeds on information, transparency, and trust. In short, capitalism requires truth. We are lost without it.

SAD GOOD-BYES

The September 2008 government takeover of Freddie Mac marked the end of an era, with all its privileges, prestige, power, and tragic fault lines. Within six months, I would finish out my own story with Freddie Mac, a company I had once been proud to work for.

The Human Toll

The horrible news spread quickly, thanks to morning radio. I was preparing to take my daughter to the orthodontist when someone reached me with the news that our acting CFO, David Kellerman, had been found dead from an apparent suicide. The date was April 21, 2009.

I stood there woodenly and leaned on the kitchen counter for support. Kellerman was "old Freddie." He'd given the company sixteen years. He was smart, well liked, and friendly to everyone. Exuding confidence, he could carry off outrageous outfits, like yellow slacks with a navy blazer and a bow tie. When Pizel was ousted, Kellerman was named interim CFO. It was a big job for such a young man—maybe too big.

My first thought was that Kellerman was the ultimate victim of our tragic tale. Into his lap had fallen all the business and accounting decisions of the past five years. The whole mess was his to sort through and make sense of. It was his to put our losses in neat columns, his to tally the billions we'd need from Treasury, and his to personally attest to the accuracy of a 300-page financial disclosure.

It was his to deal with the regulator and the myriad and unrelenting requests, reports, and outstanding issues. It was his to implement the most massive accounting change in years: bringing $1 trillion of off-balance sheet assets on balance sheet within the space of nine months. It was his to figure out how to account for all the noneconomic initiatives we were required to do to help stabilize the housing market.

Kellerman's death captured, in a way, all the little deaths we all were suffering and caught them all up in a great shroud. Our hearts left us that day. I wondered if the company could take much more.

An all-employee town hall was called for later that morning. These town hall meetings were becoming our form of group therapy.

That day, as we trudged once again over Jones Branch Drive, cameramen pointed large TV cameras at our sad, downturned faces. Passing them, I noticed that an official from FHFA had caught up to our group and was walking next to me. I thought morbidly of death as the great leveler—probably the only thing that can destroy Washington's attitude that "Where you stand depends on where you sit."

"How are you doing?" he asked extremely quietly.

"Not so well," I answered, staring at the tips of my shoes. "We're just people, all of us."

And maybe that's what it comes down to in the end: people. Weak, greedy, insecure, short-sighted—but at times capable of deep insight and great moral courage. Men and women working in the boxes and layers of organizations that orbit other boxes and other organizations in the intertwining and complex systems of money and power. Perhaps things could have turned out differently for Freddie Mac if the men and women in the boxes, in the layers, and in the jagged planetary system of Washington had all played their cards differently.

Departure

When someone dies at your workplace, you take a hard look at your job and your life. That's when I made up my mind to leave Freddie Mac—and not because they were going to pay me to leave. They didn't even offer. It had been 19 years, and I was so done. As a wide-eyed twenty-something,

I had come to Washington over two decades before to make a difference. Aside from taking a few stabs at the dark side enveloping my company, I felt pretty ineffectual. That's why I was astounded at my farewell party when my boss said, "Perhaps if we had listened to Susan more we wouldn't be where we are today."

Then came the day of relinquishment. I packed boxes, turned in badges and keys, and cast my eye about the place one last time. It began when a woman from Legal arrived with boxes to pack up my files. I had been strongly warned not to take any documents with me, and I had obliged. But there in the cabinets lay the last vestiges of my corporate career. Employee performance records, legislative analyses, drafts of congressional testimony, scads of negative articles and reports about the GSEs, the work I did on our response to Hurricane Katrina, the draft paragraph for President Bush's SOTU, a yellowing page from the *Atlanta Constitution*, which castigated Freddie for meddling in state politics—it was all there, now being laid to rest.

The woman from Legal had carefully recorded the contents of each file and placed them in boxes, like little children being tucked into bed after a raucous day. The boxes were sealed with packing tape and would probably be sent to a place like Iron Mountain where all truth goes to die until summoned by law firms. And yet, as I think of those files now, I know their truths cannot be contained. Truth is radioactive, it occurred to me. It will burn through whatever container we attempt to place it in. There is leakage, then seepage, and then a gushing roar.

A few hours later, a woman from Human Resources arrived to conduct the exit interview. She had sent me a checklist of items and questions a few weeks prior, so I had assembled a little pile of corporate detritus: my credit card, building pass, and cell phone. These I handed to her. Then began the questions about why I was leaving the company; after all, I had not been asked to leave, and management was curious. It was not every day that an executive walked away jobless.

I stared hard at the little boxes on the checklist. I knew what a good corporate girl would do: just make up an answer and be done with it. I glanced at the woman interviewing me, her pen poised to record my answer, and then looked down at the list again. Why *was* I leaving, exactly?

I decided to unload. What did I have left to lose?

"You all think we just want money, perks, and vacation and that we'll stay here and work even if we are miserable," I said finally. "But we're talking about how people are spending their lives. For God's sake, did we learn nothing from David's death?"

I pushed the checklist across the desk to her and crossed my arms. "If you really want to know, I am leaving because this company failed itself and its employees." My eyes misted. "I don't see a box to check for that."

The woman and I locked eyes, and she put down her pen. Her officiousness melted. Maybe she had heard something like that from other employees who were leaving. I wondered what she would tell the head of HR of our conversation.

I continued. "It's just that, well, something terrible occurred here, and we're all pretending it didn't happen. Each new CEO comes in and will have nothing to do with the past. But the past is here. We are the past. We saw it. We lived it. It's not going away until we face it and come to terms with each of our contributions to what happened."

The interview was over. She walked me down to the security guard's desk to turn in my badge. I was given a red sticker that said "Temporary." "This is so you can stay as late as you want today," she explained. Then she shook my hand, and we parted ways.

I returned to my office to retrieve a few pictures and mementos—and one last look. On the whiteboard was a diagram I'd drawn of the future of the housing finance system. I erased it.

My thoughts traveled back to my father, who felt forced out of a large corporation after 30 long years. He said that leaving a company is like pulling your hand out of a bucket of water. As soon as you leave, the water fills the emptiness of where you were. Your space is taken, and organizational life goes on without you. I could feel the waters swirling.

HOUSING'S FUTURE

In telling this complex story, my goal has not been to cast blame on any one individual, company, regulator, or political party, although there were many blameworthy decisions and actions. Rather, I have wanted to illustrate that the search for a single scapegoat—or even a single ideological narrative to explain the crisis—is a vain quest. From the housing cheerleaders to the pols, from naïve consumers to shameless predatory lenders, and from co-opted regulators to opportunistic lenders, GSEs, and Wall Street firms, the US financial crisis was a collective tragedy, the seeds of which were sown decades before. Too many said, "It's someone else's responsibility to handle this risk." Too few asked, "What is the *right* thing to do?" and then had the courage to do it, even at their own peril.

On the other hand, I agree with the view expressed by former Congressional Budget Office head Doug Holtz-Eakin and others, that if the crisis was everybody's fault then it was nobody's fault. Shirking responsibility is adolescent. A mature, healthy response would be to admit our failures and commit to learning from them. All participants in housing finance need to aim higher next time and not simply rely on rules and regulations to do the job of conscience and good judgment.

More broadly, it's time to acknowledge that the entire US housing finance system remains riddled with dangerous fault lines. These fissures are at once ideological, political, and ethical. Among them:

- We spend enormous public resources supporting middle- and upper-class homeownership, while affordable housing for the poor languishes.
- We provide market-distorting government guarantees to a housing industry that is rife with conflicting incentives and needs to be weaned from the mother's milk of government support.
- We push homeownership as a way to reverse a terrible legacy of discrimination and find that we have unwittingly hurt many people our well-intended public policies sought to assist.
- We are addicted to debt financing at all levels of society, as if simply buying and furnishing more and bigger houses is the most productive and sustainable way to create jobs.

Most profoundly, we show that we are a nation with little regard for our neighbors when lenders originate mortgages they know can't be repaid; when borrowers defraud, sue, or deliberately default in order to be relieved of debt obligations; when creditors sever the traditional alignment of interests with borrowers; and when high-powered corporations, trade associations, and individuals seek to corrupt national leaders and institutions, at the highest levels, in the excessive and relentless pursuit of personal gain. Without some radical national soul searching, we risk repeating these grave errors. Given enough competitive strain, it won't be long before these unacknowledged fissures crack open again.

Housing Policy as "Golden Mean"

For several years, policy makers have been working feverishly to set up new financing structures and new rules of the road for mortgage lending. The ideological chasm between conservatives and liberals is so raw and so wide that finding a system that knowingly and skillfully bridges these divides is absolutely critical. A search for the golden mean between our two polarizing extremes seems elusive. But here's a place to start.

Leaning Conservative

Housing policy should lean conservative when it comes to encouraging homeownership for at least three reasons. First and foremost, the home-ownership stakes are high for average families—and the cost of getting in over one's head is higher still. Better to have a slower accession into the ranks of homeowners—and fewer defaults. Housing wealth can only be transferred to the next generation if it is built and protected. Sometimes this takes a lifetime.

Second, a conservative approach to homeownership is necessary given that the entire system, from consumer to investor, is rife with moral hazard and opportunities to game the system. To manage all the various interactions—notoriously complex, legalistic, and frankly incomprehensible—requires significant regulation, oversight, and en-forcement. The more complicated the regulations, the more temptations, loopholes, and lawsuits all the way around. A system with fewer exceptions, loopholes, and offsetting factors would be preferable.

Third, a conservative approach is entirely prudent given the enormity of the risks involved—particularly the interest rate risk on 30-year fixed-rate mortgages—and the propensity to shift those risks toward the entity with the lowest capital requirements: the US government. The costs to the nation and world of another collapse of the overextended US housing market would be unthinkable.

Beyond providing a fair and reasonable level of access, the nation's mort-gage market is not the place to experiment with social policy. Quite simply, barriers to entry are needed, and sizable down payments should be required to reduce risk and moral hazard. The mortgage market used to operate on such a model, and it's time to move back toward that. A safe system is in absolutely everyone's best interest, particularly the underserved.

Leaning Liberal

By the same token, there are three important ways in which housing pol-icy needs to lean liberal. The first has to do with fairness. It is critical to ensure that nonfinancial variables like race and ethnicity, marital status, and other borrower characteristics do not impede access to homeown-ership. Research should continue to shed light on the hidden barriers to homeownership, and efforts should be made to vigorously dismantle them. Enforcement of fair lending laws is critical. Although the flow of high-risk mortgages to lower-income and minority communities was encouraged by unwitting social policy, racial targeting and discrimination plagued the subprime market. Wizened to these dangers, let's hope that FHFA, HUD, and the CFPB—and other regulators—keep this from happening again.

Another fairness issue is the need to reduce, if not eliminate, the mortgage interest tax deduction for very large mortgages—however loudly the housing lobby screams. These resources could be redirected to fund scarce housing resources, such as rental vouchers, for people who need assistance in securing shelter. I am not arguing against the desire of some to live in huge homes, although I think there are important social and environmental costs to be considered. I am arguing that taxpayers shouldn't be subsidizing their mansions.

Second, to lean liberal is to recognize that housing is a basic human need. Since the private market is interested in profits, it will not always produce the necessary supply, particularly housing for lower-income consumers. Hence, there is a role for government to play in ensuring that quality, affordable rental housing is available. FHA should be capitalized, modernized, and staffed to play a leading role going forward. In addition, increasing the supply of affordable rental housing would presumably result in lower rents, particularly in urban areas. A greater supply of quality affordable housing could, in turn, reduce political pressure to liberalize mortgage underwriting requirements simply because a monthly mortgage payment may be lower than a monthly rental payment.

Third, leaning liberal should lead to innovation and change. The sudden 30 percent drop in housing prices was sobering; let's not forget it happened. With so many homeowners in a weakened financial condition, this could be an opportunity to institute user-friendly rent-to-own programs, equity sharing, and other approaches to sustainable homeownership. To be sure, these programs cut against the national grain of ownership and are not easy to implement. Yet they need to move up on the policy agenda; most housers I know are smart and can figure these things out. The most urgently needed innovation is for broader use and availability of quality prepurchase counseling. Almost everyone in the industry believes this is a good thing because counseling lowers defaults, but no one wants to pay for it. Since having more financially literate consumers would benefit the entire mortgage industry, all should chip in to make it happen.

Beyond ideology, a national shift from excessive debt toward savings, including for a decent down payment, is critical. Homeownership, according to a number of experts, is overrated as a get-rich-quick investment.

We also need to steer away from overconsumption of housing in favor of investments in more productive sectors of the economy. Savings from the MID could be redirected to helping underwrite the cost of higher education; strapped graduates may not be able to buy houses without debt relief. Public policy and tax policy have important roles to play in bringing this about, as well as monetary policy. How long will the Fed drag its feet on raising interest rates? At what point does artificially cheap mortgage money result in another overheated housing market? What about rewarding saving over debt?

GSE Reform

Fundamental adjustments in housing policy, combined with getting a grip on our national obsession with our homes and indebtedness, would go a long way to mend the deep fissures that contributed to the greatest financial eruption in world history. These changes also would provide a firmer foundation—and more civil dialogue—around the future of Freddie Mac and Fannie Mae. Finding a golden ideological mean is absolutely critical to rebuilding a sustainable system.

Conservatives care about market efficiency and limited government, so they like to think that the private sector can go it alone when it comes to the housing market—that no government guarantees or involvement are necessary. In a perfect world with perfect information where all risks could be priced, that might be possible. But that's not the world we live in. As long as consumers are willing to enter into long-term commitments to pay for their homes, there will be risk. Somebody has to bear it: borrowers, creditors, government, or some combination thereof. Despite their recent problems, the GSEs have developed significant technical know-how and expertise in managing risk. Further, they are now public assets and have strong books of business that will generate stable returns going forward. There is an urgent need to reform them before a growing talent drain materially weakens them, before their systems are completely obsolete, before their capital is depleted.

Liberals care a lot about affordable housing and fairness, which is why they raise concern over differences in homeownership rates across racial and ethnic groups. Although the nation's growing wealth gap is worrisome, seeking to solve it through easy access to homeownership—however politically attractive that might be—can be ultimately destructive, as recent experience has shown. Homeownership is not for everyone at every moment in time, and there are some housing structures and neighborhoods that are simply too risky to finance en masse. People must have stable employment and a fair bit of money put away in savings before they take on the responsibilities of owning a home and fixing the roof, the toilet, and so on. It's OK for people to rent their homes for a while or forever. Lower-income families will have lower homeownership rates for a while, or even for a long time. Our nation's racial travesties continue to reverberate today. If we really want to make more people homeowners, then we must go upstream and address the inequalities in the education and labor markets. There is no quick fix.

Consumers need to slow down and exert greater self-control. Amassing debt to get things earlier in life is not always a good thing. Houses are not the great investment they once were—if they ever were, particularly in areas with weak house-price growth. Individuals need to take greater responsibility for becoming financially literate. Read the fine print. Focus on building home equity for the future, not on spending it today.

Taken together, what we are talking about is a both/and approach to housing policy that works for both conservatives and liberals. To borrow from Harvard social scientist Robert Putnam, fixing housing finance is a "purple problem," in that both red-state conservatives and blue-state liberals have unique insights, perspectives, and solutions to offer.[1]

Live or Die?

We now come to the six-million-dollar question: What should be done with Freddie Mac and Fannie Mae? While there are many permutations to the various reform proposals, and coalitions are constantly calving like icebergs, I have grouped the two most distinct camps.

Recap and Release

In this odd set of bedfellows are vastly powerful hedge funds, small banks, and consumer groups that want a return of the status quo, with adjustments. Left to their devices, they would return the chastened companies to their privileged place as pillars of the greatest housing finance system in the world. This would involve the government allowing the GSEs to begin to amass capital—or giving them fresh stocks—and selling them back to their shareholders. Rewarding the hedge funds with billions would be a bitter pill, but that may be the price to get private capital to reenter the housing mainstream and play ball. Assuming the GSEs are stripped of their government guarantee as part of this transaction, mortgage rates would likely rise. A big question is by how much? Would mortgage-backed security investors really believe the government had truly stepped away, or would the new GSE managers enjoy the same "big, fat gap" that the implicit guarantee provided their predecessors? Would it really be different from the system now lying on its back?

Wind Down and Replace

This option gives full vent to congressional and public fury to punish the entities by dismembering them limb by limb. In this scenario, a new agency would be created to provide government insurance on a slice of the risk of mortgage-backed securities issued by banks and other financial institutions. Fees would be set by the new entity. Would they be high enough to cover risk? The big banks are only slightly less hated than the GSEs. Can we trust them to manage mortgage credit risk and avoid another race to the bottom? Will small lenders be able to compete? Will the new insuring entity be able to resist political pressure to lower insurance fees?

In March 2016, a coalition of housing luminaries published a paper through the Urban Institute entitled "A More Promising Road to GSE Reform."[2] Forsaking illusions of grand reform, the authors advocate building on FHFA's plodding efforts to combine the GSE security platforms and offload credit risk to willing private market investors. In place of the quasi-governmental GSEs, the new single entity, the National Mortgage Reinsurance Corporation, would be a full-fledged government corporation like Ginnie Mae. It would continue to buy conventional mortgages, and its mortgage securities would carry explicit government backing, as they have since 2008. To keep taxpayer risk to a minimum, the NMRC would be required to transfer all noncatastrophic credit risk to the capital markets and charge a g-fee commensurate with risk. The net entity would still need to meet affordable housing goals and duty-to-serve requirements.

The plan sounds do-able, and policy makers are tired. But the risks of moral hazard remain unaddressed. Everyone loves a full government guarantee, as it lets them off the hook, and the government's cost of capital hardly reflects the real risks inherent in mortgage lending. If Dodd-Frank had truly fortified the primary market by requiring lenders to retain capital, such a plan might have a chance. But as described earlier, DFA's risk retention precautions were eviscerated by the mortgage and housing trade groups. Without significantly tightening the qualified residential mortgage requirement (QRM), mortgage credit risk will again concentrate with the GSEs—or their successors. And what of continued pressure to make mortgage money cheaper and more available to underserved groups through low-down-payment loans and other liberalized terms? Are we really going to do that again?

I'll give the last word to Mark Calabria with the CATO Institute:

> Our current system of mortgage finance is fundamentally flawed. It has not delivered sustainable increases in homeownership. It has not delivered financial stability (obviously). It has left homeowners drowning in debt and driven house prices beyond the reach of the middle class. We should stop driving in circles trying to tweak the status quo. If that means being less pragmatic, then so be it. There is simply too much at stake to settle for anything other than fundamental reform, whether such is politically promising or not.[3]

Conclusion

The GSEs failed. Their business model was flawed. Taxpayers have already paid in $187.5 billion; more could be coming. Twenty years of government studies warned this could happen. It did. It's time to get beyond the recriminations and create a new system for the next generation of homeowners—one that rewards saving for down payments, shifts tax benefits to the middle class, encourages the building of affordable, environmentally sustainable, energy-efficient homes, and supports a healthy rental market. Tinkering with the status quo may seem to be the easier route, but it is likely to yield the same disastrous results. Bipartisan action begins with agreement on fundamental principles.

Homeownership remains a national priority. While we should begin shifting resources and incentives to create other viable choices, owner-occupied housing will remain a desirable norm. But that requires vast quantities of liquidity. In the first quarter of 2016, GSE securities accounted for 45 percent of the $10 trillion in single-family mortgage debt outstanding.[4] The GSEs are backing at least 80 percent of new mortgages and have processed 3.4 million HARP refinances. Something this central to American life requires government participation. We simply can't expect private investors to pay for it, to provide for it, and to manage it. That said, to temper animal instincts and minimize moral hazard, all players—from borrower to lender to investor—must have skin in the game.

We must acknowledge and accurately price for risk. If homeownership is going to be widely affordable, then long-term, fixed-rate mortgages must remain in place. They are the lifeblood of this system, but they also add risk. The price of a mortgage should reflect this risk. If we want to help more people become homeowners, there are better ways to do it than through "spongy conduit" institutions, liberalized underwriting standards, housing goals, hidden tax expenditures, or other artificial means. Rather, we should give direct subsidies that are accountable to the democratic process. For example, instead of lowering down payments to 3 percent, why not provide down payment assistance? At least this would get the incentives right and minimize default risk.

No one will believe that the US government will not bail out housing again, so some sort of guarantee is needed. Government insurance against catastrophic loss, combined with greater skin in the game for all participants, should be adequate to draw private capital to our shores. Since politics will always be a threat to ensuring that fees remain commensurate with risk, greater pricing transparency is needed, as with any public utility.

We need an honest reckoning of what's gone before. Although homeownership is clearly a national policy objective, as a major instrument of that policy, the GSEs have long been the weak link. From their shady, off-budget beginnings, the GSEs have suffered from a lack of legitimacy and bipartisan support, which made Congress easy prey. The GSEs sat atop dangerous fault lines, and their vast subsidies and risks have long been submerged from public view. Perhaps it was not a bad deal to pay $187.5 billion for the decades of homeownership we've enjoyed on the cheap. The tsunami could have been far worse. Many hands contributed to their demise.

It is time to come clean on all the government pins in the GSE voodoo doll. Although the GSEs have repaid their debt to society by more than $50 billion, the government continues to milk billions from the reserves they need to weather a future downturn. A careful read of the 2017 president's budget reveals all the government hooks into these entities. In 2016, the GSEs will contribute $40 billion off their g-fee income toward deficit reduction. They will pay $343 million into government-mandated housing funds, which they have no control over. Then they will hand over remaining profits of $240 billion; the budget assumes these payments will continue through 2026. These amounts are above and beyond their federal income taxes, among the nation's largest. Before redistributing GSE profits, the entities actually need to make some.

Continued gridlock over GSE future is withering public investment. Freddie Mac and Fannie Mae have had to tread water in a shark-infested ocean while Congress argues about their future. The situation is unsustainable. As has been noted, the GSE capital buffers will be depleted by 2018, processing systems are growing obsolete, and attrition in their highly trained staff is already underway. Without reform, a loss of market confidence becomes increasingly possible. The GSEs are like old cars needing repairs. Fix them or sell them while they have value, while they can still run.

WHEREFORE ETHICS?

Searching for a single smoking gun to explain the financial crisis is a fool's errand. All the hands, set-ups, and agendas—combined with massive movements of capital from all parts of the world—put this crisis in the epic category in terms of size, impact, and contributing factors. While not exhaustive by any means, this book has sought to unpack the different levels of fracture—philosophical and ideological, policy and political.

Some practical suggestions have been provided to move toward a sustainable housing policy befitting a grown-up nation. Americans should not have to live in cardboard boxes or sleep on park benches. And those Americans who choose to live in mansions should not expect support from the federal government. The urgent need to reform the GSEs gives us a unique opportunity to change a few more things than just the name of the organizations that provide us all that low-cost liquidity. But what of ethics—national, public, corporate, and personal?

Fall from Grace

In chapter 1, I quoted from the government's 2011 *Financial Crisis Inquiry Report*. While the report continues to be a lightning rod for bitter partisan wrangling over whether it was Wall Street or housing policy that caused the crisis, it has been easy to overlook an indictment that very few would disagree with—that there was a "systematic breakdown in accountability and ethics."[1]

Ethics is a touchy subject to broach because it might veer toward preachiness, morality, and old-fashioned notions of character, virtue, and, worst of all, religion. But speak of ethics we must. It is the foundation—the ground floor—of all of our national institutions, our national reputation and integrity, and each individual's fondest hopes and dreams.

Even if policy makers were able to properly reform the GSEs and set up the perfect housing finance system, unethical behavior—writ large—can ruin everything. It almost did.

Consideration of ethics intersects the discussion of regulations in a curious way. Quoting from Federalist 51, "if men were angels, no government would be necessary." Since the nation's founders were clear-eyed enough to understand the destructive power of self-interest, they devised a constitutional structure to separate powers, check interest with interest, prevent faction, and bring order by passing laws, writing rules, and empowering judges to enforce them.

As important as this framework is to national life, it was never intended to take the place of virtue and moral judgment. Indeed, it cannot bear such a responsibility. In the much-quoted words of second president John Adams, "Our Constitution was made only for a moral and religious people. It is wholly inadequate to the government of any other." Perhaps the decline of moral reflection is one reason the constitutional order, including our political discourse, seems at times to be imperiled. We simply expect too much of it.

The old housing finance system—that got badly taken advantage of— had a lot of grace, which meant the industry was allowed to operate on a wide berth of public trust. Before the crisis there were relatively few (or outmoded) regulations governing exactly how consumers, lenders, and GSEs would deal with each other on the field. Credit rating agencies would also fall into this camp. Loosely regulated, the system operated instead on traditional methods of doing business, traditional underwriting guidelines, and trust. In short, it was a system of self-regulation, not perfect, but something to be prized.

Outmoded and non-existent regulations were certainly not optimal for a complex housing finance system like ours, but a poor regulatory structure alone did not create the disaster we've just experienced. People did. Institutions and their employees traded wickedly on that berth of grace and, in the end, lost it. Rampant competition brought on by Wall Street—combined with the GSEs' unwavering focus on defending their valuable charters and protecting market share—resulted in a massive ethical breakdown on multiple fronts. The sins of the GSEs cost them their business franchise, their autonomy, and quite possibly their future existence. To use theological terms, they fell from grace and now live under serious law.

Consumers and lenders also live under more law than they would like. Today mortgages can take forever to originate because the required documentation is voluminous and lenders are terrified they are going to be sued. Consumers chafe because they have to prove everything down to the last penny—no one trusts them. And the average loan file is well in excess of 500 pages. Lender compliance departments are swelling with new employees. Everybody is checking on everybody else.

Even regulators can't be trusted. The 2008 GSE reform law created a regulator to watch over the regulator. Keeping a sharp eye on FHFA, who keeps watch over the GSEs, is the FHFA Office of Inspector General.

Progressives put a lot of stock in new regulations, notwithstanding the proven tendency of people and institutions to find ingenious ways to go around them. Conservatives deplore the surfeit of new regulations as a drag on market innovation and adding unnecessary costs. But without greater attention to ethics, particularly the internal kind, what else is there to check overly self-interested behavior?

Deeper Still

Ideological, political, and policy divides must be mended, but they will not be enough to keep the mortgage market from collapsing again without attention to ethics. Deeper reforms are needed, reforms that penetrate to the core of the capitalistic system, the political scrum, and each individual firm, employee, consumer, and heart.

How do we get there? The answers are in the rearview mirror. In the words of Jim Wallis, "we don't have any blueprints for a new system, and we should not look for any. At best, what we have are some spiritual guideposts and road maps."[2]

Perhaps the earliest place to look is Aristotle, whose virtue ethics is enjoying a renaissance among political philosophers. Aristotle believed that the purpose of life in the *polis*, or city state, is to form good citizens and to cultivate good character. This view of the good life—which produced good people, as opposed to good things—differs from the modern reasons for participation in politics. According to Harvard's Michael Sandel, relying simply on our constitutional "framework of rights that is neutral among ends" can blind us to the need for virtue, relationships, and community.[3]

Even more dissonant with modern culture, Aristotle believed that happiness is not a state of mind but a way of being. We become happy, he said, when the soul's activity accords with virtue. In short, when we do the right thing, we are happy. Choosing the good is not innate; it must be learned. And so we practice; "we become just by doing just acts, temperate by doing temperate acts." Since civic virtue depends on the virtuous habits of its people, "the purpose of law is to cultivate habits that lead to good character."[4]

Wishful thinking? Writing a few years before the financial crisis, Chicago school economist Deirdre McClosky, in *The Bourgeois Virtues: Ethics for an Age of Commerce*, called for an "ethical reinvestment" reminiscent of Aristotle: "We need to defend a defensible capitalism. We citizens of the bourgeois towns need to rethink our love and courage. We need to nourish the commercial versions of temperance, justice and prudence that were admired during the eighteenth century . . . and we need to find a safe home for faith and hope."[5]

Speaking of the eighteenth century, consider the ethical reflections of the patron saint of free markets and the invisible hand, Adam Smith. In the *Theory of Moral Sentiments*, which he considered a greater work than *Wealth of Nations*, Smith foresaw that virtue would be a critical ingredient for good sustainable commerce—and that corporate virtue had its roots in the community. To keep invidious self-interest in check, Smith believed that business leaders should make their decisions with the self-awareness of an "impartial spectator," which could be summoned by the use of moral imagination. Referring to the spectator as the fictitious "man within the breast," Smith reasoned that if people would view their contemplated strategies and actions through the eye of some disinterested observer, leaders would be more likely to choose the public interest over private—and the world would be a much better place. This is because, he reasoned, people desire not only "to be loved, but to be lovely."[6]

Smith biographer Nichols Phillipson writes, "In learning how to 'humble the arrogance of [our] self-love,' and bring it down to something which other men can go along with, we have taken the first step on the road to a life of virtue. We have learned how to judge our own conduct and how to live independently of the opinions of others."[7]

In short, ethical people don't just follow reason, emotion, or the herd; they follow some internal compass. Call it conscience, common sense, or an inner deity, the ethical person will hearken to this voice over the passions and clamoring of the marketplace—or at least try to do so.

Assuming the captains of finance are willing to suspend their valuation models and ask what is the right thing to do, they should take the next step and use moral imagination to conjure up a relevant spectator. For example, a creditor could envision a borrower seeking a mortgage. Perhaps it is a low-income borrower, a mom and pop investor, or a foreign central bank. These mental exercises would supply the needed human face and outside perspective lacking in most corporate boardrooms. Imagining this personage as an impartial spectator (who otherwise probably didn't have any say in the matter) would serve as a limiting force on the damaging effects of unbridled self-interest.[8]

Scottish poet Robert Burns said as much in his humorous poem entitled "To a Louse," one of which was crawling on the shoulder of a woman who thought she was dressed to the nines. Reflecting on the difference in her view of herself and the real, external view, he penned, "O would some power the giftie gie us to see ourselves as others see us."

Other variations of this concept are what many around in DC call the *Washington Post* "smell test" (How would you feel about having this decision, for example, reported on the front page of the newspaper?) Christians might ask, "What would Jesus do?"

Certainly these mechanisms have their own flaws and limits. Even Smith acknowledged that his impartial spectator was an imperfect ethical gauge, formed as it was by the society at large. The WWJD mantra likewise has its weaknesses, as people's understanding of the teachings of Jesus is obscured by generations of religious teachings and growing secularism. And virtue itself, while laudable, is difficult to acquire or even comprehend. In a postmodern and skeptical age, even defining what virtue is can be problematic and viewed as judgmental.

Notwithstanding these weaknesses, trying to grapple with questions of ethics is far better than ignoring them altogether. Freddie Mac's leaders would have benefited from having an impartial spectator in mind when key decisions were being made. The firm was fixated on itself, on survival, and on beating Wall Street when it should have been thinking about borrowers and investors—the people who were depending on the firm to do the right thing.

Organizational Life

Ethics is not the sole responsibility of leaders. Middle management and rank-and-file employees also need to embrace an ethical stance as critical to organizational success.

Unfortunately, in professional spheres ethics has been defined so narrowly as to be almost useless in dealing with the mega-failures discussed in this book. To wit, my students and I marvel at the so-called "pizza rule" promulgated by the Senate Ethics Committee.[9] Professional ethics and codes of conduct have their place, but they are unreliable barometers of an ethical culture. In the book *Unmasking Administrative Evil*, authors Adams and Balfour describe how ethical failures can occur when "ordinary people may simply be acting appropriately in their organizational role . . . and at the same time participating in what a critical and reasonable observer, well after the fact, would call evil."[10] In other words, bad things happen even while employees think they are doing a good job. Administrative evil is a modern problem related to large complex structures and the increasing use of technology (over human judgment). Wall Street's dehumanizing tendency to see mortgages as simply cash flows to be sliced and diced might be a good example of this.

A second problem known as moral inversion occurs when "something evil is redefined convincingly as good." Freddie Mac's purchase of non-traditional mortgages—in the name of expanding homeownership—has elements of moral inversion. Our negative past experience with low-documentation loans should have been enough to warn us away. However, once the public square rebranded those loans as good, Freddie bought them in record numbers.

Unfortunately, detecting and correcting ethical blind spots is not easy because they are masked. For starters, we are such a tolerant people that we loathe using the word "evil" to describe anything short of downright heinous. Holding a meeting where everyone agrees to buy a certain type of mortgage (that is legal and consumers seem to want) hardly seems to warrant the epithet of evil. It certainly did not seem so at the time, but that's what happens when groupthink is prevalent, historical consciousness is minimized, and dissent is discouraged or punished.

Second, organizational structure can diffuse individual responsibility to such a point that no one feels any ethical ownership for a decision. Components of the modern bureaucracy—hierarchy, span of control, and division of labor—may be efficient, but they diffuse responsibility and accountability. The structure of the securitization process is similarly cloaked in efficiency; because risk is sectioned into minute packages and diffused through the capital markets, no one feels the full weight of responsibility.

Other masks include pride—moral blindness—as well as the lack of distance or perspective. According to Adams and Balfour, "identifying administrative evil is most difficult within one's own culture, historical time period," and organization.[11] The geographic and temporal distance between a lender originating a mortgage and a GSE acquiring it sight-unseen 60 days later masked the reality of what was really going on. That's why it took consumer advocates, with their greater proximity, to help Freddie Mac see what it could not from our 50,000-foot vantage point. Denial is another mask. The failure to even engage in questions of morality simply compounds the problem. And if someone does say that the emperor has no clothes, the outcome usually is not a good one for the truth-teller, at least in the short term. Freddie Mac's former chief credit officer expressed his views on the growing riskiness—and sordidness—of the company's books of business and was soon asked to seek employment elsewhere.

Well-meaning public policy also can become an instrument of evil when it is fixed on an instrumental or technical goal (which can rule out good judgment and ethical considerations). I would put the GSE affordable housing goals in this category. Regulators and the public became fixated on an annual ratio, a single number, at the expense of the distorting impact of the goals on the housing market and the GSEs themselves.

The sad fact is that "efficient and legitimate institutions can be used for constructive or destructive purposes."[12] To prevent this, responsibility rests with both leaders and employees who understand their role and identity in such a way that they can resist seductive and cunning temptations endemic to modern, complex organizations and systems.

A Few Suggestions

How can one assess one's organization or public policies for moral blind spots? First, leaders need to commit to regularly take stock of their organization's culture. How much groupthink is occurring? What are the different norms and values employees espouse? As previously described, Freddie Mac's warring cadres of Wall Street traders and housers exacerbated the firm's normative fault lines. What are the power dynamics? Are employees intimidated, or will they speak up? What is happening at the bottom of the organization? Why didn't Freddie Mac's business leaders link the insights of the fraud unit to corporate strategy? Leaders should not sequester themselves in a C-suite but rather walk the floor. There should be a mechanism (other than a complaint box) for drawing ideas and issues out of the workforce. For example, management could create a shadow board comprising a diverse group of younger leaders; it would be tasked with the same issues being handled by the official board of directors. Not only is this excellent training for the next generation of leaders, but discrepancies in decisions could prove to be highly instructive and could help unmask dangerous currents.

Second, CEOs need to guard against overconfidence and optimism. Paradoxically, the very character traits that make these men and women well suited for corporate leadership are also their Achilles heel. Optimists need to seek out contrarian voices and listen to them. Ethics is greater than mere compliance, and leaders must recognize the difference. They also need to recognize that the external environment of today's large public organizations is multi-tiered and thick with moral complexity. More ethical reflection, not less, is critical for successfully navigating away from the shoals of self-inflicted ethical disaster. Yet we resist this suggestion as quaint. Writing several decades ago, public management theorist Dwight Waldo wisely observed that "The scientific mentality that is largely responsible for the Organization Revolution simultaneously makes it difficult to take ethical matters seriously."[13]

Third, an organization should take into account a law's spirit or intent, as opposed to merely complying with it. Freddie Mac's accounting and political scandals demonstrate the perfidy of being too clever by half. Nothing goes over worse following a scandal than saying "well, it wasn't illegal." The public instinctively knows that is not enough and is relentlessly unforgiving on that score.

Conclusion

Analyzing the various competing policies, politics, and ideologies—as well as the players, ranging from consumers to lenders, from GSEs to Wall Street firms, and from regulators to lawmakers—it is clear that greater attention to ethics on the part of the GSEs and others, as well as moral courage, possibly could have lessened the blow of the collapse of the US housing market, if not prevented it altogether. If only the mortgage industry, with its many decades of experience, had presented a united front against Wall Street's cavalier approach to risk and disregard for borrowers who were lured into bad loans they could neither afford nor keep, things might have been very different.

Justice should be done, but let's not fool ourselves that new laws or lawsuits, or even putting people in jail, will be enough to keep this from happening again. We also need to revisit old ideas about virtue and moral imagination.

Most important, everyone would benefit from stronger *internal* government to manage the manifold devices and desires of the human heart. We would do well to recall what Lord Moulton wrote in a 1924 essay in the *Atlantic Monthly* and Martin Luther King quoted in 1968: because laws are inadequate (and even unjust) we must supplement them with "obedience to the unenforceable."[14] That kind of law is unwritten. It does not come from elected officials or regulators but from believing in something bigger than ourselves, something more moral than our hearts, an unseen judge of action and inaction who someday will call things into account. Only something like the old-fashioned fear of God has the power to induce people to do the right thing even when there is a lot of money on the table and nobody is looking—at least not right then.

Key Acronyms

A-minus   mortgage posing slightly more credit risk than an A-quality loan

Alt A   mortgage with low or reduced documentation or other "alternative" terms

ARM   adjustable rate mortgage

CBO   Congressional Budget Office

CRA   Community Reinvestment Act

CRL   Center for Responsible Lending

DFA   Dodd-Frank Act

FCIC   Financial Crisis Inquiry Commission

FDIC   Federal Deposit Insurance Corporation

FHA   Federal Housing Administration

FHFA   Federal Housing Finance Agency

FHLMC   Federal Home Loan Mortgage Corporation (Freddie Mac)

FNMA   Federal National Mortgage Association (Fannie Mae)

FRB   Federal Reserve Board (the "Fed")

GAO   Government Accountability Office

GNMA   Government National Mortgage Association (Ginnie Mae)

GSE   government-sponsored enterprise

HAMP   Home Affordable Modification Program

HARP   Home Affordable Refinance Program

HELOC   home equity line of credit

HERA   Housing and Economic Recovery Act of 2008

HFSC   House Financial Services Committee

HOEPA   Home Owners Equity Protection Act of 1994

HUD   US Department of Housing and Urban Development

IMF   International Monetary Fund

LTV   loan-to-value ratio

MBA	Mortgage Bankers Association	**PLS**	private-label security
MBS	mortgage-backed security	**PSPA**	Preferred Stock Purchase Agreements
MI	mortgage insurance	**PwC**	Price, Waterhouse, Coopers accounting firm
MID	mortgage interest tax deduction	**QM**	qualified mortgage
NINA	no income, no asset documentation mortgage	**QRM**	qualified residential mortgage
NTM	nontraditional mortgage	**SBC**	Senate Banking Committee
NWS	net-worth sweep		
OCC	Office of the Comptroller of the Currency	**SEC**	Securities and Exchange Commission
OFHEO	Office of Federal Housing Enterprise Oversight	**SISA**	stated income, stated assets documentation mortgage
OMB	Office of Management and Budget	**S&L**	savings and loan institution
OTS	Office of Thrift Supervision	**TARP**	Troubled Asset Relief Program
PC	Freddie Mac mortgage participation certificate	**UPB**	unpaid principal balance

Notes

Prologue. Acknowledging the Obvious

1. Analytical Perspectives, Budget of the United States Government, Fiscal Year 2017 (Washington, DC: Government Printing Office, 2016), 312. www.whitehouse.gov /sites/default/files/omb/budget/fy2017/assets/ap_20_credit.pdf.

2. Ibid.

3. Tara Rice and Jonathan Rose, "When Good Investments Go Bad: The Contraction in Community Bank Lending after the 2008 GSE Takeover," International Finance Discussion Paper 1045, March 2012, 4. www.federalreserve.gov/pubs/ifdp/2012/1045 /ifdp1045.pdf.

4. These securities were sold at a profit by March 2012 and netted taxpayers a budgetary gain of $11.9 billion. Analytical Perspectives, Budget of the United States Government, Fiscal Year 2017 (Washington, DC: Government Printing Office, 2016), 313.

5. Federal Housing Finance Agency, "Treasury and Federal Reserve Purchase Programs for GSE and Mortgage-Related Securities," data as of May 5, 2016. See tables 3 and 4. www.fhfa.gov/DataTools/Downloads/Pages/Treasury-and-Federal-Reserve -Purchase-Programs-for-GSE-and-Mortgage-Related-Securities.aspx.

6. Federal Reserve Board, "Federal Reserve Statistical Release: Factors Affecting Reserve Balances," June 23, 2016. See table 5. As of June 22, 2016, the combined face value of MBSs issued by Fannie Mae, Freddie Mac, and Ginnie Mae was $1.758 trillion. Total FRB assets were $4.482 trillion. www.federalreserve.gov/releases/h41/current /h41.htm#h41tab2.

Chapter 1. Reckoning Day

1. As described on p. 5 of the 2011 SEC complaint against CEO Richard F. Syron, Patricia L. Cook, and Donald J. Bisenius, "On September 7, 2008, FHFA, as conservator, adopted a resolution eliminating the par value of Freddie Mac's common stock, increasing the number of shares of Freddie Mac common stock authorized for issuance to four billion, preventing Freddie Mac from making any payment to purchase or redeem its capital stock or pay any dividends to holders of Freddie Mac's common stock, and limiting the voting rights of holders of Freddie Mac's common stock." www.sec.gov /litigation/complaints/2011/comp-pr2011-267-freddiemac.pdf.

2. W. Scott Frame, "The 2008 Federal Intervention to Stabilize Fannie Mae and Freddie Mac," Federal Reserve Bank of Atlanta Working Paper 2009-13, April 2009, 1.

3. US Treasury Department Office of Public Affairs, "Fact Sheet: Treasury Senior Preferred Stock Purchase Agreement," September 7, 2008.

4. *Mary Poppins*, directed by Robert Stevenson (Burbank, CA: Disney Studios, 1964).

5. The Senior Preferred Stock Purchase Agreement (PSPA) sought to provide "significant protections for the taxpayer, in the form of senior preferred stock with a liquidation preference, an upfront $1 billion issuance of senior preferred stock with a 10 percent coupon from each GSE, quarterly dividend payments, warrants representing an ownership stake of 79.9 percent in each GSE going forward, and a quarterly fee starting in 2010." US Treasury, "Fact Sheet."

6. The GSEs' required 10 percent quarterly dividend has been viewed by some investors as particularly severe. In contrast, although the bailout of the massive insurance company American International Group originally required a 10 percent coupon on a combined (Federal Reserve and Treasury) $182 billion infusion, Treasury later relented. In December 2012, the US government sold its remaining shares in AIG and pocketed $23 billion in positive return, according to the government. See Treasury press release dated December 11, 2012, at www.treasury.gov/press-center/press-releases/Pages /tg1796.aspx.

7. Henry M. Paulson, *On the Brink: Inside the Race to Stop the Collapse of the Global Financial System* (New York: Hachette Book Group, 2010), 170.

8. *Financial Crisis Inquiry Report* (New York: Public Affairs, 2011), xxii–xxiii.

9. House Financial Services Committee, Subcommittee on International Monetary Policy and Trade, "The U.S. Housing Finance System in the Global Context: Structure, Capital Sources, and Housing Dynamics." See webcast at 1:25:43 and following, www .financialservices.house.gov/calendar/eventsingle.aspx?EventID=263451.

10. *Financial Crisis Inquiry Report*, xxiii.

11. US Government Accountability Office, "Report to Congress: Financial Crisis Losses and Potential Impacts of the Dodd Frank Act," January 2013, 21. www.gao.gov /assets/660/651322.pdf.

12. Ibid., 20.

13. *National Foreclosure Report*, September 2015, CoreLogic, 3. www.corelogic.com /research/foreclosure-report/national-foreclosure-report-september-2015.pdf.

14. Center for Responsible Lending, "Collateral Damage: The Spillover Costs of Foreclosures," by Debbie Gruenstein Bocian, Peter Smith, and Wei Li, October 24, 2012. www.responsiblelending.org/mortgage-lending/research-analysis/collateral-damage .pdf. According to the report, "Families affected by nearby foreclosures have already lost or will lose $21,077 in household wealth, representing 7.2 percent of their home value, by virtue of being in close proximity to foreclosures. Families impacted in minority neighborhoods have lost or will lose, on average, $37,084 or 13.1 percent of their home value."

15. Debbie Gruenstein Bocian, Wei Li, and Keith Ernst, "Foreclosures by Race and Ethnicity: The Demographics of a Crisis," Center for Responsible Lending, 2010.

16. RealtyTrac, "National Real Estate Trends and Market Information," April 2013. Data retrieved on May 9, 2013 at www.realtytrac.com/statsandtrends/foreclosuretrends.

17. See Atif R. Mian, Kamalesh Rao, and Amir Sufi, "Household Balance Sheets, Consumption, and the Economic Slump," Chicago Booth Research Paper No. 13-42, February 27, 2013. The authors found that consumer spending for automobiles was correlated with the degree to which a borrower's mortgage was underwater. Thus, for example, in areas where less than 15 percent of homeowners were underwater, only a small decline in spending was observable, compared to much larger spending declines in areas where more than half of homeowners were underwater.

18. Annamaria Androitis, "Home-Equity Lines of Credit See Jump in Delinquencies," *Wall Street Journal*, June 8, 2015. www.wsj.com/articles/home-equity-lines-of-credit-see -jump-in-delinquencies-1433777432.

NOTES TO PAGES 14–17 | 259

19. According to Governing.com, seven cities and localities have filed for Chapter 9 bankruptcy since 2010, of which three filings were subsequently dismissed. In 2012, Stockton, California, became the largest city to file for bankruptcy protection. www.governing.com/gov-data/municipal-cities-counties-bankruptcies-and-defaults.html.

20. US Government Accountability Office, "Report to Congress: Financial Crisis Losses and Potential Impacts of the Dodd Frank Act," January 2013, 15. www.gao.gov/assets/660/651322.pdf.

21. Tyler Atkinson, David Luttrell, and Harvey Rosenblum, "How Bad Was It? The Costs and Consequences of the 2007–09 Financial Crisis," Staff Papers, Dallas Federal Reserve, No. 20, July 2013.

22. US Government Accountability Office, "Report to Congress: Financial Crisis Losses and Potential Impacts of the Dodd Frank Act," January 2013, 26.

23. Standard & Poors, "United States of America Long-Term Rating Lowered To 'AA+' On Political Risks And Rising Debt Burden; Outlook Negative," August 5, 2011, 3. www.washingtonpost.com/wp-srv/politics/documents/spratingreport_080611.pdf.

24. Gwladys Fouche, "Subprime Chill Reaches the Arctic," *The Guardian*, June 30, 2008. www.guardian.co.uk/business/2008/jun/30/subprimecrisis.creditcrunch.

25. Ezra Klein and Evan Soltas, "Americans Haven't Rebuilt 91 Percent of Their Wealth. They've Rebuilt Less Than 45 Percent," *Washington Post*, May 31, 2013.

26. International Monetary Fund, "United States: Selected Issues," August 2012, 8. www.imf.org/external/pubs/ft/scr/2012/cr12214.pdf.

27. Analytical Perspectives, Budget of the United States Government, Fiscal Year 2017 (Washington, DC: Government Printing Office, 2016), 313. www.whitehouse.gov/sites/default/files/omb/budget/fy2017/assets/ap_20_credit.pdf.

28. Ibid.

29. Brian Collins, "Lawmakers Object to Discounts on Nonperforming Loan Sales," *National Mortgage News*, March 24, 2016. www.nationalmortgagenews.com/news/compliance-regulation/lawmakers-object-to-discounts-on-nonperforming-loan-sales-1074440-1.html.

30. See Department of Treasury press release dated December 11, 2012. www.treasury.gov/press-center/press-releases/Pages/tg1796.aspx.

31. Federal Housing Finance Agency, *2014 Report to Congress*, 1. www.fhfa.gov/AboutUs/Reports/ReportDocuments/FHFA_2014_Report_to_Congress.pdf.

32. Federal Housing Finance Agency, *2015 Report to Congress*, 18. www.fhfa.gov/AboutUs/Reports/ReportDocuments/FHFA_2015_Report-to-Congress.pdf.

33. Joe Light and Austen Hufford, "Freddie Mac Swings to Loss, Won't Make Dividend Payment," *Wall Street Journal*, May 3, 2016. www.wsj.com/articles/freddie-mac-swings-to-loss-wont-make-dividend-payment-1462281293.

34. Federal Housing Finance Agency, *2015 Report to Congress*, 18. www.fhfa.gov/AboutUs/Reports/ReportDocuments/FHFA_2015_Report-to-Congress.pdf.

35. Ibid., 17.

36. Federal Housing Finance Agency, *2015 Report to Congress*, 16. www.fhfa.gov/AboutUs/Reports/ReportDocuments/FHFA_2015_Report-to-Congress.pdf.

37. Bethany McLean, *Shaky Ground: The Strange Saga of the US Mortgage Giants* (New York: Columbia Global Reports, 2015), 121.

38. Federal Housing Finance Agency, "Senior Preferred Stock Purchase Agreements." www.fhfh.gov/conservatorship/pages/senior-preferred-stock-purchase-agreements.aspx.

39. McLean, *Shaky Ground*, 121.

40. Gretchen Morgenson, "Fannie, Freddie and the Secrets of a Bailout with No Exit," *New York Times*, May 5, 2016. www.nytimes.com/2016/05/22/business/how-freddie-and-fannie-are-held-captive.html.

41. See, for example, "The Continued Profitability of Fannie Mae and Freddie Mac Is Not Assured," Office of Inspector General of the Federal Housing Finance Agency (March 2015), and the Urban Institute's report entitled "What to Make of the Dramatic Fall in GSE Profits?" (March 2015).

42. Federal Housing Finance Agency, *2015 Report to Congress*, 18. www.fhfa.gov/AboutUs/Reports/ReportDocuments/FHFA_2015_Report to Congress.pdf.

43. Melvin L. Watt, FHFA Director, "Prepared Remarks before the Bipartisan Policy Committee," February 18, 2016. www.fhfa.gov/Media/PublicAffairs/Pages/Prepared-Remarks-Melvin-Watt-at-BPC.aspx.

44. On April 12, 2016, Rep. Mick Mulvaney (R-SC) introduced H.R. 4913, known as the Housing Finance Restructuring Act of 2016. On May 10, 2016, the National Taxpayers Union and eleven other groups signed an "Open Letter to the House and Senate: Protect the Financial System and Taxpayers from Another Fannie/Freddie Bailout—Enact the Housing Finance Restructuring." www.ntu.org/library/doclib/H.R.-4913-Fannie-and-Freddie-Reform-Coalition-Letter.pdf.

45. Letter addressed to FHFA Director Melvin Watt and Treasury Secretary Jack Lew dated June 1, 2016 and signed by 32 members of Congress. www.dsnews.com/wp-content/uploads/2016/06/Democrat-Letter.pdf.

46. Gretchen Morgenson, "A Revolving Door Helps Big Banks' Quiet Campaign to Muscle Out Fannie and Freddie," *New York Times*, December 7, 2015. www.nytimes.com/2015/12/07/business/a-revolving-door-helps-big-banks-quiet-campaign-to-muscle-out-fannie-and-freddie.html?_r=0.

47. David H. Stevens, "Why We Need to Move Past 'Recap and Release,'" *The Hill*, June 13, 2016. http://thehill.com/blogs/congress-blog/economy-budget/283271-why-we-need-to-move-past-recap-and-release. David Stevens is the current president and CEO of the MBA.

48. In a 2010 FHFA study, the credit quality and performance of mortgages purchased by the GSEs are compared to those used in private label securitizations. By almost every measure, GSE loan performance was considerably better than that for non-GSE loans. Federal Housing Finance Agency, "Data on the Risk Characteristics and Performance of Single-Family Mortgages 2001–2008," September 13, 2010. www.fhfa.gov/PolicyProgramsResearch/Research/Pages/Data-on-the-Risk-Characteristics-and-Performance-of-Single-Family-Mortgages-2001–2008.aspx.

Industry analysts have made the same observation. In an *American Banker* op-ed, mortgage analyst Laurie Goodman is quoted as saying, "private label securitizations issued during 2005–2007 incurred a loss rate of 24%, whereas the GSE loss rate for

2005–2007 vintage loans was closer to 4%." David Fiderer, "GSE Critics Ignore Loan Performance," *American Banker*, May 17, 2013. www.americanbanker.com/bankthink /gse-critics-ignore-loan-performance-1059187-1.html.

49. *Financial Crisis Inquiry Report*, x. Wallison's point about ill-conceived government housing policy resurfaced at the end of 2012 in light of the announcement that the Federal Housing Administration, the only other source of mortgage finance these days, was basically insolvent. Wallison's colleague at AEI, Edward Pinto (a former Fannie Mae chief risk officer), analyzed FHA's post-crisis books of business and found a surprisingly high level of weak loans and high expected foreclosure rates. Worse, the highest risk loans are financing homes in poorer or high-minority neighborhoods, which bodes ill for recovery in those communities anytime soon. While liberal-leaning economists were quick to challenge Pinto's analysis, it's not the first time we've heard this complaint about well-meaning government policies gone awry. In the early 1990s, a consumer advocate named Gale Cincotta made the same argument to Freddie Mac staff about FHA and the same impassioned plea (but from the other side of the aisle): you are not "helping" our communities by giving us easy money.

50. Doug McKelway, "What to Cut: Calls to Shed Debt-Burdened Fannie, Freddie," FoxNews.com, March 28, 2013. www.foxnews.com/politics/2013/03/28/what-to-cut -calls-to-shed-debt-burdened-fannie-freddie/#ixzz2PFweaI38.

51. "*Special Report* Falsely Suggested Fannie and Freddie Chief Perpetrators of Financial Mess, Rep. Frank Opposed Stricter Oversight," Newscorpwatch, October 1, 2008. www.newscorpwatch.org/research/200810010014.

52. Arnold Kling, "The Financial Crisis: Moral Failure or Cognitive Failure?" *Harvard Journal of Law and Public Policy* 33 (2010): 508–510. www.harvard-jlpp.com /33-2/507.pdf.

53. "Remarks by Counselor to the Secretary for Housing Finance Policy Dr. Michael Stegman before the Goldman Sachs Third Annual Housing Finance Conference," March 5, 2015. www.treasury.gov/press-center/press-releases/Pages/jl9987.aspx.

Chapter 2. Homeownership: Dream or Nightmare?

1. Maya Angelou, *All God's Children Need Traveling Shoes* (New York: Vintage Books, 1991).

2. *Gone with the Wind*, directed by Victor Fleming (Hollywood, CA: Metro-Golden Mayer, 1939).

3. Charles Sheldon, *In His Steps* (New York: Barbour and Company, 1984), 9.

4. Bipartisan Housing Commission, "Housing America's Future, New Directions for National Policy," 40. http://bipartisanpolicy.org/wp-content/uploads/sites/default /files/BPC_Housing%20Report_web_0.pdf.

5. Ibid., 16.

6. Susan Wharton Gates, "FHA at a Crossroads," *Secondary Mortgage Market Magazine*, Freddie Mac, Vol. 11, No. 3.

7. Sam Ro, "Robert Shiller Destroys the Idea of Investing in a Home," *Business Insider*, February 7, 2013. www.businessinsider.com/robert-shiller-home-investment -a-fad-2013-2#ixzz2SphwFBl7.

8. Margot Adler, "Behind the Ever-Expanding American Dream House," National Public Radio, July 4, 2006. www.npr.org/templates/story/story.php?storyId=5525283. See also Timothy Hurst, "30-Year Growth Spurt Ends for Average American House Size," Ecopolitology, February 21, 2010. http://ecopolitology.org/2010/02/21/30-year-growth-spurth-ends-for-average-american-house-size/.

9. Bipartisan Housing Commission, "Housing America's Future," 39.

10. Quotations are taken from Richard Green and Michelle White, "Measuring the Benefits of Homeowning: Effects on Children," Journal of Urban Economics 41 (1997): 441–442.

11. Richard Green and Michelle White found that children of homeowning parents are less likely to drop out of school or to have children as teenagers. "Measuring the Benefits of Homeowning: Effects on Children," Journal of Urban Economics 41 (1997): 441–461. Donald Haurin, Toby Parcel, and R. Jean Haurin found that homeownership improves the educational attainment of children while reducing behavioral problems. "The Impact of Homeownership on Child Outcomes," Joint Center for Housing Studies, Harvard University, October 2001.

12. Bipartisan Housing Commission, "Housing America's Future," 21. The data were drawn from a study by the National Association of Homebuilders. See Helen Fei Liu and Paul Emrath, The Direct Impact of Home Building and Remodeling on the US Economy (Washington, DC: National Association of Home Builders, 2008).

13. Ibid., 21. The report notes that "if residential fixed investment reflected its historical average, the current rate of economic growth could double."

14. According to the National Alliance to End Homelessness, in 2012 the national homeless rate was 20 homeless people per 10,000 people in the general population; among veterans it was 29 homeless per 10,000. A point-in-time estimate taken in January 2012 found more than 630,000 people homeless, a slight decline from 2012. However, declining median income, rising rents, and increases in those living in poverty suggest that improvements may not be sustainable. In 2011, the national poverty rate was 15.9 percent, representing more than 48 million people. Homelessness Research Institute and National Alliance to End Homelessness, "The State of Homelessness in America 2013," 3. http://b.3cdn.net/naeh/bb34a7e4cd84ee985c_3vm6r7cjh.pdf.

15. Andrew Oswald, "Economist Debates: Home-Ownership," The Economist, September 19, 2012. www.economist.com/debate/days/view/882/print. "In a sensibly functioning economy it is easy for people to move around to drop into the vibrant job slots thrown up by technological change. That movement is particularly necessary for the young, who are looking for their early jobs. High home-ownership in a nation is like a treacle blanket thrown over the surface of the country and economy. With a high degree of owner-occupation, everything slows. Folks get stuck. Worse, they become long-distance commuters and clog up the motorways for their neighbours. Renters can up sticks and go to new jobs. In that way they do the economy a favour. Milton Friedman knew this. In a famous speech published in the 1968 American Economic Review he said that the equilibrium rate of unemployment depends on the flexibility of the housing market."

16. Analytical Perspectives, Budget of the United States Government, Fiscal Year

2017, 229. www.whitehouse.gov/sites/default/files/omb/budget/fy2017/assets/ap_14 _expenditures.pdf

17. The four rental subsidies are: exception from passive loss rules for $25,000 of rental loss, credit for low-income housing investments, accelerated depreciation on rental housing, and exclusion of interest on rental housing bonds.

18. Seth Hanlon, "Tax Expenditure of the Week: The Mortgage Interest Deduction," Center for American Progress, January 26, 2011. www.americanprogress.org/issues /open-government/news/2011/01/26/8866/tax-expenditure-of-the-week-the-mortgage -interest-deduction.

19. For an excellent explanation of the history of the MID, regressivity, and policy recommendations, see Eric J. Toder, co-director of the Urban-Brookings Tax Policy Center, "Testimony before the Committee on Ways and Means, United States House of Representatives, Hearing on Tax Reform and Residential Real Estate," April 25, 2013. www.taxpolicycenter.org/UploadedPDF/1001677-Toder-Ways-and-Means-MID.pdf.

20. Diana Olick, "Americans Are Tapping Into Home Equity Again," CNBC, February 8, 2013. www.cnbc.com/id/100446233.

21. Analytical Perspectives, Budget of the United States Government, Fiscal Year 2017, 229. www.whitehouse.gov/sites/default/files/omb/budget/fy2017/assets/ap_14 _expenditures.pdf.

22. Eric J. Toder, Institute Fellow, Urban Institute, and Co-Director, Urban-Brookings Tax Policy Center, Testimony Before the Committee on Ways and Means, United States House of Representatives Hearing on Tax Reform and Residential Real Estate, April 25, 2013, 6. www.taxpolicycenter.org/uploadedpdf/1001677-toder-ways -and-means-mid.pdf.

23. International Monetary Fund, "United States: Selected Issues Paper," July 2010, 44. www.imf.org/external/pubs/ft/scr/2010/cr10248.pdf.

24. Ibid., 46.

25. Congressional Budget Office, "Federal Subsidies and the Housing GSEs," May 2001, 2, table 1. www.cbo.gov/sites/default/files/cbofiles/ftpdocs/28xx/doc2841/gses .pdf. In a footnote, CBO quotes a former Federal Reserve chairman as noting, "The GSE subsidy is unusual in that its size is determined by market perceptions, not by legislation. Indeed the prospectuses of the debentures issued by GSEs explicitly state that they are not backed by the full faith and credit of the United States government. Accordingly, the extent to which the subsidy is exploited is determined by the extent to which GSEs choose to issue debt and mortgage-backed securities, not by legislation." Letter to Congressman Richard H. Baker, August 25, 2000.

26. Ibid.

27. Alan Greenspan, "Regulatory Reform of the Government-Sponsored Enterprises," Testimony Before the Committee on Banking, Housing, and Urban Affairs, US Senate, April 6, 2005. www.federalreserve.gov/boarddocs/testimony/2005/20050406/default .htm.

28. Subsequent research by the Federal Reserve would further reduce the value of the subsidy passed through to homeowners—and attendant impact on homeownership rates. See "The GSE Implicit Subsidy and the Value of Government Ambiguity," by

Wayne Passmore, Board of Governors of the Federal Reserve System. As Passmore notes, "I conclude that the value of the federal government's ambiguous relationship to GSE shareholders is positive, very large, and does not seem to result in an increase in home-ownership. See FRB staff working paper 2005–05 available at www.federalreserve.gov /pubs/feds/2005/200505/200505pap.pdf.

29. US Department of Commerce, *Residential Vacancies and Homeownership in the Fourth Quarter 2015.* www.census.gov/housing/hvs/files/currenthvspress.pdf.

30. Suzanne Mettler, *The Submerged State: How Invisible Government Policies Undermine American Democracy* (Chicago: University of Chicago Press, 2011), 23.

31. Ibid., 26.

32. Bipartisan Housing Commission, "Housing America's Future," 21.

33. James Truslow Adams, *The Epic of America* (New York: Little Brown and Company, 1931).

Chapter 3. Securitization Breakdown

1. *It's a Wonderful Life*, directed by Frank Capra (Culver City, CA: RKO Radio Pictures, 1946).

2. W. Scott Frame and Lawrence J. White, "Fussing and Fuming Over Fannie and Freddie: How Much Smoke and How much Fire?" Federal Reserve Bank of Atlanta, Working Paper 2004-26, 2004, 5. www.frbatlanta.org/filelegacydocs/wp0426.pdf.

3. Ibid. According to Scott Frame, economist with the Federal Reserve Bank of Atlanta, "A major motivation for the conversion of Freddie Mac to a publicly traded company was the belief that a wider potential share-holding public would raise the price of the shares held by the then ailing S&L industry and thus improve the balance sheets of the latter."

4. *The Financial Crisis Inquiry Report* (New York: Public Affairs, 2011), 316.

5. Ibid., 45.

6. Arnold Kling, "The Financial Crisis: Moral Failure or Cognitive Failure?" *Harvard Journal of Law & Public Policy* 33 (2010): 513.

7. Edward J. DeMarco, Acting Director, Federal Housing Finance Agency, "An Update from the Federal Housing Finance Agency on Oversight of Fannie Mae, Freddie Mac and the Federal Home Loan Banks," Statement before the US Senate Committee on Banking, Housing and Urban Affairs, April 18, 2013, 8. www.fhfa.gov/webfiles /25114/DeMarcoSenateBankingTestimony41813.pdf.

8. Housing Wire, "New FHFA Director Stops Rate Hikes Short," December 23, 2013. www.housingwire.com/articles/28387-new-fhfa-director-stops-rate-hikes-short.

9. In December 2011, Congress passed the Temporary Payroll Tax Cut Continuation Act, which directed FHFA to increase GSE guarantee fees by at least 10 basis points, on average, to fund a two-month extension of the payroll tax cut.

10. Analytical Perspectives, Budget of the United States Government, Fiscal Year 2017, 312. These amounts are above and beyond the billions the GSE are remitting to the government under the terms of the Third Amendment. www.whitehouse.gov/sites /default/files/omb/budget/fy2017/assets/ap_20_credit.pdf.

11. On March 14, 2013, the "Jumpstart GSE Reform Act" was introduced in the

Senate Banking Committee by US Senators Bob Corker, R-TN, Mark Warner, D-VA, David Vitter, R-LA, and Elizabeth Warren, D-MA.

12. "Corker, Warner, Vitter and Warren Introduce 'Jumpstart GSE Reform Act,'" March 14, 2013. www.corker.senate.gov/public/index.cfm/news?ID=76f378c0-c1f9-4316-8023-014b4db2ae8d.

13. Analytical Perspectives, Budget of the United States Government, Fiscal Year 2017, 314.

14. "Freddie Mac First Quarter 2013 Financial Results Supplement," May 8, 2013, 17. www.freddiemac.com/investors/er/pdf/supplement_1q13.pdf.

15. Fannie Mae 10-Q for the quarterly period ended March 31, 2013. www.fanniemae.com/resources/file/ir/pdf/quarterly-annual-results/2013/q12013.pdf.

16. Federal Housing Finance Agency, *2014 Report to Congress*, 8.

17. Ibid., 17.

18. QRM rule released March 2011 by the Federal Deposit Insurance Corporation and the Federal Reserve.

19. Alan Ziebel, "Bair to Regulators: Don't 'Eviscerate' Mortgage Rules," *Wall Street Journal*, November 6, 2013. http://wsj.com/washwire/2013/11/01/sheila-bair-dont-eviscerate-mortgage-rules.

20. Floyd Norris, "Mortgages Without Risk, at Least for the Banks," *New York Times*, November 28, 2013.

21. Brenna Swanson, "Fannie and Freddie Officially Approve 3% Down Payment Mortgages," *Housing Wire*, December 8, 2014. www.housingwire.com/articles/32269-fannie-and-freddie-officially-approve-3-down-payment-mortgages.

Chapter 4. Charter Confusion

1. Richard W. Stevenson, "House Banking Chief Wants Freddie Mac Bond Inquiry," *New York Times*, April 11, 1987.

2. Bethany McLean and Joe Nocera, *All the Devils Are Here: The Hidden History of the Financial Crisis* (New York: Penguin, 2010), 47.

3. "Freddie Mac Information Statement and Annual Report to Stockholders for Fiscal Year ended December 31, 2004," *Freddie Mac 2004 Annual Report*, 11. www.freddiemac.com/investors/ar/pdf/2004annualrpt.pdf.

4. For a fuller description of Freddie Mac's incentive compensation program, see Office of Federal Housing Oversight, "Report of the Special Examination of Freddie Mac," December 2003, 60. www.fhfa.gov/SupervisionRegulation/LegalDocuments/Documents/Litigation/v_Leland_Brendsel/brendseldeclareexa.pdf.

5. Ibid.

6. This was the case in 2008 when fear of a collapsing market caused investors to flee the US housing market for the safety of other instruments, such as US Treasuries. Falling demand for mortgages causes yields to rise—and borrowers pay higher mortgage rates as a result.

7. As former Fannie Mae CFO Tim Howard recounts in his book *Mortgage Wars*, there was no love lost between the GSEs and the MI companies, which owed their existence to lobbying prowess. Howard dubbed the MIs "Government Mandated

Enterprises," or "Gimmies" for short. Timothy Howard, *The Mortgage Wars* (New York: McGraw Hill Education, 2014), 92–94.

8. The GSE conforming loan limit is set annually by the Federal Housing Finance Agency. www.fhfa.gov/GetFile.aspx?FileID=135.

9. In 2008, to keep mortgage money flowing following the housing crash, the loan limit was raised to $729,250 in areas of the country deemed to be "high cost." This provided greater financing in higher-cost states like California and Massachusetts.

10. Federal Housing Finance Agency, "2016 Maximum Conforming Loan Limits Established for Fannie Mae and Freddie Mac," November 25, 2015. www.fhfa.gov/Media /PublicAffairs/Pages/2016-Maximum-Fannie-and-Freddie-Conforming-Loan-Limits -Established.aspx.

11. See *Freddie Mac Charter*, Sec. 305(a)(2). www.freddiemac.com/governance/pdf /charter.pdf.

12. Other factors appear to have more influence in explaining default rate differences between borrower income groups. For example, pre- and post-purchase mortgage counseling has been shown to reduce borrower default rates.

13. By the time the GSEs were placed in conservatorship in 2008, the housing goals were considerably more onerous, accounting for well over 50 percent of business activity.

14. *Financial Crisis Inquiry Report* (New York: Public Affairs, 2011), 309.

15. Until the financial crisis hit, bank regulators were ready to allow lower bank capital ratios consistent with those included in the Basel II Accord in an effort to remain competitive with European banks. This would have made bank capital requirements for large banks at or below comparable GSE capital requirements for mortgages.

16. Thomas H. Stanton, "Government-Sponsored Enterprises and Changing Markets: The Need for an Exit Strategy," *The Financier: ACMT* 2, no. 2 (May 1995): 30. www.thomas-stanton.com/pubs/gse/GSE-Need_for_an_Exit_Stragety.pdf.

17. Ronald C. Moe, "The Emerging Federal Quasi Government: Issues of Management and Accountability," *Public Administration Review* 61, no. 3 (May/June 2001): 290–312.

18. Congressional Budget Office, "Controlling the Risks of Government Sponsored Enterprises," April 1991, xvii.

19. Congressional Budget Office, "Updated Estimates of the Subsidies to the Housing GSEs," April 8, 2004. www.cbo.gov/sites/default/files/cbofiles/ftpdocs/53xx /doc5368/04-08-gse.pdf.

20. Adam J. Levitin and Susan M. Wachter, "Why Housing?" *Housing Policy Debate* 23, no. 1 (2013): 5–27.

21. *Financial Crisis Inquiry Report* (New York: Public Affairs, 2011), 321.

Chapter 5. Affordable Housing

1. In HERA, the GSE reform legislation enacted in July 2008, responsibilities for mission and safety soundness were combined under one regulator, the Federal Housing Finance Agency.

2. Freddie Mac press release, February 13, 2004. The link to the press release on Freddie Mac's website is no longer functional.

3. Alex Berenson, "$6 Billion Loan Deal by Freddie Mac Examined by US," *New York Times*, March 27, 2004. www.nytimes.com/2004/03/27/business/6-billion-loan -deal-by-freddie-mac-examined-by-us.html.

4. Rob Blackwell, "Freddie and HUD Not Seeing Eye to Eye on Goals," *American Banker*, May 20, 2004. www.americanbanker.com/issues/169_98/index.html?issue _month=01&issue_day=02&issue_year=2011.

5. CEO Syron announced Freddie Mac's HMDA commitment in a speech to the LBJ School of Public Affairs at the University of Texas on May 13, 2004. The link to the speech on Freddie Mac's website is no longer functional.

6. See, for example, Dennis Glennon and Mitchell Stengel, "An Evaluation of the Federal Reserve Bank of Boston's Study of Racial Discrimination in Mortgage Lending," Office of the Comptroller of the Currency Working Paper 94-2, April 1994. In this paper, OCC researchers examined the criticism of the original Boston Fed study and gave a "qualified confirmation of the results" pending further research. www.occ.gov /publications/publications-by-type/economics-working-papers/1999-1993/working -paper-1994-2.html. In 1999, the Urban Institute also considered the critiques of the original study in "Mortgage Lending Discrimination: A Review of Existing Evidence," 43–84. The UI analysis generally supports the original study, concluding that "the large differences in loan denial between minority and white applicants identified by Munnell et al. cannot be explained by data errors, omitted variables, or the endogeneity of loan terms." www.urban.org/UploadedPDF/mortgage_lending.pdf.

7. Alicia H. Munnell, Lynn E. Browne, James McEneaney, and Geoffrey M. B. Tootell, "Mortgage Lending in Boston: Interpreting HMDA Data," Federal Reserve Bank of Boston Working Paper No. 92-7, October 1992, 2. www.bos.frb.org/economic /wp/wp1992/wp92_7.pdf.

8. Years later, consumer advocates urged the GSEs to give underwriting credit to immigrant borrowers who sent remittances back to their home countries and to apartment dwellers who paid their utility bills on time. Freddie Mac economists considered these requests but invariably concluded that to be a successful homeowner, a borrower needs to have skin in the game in the form of a down payment; needs to make enough money to afford the monthly payments plus a reserve for the unexpected costs; and needs a decent record handling credit—which is more than simply paying bills on time.

9. *Financial Crisis Inquiry Report* (New York: Public Affairs, 2011), 127.

10. Ibid., 224.

11. Ibid., 184. Similar reasons are recounted by "dozens of current and former Fannie Mae employees and regulators."

12. Ibid., 187.

13. See, for example, *Housing America's Future: New Direction for National Policy*, 66.

14. Analytical Perspectives, Budget of the United States Government, Fiscal Year 2017, 311–312.

15. Ibid., 314. The three funds are the Housing Trust Fund, the Capital Magnet Fund, and the HOPE Reserve Fund. FHFA, Treasury, and HUD are charged with allocating, administering, and distributing the funds in accordance with the statutory purpose of each fund.

16. Ibid.

Chapter 6. Subprime Semantics

1. The GSE charters specified that the operations of the GSEs were "confined so far as practicable to residential mortgages which are deemed by the Corporation to be of such quality, type and class as to meet generally the purchase standards imposed by private institutional mortgage investors." See *Freddie Mac Charter*, Sec. 305 (a)(1).

2. Joshua Rosner, "Fannie Mae and Freddie Mac: How Government Housing Policy Failed Homeowners and Taxpayers and Led to the Financial Crisis," Testimony before the Subcommittee on Capital Markets and Government Sponsored Enterprises. http://financialservices.house.gov/uploadedfiles/hhrg-113-ba16-wstate-jrosner-20130306.pdf.

3. David S. Hilzenrath, "Buffett Testifies That He Saw Early Signs of Freddie Mac's Woes," *Washington Post*, October 31, 2007. www.washingtonpost.com/wp-dyn/content/article/2007/10/30/AR2007103002292.html.

4. *Financial Crisis Inquiry Report*, 123.

5. Roberto G. Quercia, Allison Freeman, and Janneke Ratcliffe, *Regaining the Dream: How to Renew the Promise of Homeownership for America's Working Families* (Washington, DC: Brookings Institution Press, 2011), 44.

6. Rakesh Kochar, Ana Gonzalez-Barrera, and Daniel Dockterman, "Minorities, Immigrants and Homeownership; Through Boom and Bust," Pew Hispanic Center, May 12, 2009. See figure 14. www.pewhispanic.org/2009/05/12/through-boom-and-bust.

7. Ylan Q. Mui, "For Black Americans, Financial Damage from Subprime Implosion Is Likely to Last," *Washington Post*, July 12, 2012. www.washingtonpost.com/business/economy/for-black-americans-financial-damage-from-subprime-implosion-is-likely-to-last/2012/07/08/gJQAwNmzWW_story.html.

8. A summary of allegations is available at www.sec.gov/litigation/complaints/2011/comp-pr2011-267-freddiemac.pdf. Of note, "While Freddie Mac disclosed during the Relevant Period [March 2007 to August 2008] that the exposure of its Single Family Guarantee business to subprime loans was between $2 billion and $6 billion, or between 0.1 percent and 0.2 percent, of Freddie Mac's Single Family Guarantee portfolio—its exposure to subprime was materially greater. As of December 31, 2006, Freddie Mac's Single Family Guarantee business was exposed to approximately $141 billion (or 10 percent of the portfolio) in loans the Company internally referred to as 'subprime,' 'otherwise subprime' or 'subprime-like' and its exposure grew to approximately $244 billion (or 14 percent of the portfolio) by June 30, 2008, as the Company sought to win back lost market share by increasing its acquisition of such loans."

9. Edward J. Pinto, "Examining the Proper Role of the Federal Housing Administration in our Mortgage Insurance Market," Statement before the Committee on Financial Services US House of Representatives, February 6, 2013, 10.

http://financialservices.house.gov/uploadedfiles/hhrg-113-ba00-wstate-epinto-20130206.pdf.

10. Ibid. See especially p. 17 of PowerPoint presentation included in testimony.

Chapter 7. Political Capture

1. Bethany McLean and Joe Nocera, *All the Devils Are Here: The Hidden History of the Financial Crisis* (New York: Penguin Group, 2010), xi.

2. *Freddie Mac 2005 Annual Report*, 36. See table 17, "Characteristics of Mortgage Loans and Mortgage-Related Securities in the Retained Portfolio." www.freddiemac .com/investors/ar/pdf/2005annualrpt.pdf.

3. *Freddie Mac 2005 Annual Report*, 49. See table 29, "Debt Security Issuances by Product, at Par Value."

4. See, for example, David H. Stevens, "Sustainable Housing Finance: Perspectives on Reforming FHA," Testimony before the Subcommittee on Housing and Insurance, Committee on Financial Services, US House of Representatives, April 10, 2013. "In short, the social consequences of increasing the minimum [FHA] down payment requirement could be dramatic. An increase would unnecessarily delay home purchase for many Americans who might be successful homeowners, with the greatest impact falling on the underserved. In particular, a tiered down payment structure would place a greater financial burden on borrowers who may have the least amount of savings." www.mbaa.org/files/News/InternalResource/84168_StevensFHATestimony041013.pdf.

5. Treasury "line of credit" is a misnomer. Actually, the legislative language specified that the Treasury department was authorized to advance to the GSEs amounts up to $2.25 billion.

6. Mike Soroghan, "Official's Testimony on GSEs Shakes Bond Market," *Real Estate Finance Today*, March 27, 2000.

7. Written Statement of Leland C. Brendsel, Chairman and CEO, Freddie Mac, before the Subcommittee on Capital Markets, Securities and Government-Sponsored Enterprises, of the Committee on Banking and Financial Services, US House of Representatives, May 16, 2000. http://archives.financialservices.house.gov/banking /51600bre.shtml.

8. The death of former British Prime Minister Margaret Thatcher in 2013 led to reflections on her housing policy, which was a blend of "social conservatism and neo-liberalism." Key aspects were the sale of the nation's stock of public housing and increased subsidies for homeownership, akin to the US mortgage interest tax deduction. While many profited from her "right to buy" initiative, some view these policies as "sowing the seeds" of the United Kingdom's housing crisis. See Kevin Gulliver, "Thatcher's Legacy: Her Role in Today's Housing Crisis," Housing Network Blog, *The Guardian*, April 17, 2013. www.guardian.co.uk/housing-network/2013/apr/17/margaret -thatcher-legacy-housing-crisis.

9. As described years later in a *Wall Street Journal* editorial, Freddie's stable of conservative consultants included former Senator Al D'Amato, Congressman Vin Weber, and then-House Majority Leader Tom Delay's former chief of staff, Susan Hirshmann. "As we know by now, Fan and Fred tried to buy everybody in town from both political parties, and the companies did it well enough to make themselves immune from regulatory scrutiny." "Whitewashing Fannie Mae," *Wall Street Journal*, December 11, 2008. www.wsj.com/articles/SB122895461803096429.

10. State of the Union Address, February 12, 2013. www.whitehouse.gov/the-press -office/2013/02/12/president-barack-obamas-state-union-address-prepared-delivery.

11. Zachary A. Goldfarb, "Obama Administration Pushes Banks to Make Home Loans to People with Weaker Credit," *Washington Post*, April 2, 2013. www

.washingtonpost.com/business/economy/obama-administration-pushes-banks-to
-make-home-loans-to-people-with-weaker-credit/2013/04/02/a8b4370c-9aef-11e2
-a941-a19bce7af755_story.html.

12. Emily Badger, "Around Atlanta, the Housing Recovery's Great Divide is in Stark Black and White," *Washington Post*, May 1, 2016. www.washingtonpost.com/graphics /business/wonk/housing/atlanta.

Chapter 8. Who's Ultimately Responsible?

1. *Financial Crisis Inquiry Report* (New York: Public Affairs, 2011), 94.

2. Ibid., 96.

3. Subsequent research funded by the Center for Community Capital found that "the coverage of HOEPA law was quite limited and virtually no mortgages were originated that were covered by HOEPA's high-cost threshold, likely because the HOEPA threshold was quite high and also because subprime lenders learned how to avoid it." Lei Ding, Roberto G. Quercia, Carolina K. Reid, and Alan M. White, "The Preemption Effect: The Impact of Federal Preemption of State Anti-Predatory Lending Laws on the Foreclosure Crisis," Research Report, Center for Community Capital, August 27, 2010, 7. http://ccc.unc.edu/contentitems/the-impact-of-federal-preemption-of-state-anti -predatory-lending-laws-on-the-foreclosure-crisis.

4. *Financial Crisis Inquiry Report*, 112. "In August 2003 the OCC issued its first preemptive order, aimed at Georgia's mini-HOEPA statute, and in January 2004 the OCC adopted a sweeping preemption rule applying to all state laws that interfered with or placed conditions on national banks' ability to lend. Shortly afterward, three large banks with combined assets of more than $1 trillion said they would convert from state charters to national charters, which increased OCC's annual budget 15%."

5. "Ga. Mortgage Law Prompts Lender Flight," Associated Press, January 22, 2003. Available at www.myplainview.com/article_f03e88a9-e5c3-5246-b81b-b210a0038dfc .html.

6. "Freeloading Freddie Mac Out of Bounds," *Atlanta Journal Constitution*, March 23, 2003.

7. Michael Hirsch, "The Predators' Ball: Fannie Mae and Freddie Mac Have Helped Defang Laws That Might Have Prevented the Subprime Mess," *Newsweek*, August 9, 2008.

8. Lei Ding, Roberto G. Quercia, Carolina K. Reid, and Alan M. White, "State Anti-Predatory Lending Laws and Neighborhood Foreclosure Rates," December 17, 2010, 7. http://clas.wayne.edu/Multimedia/DUSP/files/L_Ding/APL_Neighborhood _Impact_forthcoming.pdf.

9. Ibid., 2.

10. "Testimony of OCC Comptroller John C. Dugan before the Financial Crisis Inquiry Commission," April 8, 2010, 7. www.occ.gov/news-issuances/congressional -testimony/2010/pub-test-2010-39-written.pdf.

11. For specific requirements, see pages 9 and 10 of the OCC's final rule on Office of Thrift Supervision Integration and Dodd-Frank Act Implementation, July 20, 2011. Available at www.occ.gov/news-issuances/news-releases/2011/nr-occ-2011-95a.pdf.

12. "OCC Issues Final Rule to Implement Provisions of the Dodd-Frank Act," July 20, 2011. Available at www.occ.gov/news-issuances/news-releases/2011/nr-occ-2011 -95.html.

Chapter 9. Scandal(s)

1. See, for instance, page 5 of the so-called Baker Botts report: "At this writing, the story is not one of rampant criminal misconduct, abuse of authority for personal gain but of serious failures by senior management to discharge responsibilities entrusted to them and placed on them by the Board." "Report to the Board of Directors of Freddie Mac by Baker Botts, LLP," www.freddiemac.com/news/board_report/pdf/second.pdf.

2. According to a 2013 survey of credit unions, 93 percent of respondents cite increasing regulatory burdens as a result of DFA, and 88 percent report higher compliance costs. "NAFCU Survey: Most CUs Will Reduce or Discontinue Non-QM Mortgages," *Credit Union Times*, May 30, 2013. www.cutimes.com/2013/05/15/nafcu -survey-most-cus-will-reduce-or-discontinue-n.

3. "Report to the Board of Directors of Freddie Mac by Baker Botts, LLP," 2–3. www.freddiemac.com/news/board_report/pdf/second.pdf.

4. "Freddie Mac Announces Record Earnings for 2002 Expects Cumulative Earnings to Be Restated Upward," *PR Newswire*, January 27, 2003. www.prnewswire.com /news-releases/freddie-mac-announces-record-earnings-for-2002-expects-cumulative -earnings-to-be-restated-upward-74022577.html.

5. Eric Dash, "Fannie Mae to Restate Results by $6.3 Billion Because of Accounting," *New York Times*, December 7, 2006. www.nytimes.com/2006/12/07/business /07fannie.html?_r=0.

6. Linda Corman, "Lost in the Maze," *CFO Magazine*, May 8, 2006. The article reports that in 2005, "57 companies restated their earnings because of faulty hedge accounting, up from 27 in 2004 and 13 in 2003." www.cfo.com/article.cfm/6874855 /c_2984409/.

7. For a good discussion of the cultural divide between economics and accounting see pages 5–7 of "Report of the Special Examination of Freddie Mac," December 2003. www.fhfa.gov/webfiles/749/specialreport122003.pdf.

8. Office of Federal Housing Enterprise Oversight, "Report of the Special Examination of Freddie Mac," December 2003, ii. http://abcnews.go.com/images/Blotter /specialreport122003.pdf. For insight on how Freddie Mac employees worked with dealer counterparts to engage in noneconomic transactions, see the recorded transcript between Ray Powers of Freddie Mac and Robert Lavelle of Morgan Stanley on pages 77–79 of the report.

9. Ibid., i.

10. Ibid., iii.

11. Ibid., 71.

12. Ibid., v–vi.

13. As quoted in the 2003 "Report of the Special Investigation," "Thomas Jones, Chairman of the Audit Committee of the Board, recalled expressing his views to Leland Brendsel in March 2003 regarding the lack of audited financial statements of the

Enterprise: 'Leland, with all due respect, in my view you've put the company in a very difficult situation. You've effectively lost control of our accounting and financial reporting status and we're now sitting in a situation where we don't have audited financial statements in the market and we're one of the most critical financial entities in the capital markets. In my view it is unpardonable to not have audited financial statements that investors can rely upon and in my view in this league you don't get second chances. You've been paid a lot of money to do this job and to me it's unacceptable that we don't have audited financial statements that investors can rely upon.'" Federal Housing Finance Agency, "Report of the Special Examination of Freddie Mac," 59.

14. For the full Baker Botts report, see www.freddiemac.com/news/board_report /pdf/second.pdf.

15. "Criminal Probe Opens on Freddie Mac Conduct," June 12, 2003, *Chicago Tribune*. http://articles.chicagotribune.com/2003-06-12/business/0306120331_1 _freddie-mac-review-accounting-errors-home-mortgage-market.

16. Federal Housing Finance Agency, "Report of the Special Examination of Freddie Mac," December 2003, vi.

17. Bob Specter and Andrew Zajac, "Freddie Mac Scandals Began During Emanuel's Watch," *Chicago Tribune*, March 26, 2009.

18. The 2003 special report cited Parseghian for overseeing certain noneconomic transactions designed to smooth earnings without obtaining proper authorization. "Although Mr. Parseghian admitted that the business purpose of the linked swaps was marginal relative to their income effects, there is no evidence that he or his staff checked with Arthur Andersen before executing the swaps, and there is no written evidence that Corporate Accounting provided approval before the swaps were executed. Robert Arnall, the Arthur Andersen engagement partner, found out about the swaps after they were executed and complained to David Glenn and others . . . Mr. Arnall told them that the swaps were bare minimum on GAAP compliance and encouraged them to terminate the transactions. However, management did not unwind the transactions until much later, when nearly all of the intended effect on operating earnings had been achieved." Federal Housing Finance Agency, "Report of the Special Examination of Freddie Mac," December 2003, 47–48.

19. Jonathan Glater, "Freddie Mac Picked Chief It Knew Had Role in Its Troubles," *New York Times*, July 26, 2003. www.nytimes.com/2003/07/26/business/freddie-mac -picked-chief-it-knew-had-role-in-Its-troubles.html.

20. Pete Yost, "Freddie Mac Lobbyist Staged 50 GOP Fund-Raisers as Congress Let Legislation Die," *Associated Press*, July 18, 2003.

21. Kathleen Day, "Influence by Volume: Freddie Mac Lobbyist Got a Big Discount on GOP Fundraising Dinners at Galileo's," *Washington Post*, August 4, 2003.

22. Ibid.

23. "Complaint by Public Citizen before the Federal Election Commission," 1. www.citizen.org/documents/ACFABS.pdf.

24. Office of Federal Housing Enterprises Oversight, "Report of the Special Examination of Freddie Mac," December 2003, 59. www.fhfa.gov/webfiles/749 /specialreport122003.pdf.

25. *Financial Crisis Inquiry Report* (New York: Public Affairs, 2011), 180.

26. See "United States District Court for the Southern District of New York, US Securities and Exchange Commission v. Richard F. Syron, Patricia L. Cook and Donald J. Bisenius," December 18, 2011. The complaint alleges that the defendants "misled investors into believing that the Company had far less exposure to these riskier mortgages than in fact existed." See www.sec.gov/litigation/complaints/2011/comp-pr2011-267-freddiemac.pdf.

27. Federal Election Commission, "Freddie Mac Pays Largest Fine in FEC History," April 18, 2006. www.fec.gov/press/press2006/20060418mur.html.

28. *Financial Crisis Inquiry Report*, 319.

Chapter 10. Battle for Responsible Credit Leadership

1. For a discussion of the cognitive differences between Andrukonis and Syron at Freddie Mac see Arnold Kling, "The Financial Crisis: Moral Failure or Cognitive Failure?" *Harvard Journal of Law and Public Policy* 33 (2010): 509–510. www.harvard-jlpp.com/33-2/507.pdf.

See also *Financial Crisis Inquiry Report* (New York: Public Affairs, 2011), 179.

2. This internal Freddie Mac memo, dated October 6, 2004, was made available to the House Committee on Oversight and Government Reform following the government takeover of the firm in 2008.

3. Kenneth Harney, "No-Tell NINA Loans Are Bad for Insurers, Buyers," *Seattle Times*, April 25, 2004. http://community.seattletimes.nwsource.com/archive/?date=20040425&slug=homeharn25.

4. Freddie Mac, internal e-mail, Donna Cogswell on behalf of David Andrukonis to Dick Syron, "RE: no Income/no asset (NINA) Mortgages," September 7, 2004. The e-mail is cited as Exhibit A on p. 299 in "Jino Kuriakose, Individually and on Behalf of All Others Similarly Situated, Plaintiff, vs. Federal Home Loan Mortgage Company, Richard Syron, Patricia L. Cook, and Anthony S. Piszel, available at www.protectconsumerjustice.org/wp-content/uploads/2009/11/Freddie-Mac-lawsuit.pdf. The e-mail is also cited in Peter J. Wallison, "Dissent from the Majority Report of the Financial Crisis Inquiry Commission," January 14, 2011, American Enterprise Institute for Public Policy Research, 73. www.aei.org/files/2011/01/26/Wallisondissent.pdf.

5. Gretchen Morgenson, "A Revolving Door Helps Big Banks' Quiet Campaign to Muscle Out Fannie and Freddie," *New York Times*, December 7, 2015. www.nytimes.com/2015/12/07/business/a-revolving-door-helps-big-banks-quiet-campaign-to-muscle-out-fannie-and-freddie.html?_r=0.

6. Federal Housing Finance Agency, "Data on the Risk Characteristics and Performance of Single-Family Mortgages Originated from 2001 through 2008 and Financed in the Secondary Market," September 13, 2010, 10.

7. Chris Murphy, "Freddie Mac Looks to Move On from Accounting Fiasco," *InformationWeek*, August 21, 2006. See also a description of Touch More Loans in the SEC complaint against Syron, Cook, and Bisenius, paragraphs 21 and 45, at www.sec.gov/litigation/complaints/2011/comp-pr2011-267-freddiemac.pdf.

8. Eric Stein, Center for Responsible Lending, "Turmoil in the US Credit Markets: The Genesis of the Current Economic Crisis," Testimony Before the US Senate Committee on Banking, Housing and Urban Affairs, October 16, 2008, p. 33.

9. David Hilzenrath, "'Piggyback' Loans Allowed by Freddie Fed Mortgage Risks," *Washington Post*, December 7, 2007. www.washingtonpost.com/wp-dyn/content/article/2007/12/06/AR2007120602618_2.html?sid=ST2007120700852.

10. Ibid.

Chapter 11. One Tough Bill

1. *Financial Crisis Inquiry Report* (New York: Public Affairs, 2011), 322.

2. From 1990 to 2003, the GSEs' combined investment portfolio had grown by more than tenfold, rising from $136 billion to $1.6 trillion. See N. Eric Weiss, "Limiting Fannie Mae's and Freddie Mac's Portfolio Size," CRS Report for Congress, http://congressionalresearch.com/RS22307/document.php?study=Limiting+Fannie+Maes+and+Freddie+Macs+Portfolio+Size.

3. As part of Treasury's bailout arrangement with the GSEs, the retained portfolios of both GSEs must be reduced to $250 billion by December 31, 2018.

4. In Freddie Mac's *2006 Annual Report*, the company's official position on the Democratic proposed legislation was as follows: "The provisions of this legislation, individually and in certain combinations, could have a material adverse effect on our ability to fulfill our mission, future earnings, stock price and stockholder returns, the rate of growth in our fair value, and our ability to recruit qualified officers and directors." *Freddie Mac 2006 Annual Report*, 27. www.freddiemac.com/investors/ar/pdf/2006annualrpt.pdf.

5. Ironically, the Bush administration had tried the tactic itself, paying nongovernment commentators to support Bush education and marriage policies.

6. Stephanie Condon, "Gingrich Fends Off Questions of Freddie Mac Fees," *CBS News*, November 16, 2011. www.cbsnews.com/8301-503544_162-57325790-503544/gingrich-fends-off-questions-on-freddie-mac-fees/.

7. Associated Press, "Freddie Mac Tried to Kill Republican Regulatory Bill in 2005," October 19, 2008. www.foxnews.com/story/0,2933,440681,00.html.

8. Ibid.

9. Henry M. Paulson, Jr., *On the Brink: Inside the Race to Stop the Collapse of the Global Financial System* (New York: Hachette Book Group, 2010), 164.

10. Gretchen Morgenson and Joshua Rosner, *Reckless Endangerment: How Outsized Ambition, Greed and Corporation Led to Economic Armageddon* (New York: Henry Holt, 2011), 303.

11. As cited earlier, losses on mortgages purchased by the GSEs fared comparatively better than comparable loans that ended up in Wall Street securities.

12. One indication of the wide difference between security income earned by the two GSEs is seen in a graph of net interest income (NII) for both firms from 2011 to 2015, included in FHFA's 2015 annual report to Congress. For Fannie Mae, at the end of 2015, roughly 70 percent of NII was comprised of revenue from management and guarantee fees; revenues earned on the company's shrinking retained mortgage portfolio accounted for the remaining 30 percent. For Freddie Mac, the income sources are reversed: guarantee fee income constitutes only about 45 percent of NII, with more than half of NII coming from proceeds from the retained portfolio. See Federal Housing

Finance Agency, *2015 Report to Congress*, 15. http://www.fhfa.gov/AboutUs/Reports/ReportDocuments/FHFA_2015_Report-to-Congress.pdf.

13. Jacob Gaffney, "Fannie and Freddie Help Brighten America's Credit Outlook," *Housing Wire*, June 10, 2013. In 2011, "Standard & Poor's downgraded the US credit rating from triple-A to double-A-plus—with a negative outlook. Thanks in part to strong profits from Fannie Mae and Freddie Mac, S&P reports the outlook on the long-term rating is revised to stable from negative." www.housingwire.com/news/2013/06/10/fannie-and-freddie-help-brighten-americas-credit-outlook.

14. W. Scott Frame, Andreas Fuster, Joseph Tracy, and James Vickery, "The Rescue of Fannie Mae and Freddie Mac," Federal Reserve Bank of New York Staff Report No. 719, March 2015. www.newyorkfed.org/research/staff_reports/sr719.pdf.

15. Jena McGregor, "Senate Pushes Back on Pay Raises for Fannie, Freddie CEOs," *Washington Post*, September 21, 2005. www.washingtonpost.com/news/on-leadership/wp/2015/09/17/senate-squashes-big-raises-for-the-ceos-of-fannie-mae-and-freddie-mac.

16. "A New Housing Finance System," *Washington Post*, September 28, 2015.

17. *2014 FHFA Report to Congress*, 17. www.fhfa.gov/AboutUs/Reports/ReportDocuments/FHFA_2014_Report_to_Congress.pdf.

18. Melvin L. Watt, "Prepared Remarks before the Bipartisan Policy Committee," February 18, 2016. www.fhfa.gov/Media/PublicAffairs/Pages/Prepared-Remarks-Melvin-Watt-at-BPC.aspx.

19. Ibid.

Chapter 12. Stand Up and Say

1. *Federal Register* Vol. 71, No. 192, October 4, 2006. www.fdic.gov/regulations/laws/federal/2006/06noticeFINAL.html.

2. Ellen Schloemer, Wei Li, Keith Ernst, and Kathleen Keest, "Losing Ground, Foreclosures in the Subprime Market and Their Cost to Homeowners," Center for Responsible Lending, December 2006. www.responsiblelending.org/mortgage-lending/research-analysis/foreclosure-paper-report-2-17.pdf.

3. *Federal Register* Vol. 71, No. 192, October 4, 2006, 58613. www.fdic.gov/regulations/laws/federal/2006/06noticeFINAL.html.

4. See *Freddie Mac 2007 Annual Report*, 12. www.freddiemac.com/investors/ar/pdf/2007annualrpt.pdf.

5. SEC complaint against CEO Richard F. Syron, Patricia L. Cook, and Donald J. Bisenius. "Each defendant made, or substantially assisted others in the making of, these misleading subprime disclosures at a time when each knew, or was reckless in not knowing, that the Company was increasing its acquisition of higher-risk loans that it internally referred to as 'subprime,' 'otherwise subprime' or 'subprime-like,'" 3. www.sec.gov/litigation/complaints/2011/comp-pr2011-267-freddiemac.pdf.

6. Judith A. Kennedy, President and CEO, National Association of Affordable Housing Lenders, "Statement on Legislative Proposals on GSE Reform," House Committee on Financial Services, US House of Representatives, March 15, 2007.

7. Peter J. Wallison, "Dissent from the Majority Report of the Financial Crisis Inquiry Commission," 79. www.aei.org/files/2011/01/26/Wallisondissent.pdf.

8. Eric Stein, Center for Responsible Lending, "Turmoil in the US Credit Markets: The Genesis of the Current Economic Crisis," Testimony Before the US Senate Committee on Banking, Housing and Urban Affairs, October 16, 2008, 33.

Chapter 13. The Unraveling

1. *Financial Crisis Inquiry Report* (New York: Public Affairs, 2011), 312.

2. Chris Isidore, "Freddie Mac Scrambles for Cash, Finance Company's Shares Plunge on News That It Has Turned to Wall Street and May Cut Dividends as Losses Cut Deep into Capital," CNNMoney.com, November 20, 2007.

3. According to researchers at the Federal Reserve, "the GSEs raised a total of about $22 billion of preferred securities in 2007 and 2008, with the bulk of that being issued over a two-week period in late November and early December 2007." Tara Rice and Jonathan Rose, "When Good Investments Go Bad: The Contraction in Community Bank Lending after the 2008 GSE Takeover," Board of Governors of the Federal Reserve System, March 2012, 6. www.federalreserve.gov/pubs/ifdp/2012/1045/ifdp1045.pdf.

4. "Subprime Winner, Patricia Cook on Freddie Mac's Corporate Mission and Why It's Good for Business," *Mortgage Risk*, October 2007, 10. http://db.riskwaters.com/data /mortgagerisk/mortgage_risk_1007.pdf.

5. Freddie Mac, Supplement dated November 9, 2007 to Information Statement dated March 23, 2007. www.freddiemac.com/investors/infostat/pdf/supplement _110907.pdf.

6. Ibid.

7. Charles Duhigg, "At Freddie Mac, Chief Discarded Warning Signs," *New York Times*, August 5, 2008. www.nytimes.com/2008/08/05/business/05freddie.html ?pagewanted=all&_r=0.

8. *Financial Crisis Inquiry Report*, 316.

9. Henry J. Paulson, *On the Brink: Inside the Race to Stop the Collapse of the Global Financial System* (New York: Hachette Book Group, 2010), 3.

10. Bethany McLean, *Shaky Ground: The Strange Saga of the US Mortgage Giants* (New York: Columbia Global Reports, 2015), 21.

11. *Financial Crisis Inquiry Report*, 317. See also Tara Rice and Jonathan Rose, "When Good Investments Go Bad." At the time of the takeover, "the value of the GSEs' equity capital was positive, and so both GSEs were technically solvent . . . but both were insolvent on an economic basis. The GSEs' reported fair values of equity were much lower than the book values, and both institutions had recorded large 'deferred tax assets.'"

12. Ibid., 318.

13. Charles Duhigg, "At Freddie Mac, Chief Discarded Warning Signs," *New York Times*, August 5, 2008.

14. Ibid.

15. *Financial Crisis Inquiry Report*, 319.

16. Ibid.

17. As described in a 2013 report by the Congressional Research Service, "the goal of conservatorship is to put the company on a sound financial footing, after which the

company is returned to stockholder control. If this cannot be accomplished, the firm is placed in receivership, which is roughly the equivalent of dissolving a bankrupt company. In certain situations their receivership is mandatory and in others receivership is voluntary." N. Eric Weiss, "GSEs and the Government's Role in Housing Finance: Issues for the 113th Congress," Congressional Research Service, February 11, 2013, 2.

18. David D. Kirkpatrick and Charles Duhigg, "Loan Titans Paid McCain Adviser Nearly $2 Million," *New York Times*, September 21, 2008. www.nytimes.com/2008/09 /22/us/politics/22mccain.html.

19. Eric Stein, Center for Responsible Lending, "Turmoil in the US Credit Markets: The Genesis of the Current Economic Crisis," Testimony Before the US Senate Committee on Banking, Housing and Urban Affairs, October 16, 2008, 33.

20. As he was no longer employed by Freddie Mac, Syron's congressional testimony was not written in house.

21. US Securities and Exchange Commission, "SEC Charges Former Fannie Mae and Freddie Mac Executives with Securities Fraud," December 16, 2011. www.sec.gov /news/press/2011/2011-267.htm.

22. Joe Light and Aruna Viswanatha, "SEC Reaches Settlement with Former Freddie Mac Executives," *Wall Street Journal*, April 14, 2015. www.wsj.com/articles/sec-reaches -settlement-with-former-freddie-mac-executives-1429044796.

Chapter 15. Housing's Future

1. Robert D. Putnam, *Our Kids: The American Dream in Crisis* (New York: Simon and Schuster, 2015).

2. Jim Parrott, Lewis Ranieri, Gene Sperling, Mark Zandi, and Barry Zigas, "A More Promising Road to GSE Reform," Urban Institute, March 2016. www.urban.org /sites/default/files/alfresco/publication-pdfs/2000746-A-More-Promising-Road-to-GSE -Reform.pdf.

3. Mark A. Calabria, "'Promising Road' to GSE Reform? We've Been Here Before," *National Mortgage News*, April 19, 2016. www.nationalmortgagenews.com/news/voices /promising-road-to-gse-reform-weve-been-here-before-1076108-1.html.

4. Board of Governors of the Federal Reserve System, Mortgage Debt Outstanding, June 2016. www.federalreserve.gov/econresdata/releases/mortoutstand/current.htm.

Chapter 16. Wherefore Ethics?

1. *Financial Crisis Inquiry Report* (New York: Public Affairs, 2011), xxii.

2. Jim Wallis, *The Soul of Politics: Beyond "Religious Right" and "Secular Left"* (New York: New Press, 1995), 175.

3. Michael J. Sandal, *Justice: What's the Right Thing to Do?* (New York: Farrar, Straus and Giroux, 2009), 194–195.

4. Ibid.

5. Deirdre McCloskey, *The Bourgeois Virtues: Ethics for an Age of Commerce* (Chicago: University of Chicago Press, 2006), 32.

6. Adam Smith, *Theory of Moral Sentiments* (London: A. Millar, 1759), 83.

7. Nicholas Phillipson, *Adam Smith: An Enlightened Life* (New Haven, CT: Yale University Press, 2010), 156.

8. Smith, *Theory of Moral Sentiments*, 83.

9. US Select Committee on Ethics. See slide 3 of the presentation entitled Senate Select Committee on Ethics, Senate Official Code of Conduct at www.ethics.senate.gov /public/index.cfm/files/serve?File_id=2E0CDB90-66DF-4ED1-9A3B-9F1BC7144448.

10. Guy B. Adams and Danny L. Balfour, *Unmasking Administrative Evil* (New York: M. E. Sharpe, 2009), 8.

11. Ibid., 13.

12. Ibid., 8.

13. Dwight Waldo, *The Enterprise of Public Administration* (Novato, CA: Chandler & Sharpe Publishers, 1980).

14. Martin Luther King, *Where Do We Go from Here? Chaos or Community?* (Boston, MA: Beacon Press, 1968).

Index